What people a

Align

We are living in a time in the world when it is all too easy to feel lost or disconnected from ourselves. Harmony gives us a compass and a map to find our way home. She reminds us of the universal themes that unite us as individuals through her personal vignettes and she assists us to awaken to our own true nature. She is the compassionate therapist and gifted spiritual teacher that we need to guide us on our journey through life. This book is a gift.

Dr. Arielle Schwartz, author of *The Post-Traumatic Growth Guidebook* and *The Complex PTSD Workbook*

Harmony Kwiker is an excellent writer, and she knows her field. *Align* is one of the most comprehensive self-help books I have ever read. I believe that reading this book could offer the equivalent of several years of good psychotherapy. I will recommend it highly to both clients and professional colleagues.

Susan Campbell, Ph.D., author of *Getting Real* and *From Triggered to Tranquil*

What a wonderful book! *Align* is filled with enlightening concepts, heartfelt stories, and practical exercises all designed to help we readers know *who* we are, *why* we feel and act as we do, and *how to* transform what we need and want to change. *Align* is a rare and precious gem for spiritual seekers and a must-read for therapists and counselors of all persuasions.

Sue Patton Thoele, author of *The Mindful Woman, The Courage to Be Yourself,* and *The Woman's Book of Strength* among others

Align is a rare gem and takes the reader on an incredible journey to self-discovery and personal empowerment. Harmony Kwiker offers such a rich tapestry of practical steps to better experience the inner and outer worlds of relationships to self and others. I highly recommend this profound resource to anyone seeking self-improvement.

Lawrence Ellyard, Founder and CEO of The International Institute for Complementary Therapists and author of *The Spirit of Water*

This book is magnificent! *Align* gives us an opportunity to enhance the communication in our relationships – even the toughest relationships. This book can shift us out of common lifelong patterns of projection and reaction and bring us to a place where we are aligned with our True Self and operating with deep-seated honesty, presence and power. This book is a gift for ourselves, our spouses and everyone with whom we connect.

Deanna Reiter, author of *Dancing with Divinity* and *The Nine Scoundrels*

Many of us get lost in the theater of our projections, the conditioning of the world or in the preferences of others. Part of spiritual maturation is to deeply connect with the True Self, our core spiritual essence. In *Align: Living and Loving from the True Self*, Harmony lovingly guides the reader through this sacred process. She addresses physical, emotional, relational, communication and spiritual dynamics of authentic self-embodiment. The pages are filled with important information and deep wisdom, clearly based on years of Harmony's personal and professional development. There are practical exercises to ground the wealth of psycho-spiritual material, as well as personal sharing to make it relatable. We realize today that maximal well-being involves the spiritual as well as the physical, and *Align* is a brilliant synthesis.

Eric Meyers, author of *The Astrology of Awakening*

Harmony Kwiker takes readers on a journey discovering and aligning with their true selves. Encompassing the beautiful truths of major spiritual traditions, *Align* provides insightful exercises and stories for healing our personal and generational wounds.
Kelly Robbins, MA, author of *Trust Your Next Step: Creating the Confidence to Cut Fresh Tracks*, www.KellyRobbins.net

As a professional and growth enthusiast herself, Harmony Kwiker's book Align is an excellent bridge between counsellor and client, and spiritual growth enthusiast with Self. Align is a beautifully written book, marrying academic ideologies with real-life examples. Harmony has a thorough understanding of the human condition and *Align* is suitable for professionals seeking to expand their toolbox, and growth enthusiasts looking for a comprehensive, accessible read.
Jacqui Burnett, author of *Life's Not Yoga...or is it?*

This excellent book will be an inspiration to anyone who is wanting to explore their true nature. With great clarity and transparency the author affirms that there is nothing to fix, that we are already whole and that our infinite being is ultimately unaffected by conditioning and trauma. Highly recommended.
Martin Wells, Consultant psychotherapist in the United Kingdom National Health Service and author of *Sitting in the Stillness: Freedom from the Personal Story*

Align

Living and Loving from the True Self

Align

Living and Loving from the True Self

Harmony Kwiker

MANTRA
BOOKS

Winchester, UK
Washington, USA

JOHN HUNT PUBLISHING

First published by Mantra Books, 2022
Mantra Books is an imprint of John Hunt Publishing Ltd., No. 3 East Street, Alresford
Hampshire SO24 9EE, UK
office@jhpbooks.com
www.johnhuntpublishing.com
www.mantra-books.net

For distributor details and how to order please visit the 'Ordering' section on our website.

ISBN: 978 1 80341 058 6
978 1 80341 059 3 (ebook)
Library of Congress Control Number: 2021950816

A CIP catalogue record for this book is available from the British Library.

Design: Matthew Greenfield

UK: Printed and bound by CPI Group (UK) Ltd, Croydon, CR0 4YY
Printed in North America by CPI GPS partners

We operate a distinctive and ethical publishing philosophy in
all areas of our business, from our global network of authors to
production and worldwide distribution.

Contents

Harmony Kwiker, MA

Dedication

This book is dedicated to my beloved husband,
Christopher Arnold.
Your presence in my life is a sacred gift.

Reveal: Embody the True Self beyond Trauma and Conditioning,
by Harmony Kwiker, MA. 978-0692179765

Acknowledgments

I would like to express my deepest gratitude for the people in my life who helped to bring this book into being: my children, Mylah and Tobin, whose developing sense of self teaches me about the essence of humanity; my dad, Dr. Michael Kwiker, DO, whose dedication to life-long learning reminds me that we are continually evolving; my mom, Elizabeth Kwiker, who left this dimension at the young age of 57 but used every moment of her life to bring healing to this planet; my husband, Christopher Arnold, whose passion for relational leadership empowers everyone in his presence; Naropa's MTC chair, Peter Grossenbacher, PhD, for guiding our department with grace and humility; my editor, BreAnne Meyer, for her deep wisdom and brilliant feedback—this book would not be what it is without you; and my publishers at Mantra Books for your dedication to inspiring readers with mind/body/spirit books.

I would also like to acknowledge my students who show up with a passion and devotion to transpersonal psychotherapy. Your questions, insights, and appreciations supported the creation of this book. I would also like to express my gratitude for my clients who vulnerably show themselves to me as they do the transformational work of coming back home to their alignment. I will forever be inspired by you.

Introduction

I've been a student of healing and transformation for my entire life. I was born into a family of healers who valued personal growth, transformation, and holistic health modalities. My mom was a powerful coach and healer who embodied her deeper wisdom in a way that transcended traditional therapy. My dad is a doctor of osteopathy, and he has been a pioneer in functional medicine since the early 1970s. As I watched the impact my parents had on the community they served, I wondered what kind of healer I would become.

When I chose a traditional path of clinical psychology, my family and friends were surprised. I was surprised, too. I had seen and experienced potent healing transpire from alternative modalities and admired my parents for paving their own path. I had experienced my direct connection with deeper wisdom sitting in meditation, practicing breathwork, and experiencing energetic healings. I had tried traditional counseling, and I was disappointed in the limitations of talk therapy. It seemed to me that talk therapy focused on pathology and not on deep healing. However, I wanted to discover how to bring the depth of transformation made possible by alternative modalities into the more conventional environment of counseling.

Through my years of study and practice, I have learned that a person is only a healer to the extent they remind their client or patient that they are already whole. In a counseling setting, this means that I hold the space of a clear mirror for a client to see the ways they orient towards their wounds. As they see themselves with more clarity, they remember their essential self and naturally find their way back to their wholeness. Without trying to fix them or change them in any way, deep transpersonal counseling is about being the presence that guides a client back to who they really are.

We are all born of our essence, which is the spiritual wholeness that is our birthright. Our essence is our crystalline energy body that remains untouched by the experiences we have in life. As we experience our childhood, we collect evidence about our own existence and safety in the world. The way our caregivers look at us, speak to us, and treat us influences the way we see ourselves, think about ourselves, and treat ourselves. The way the people around us live their lives, treat other people, and engage with themselves also influences our learned ways of interacting with our environment.

From these early experiences, we develop habitual ways of thinking and behaving that continue to impact the way we feel about ourselves, other people, and the world around us. Left unexamined, our conditioned patterns will persist throughout adulthood and we will build a life based on outdated ways of thinking and behaving. This is a painful, limiting way to live our lives. Not being fully present with ourselves and the world, our unexamined and unresolved experiences of the past dictate our current experience of life.

At our core, our essential self remains within us untouched by our conditioning. Our personality is the character expression of our learned ways of being and obscures our essence. As we do the work of self-development, we seek the path back to our essence while simultaneously indulging the barriers that we have built around it. We prevent ourselves from fully embodying the truest part of our inner world and feel imprisoned by our habitual ways of being. Because our patterns are the way we've learned to navigate the world, we cling to them for a sense of control. However, since we feel limited by the old patterns, we simultaneously look for new ways to be in the world.

Once we become aware that we are living from the limitations of our learned patterns, we may seek support and cultivate practices in an effort to come back to our essence. As we develop more awareness around our essential self, we long to know how to fully embody this source of inner peace. However, when we experience emotional pain and conflict, limiting thoughts and patterns of our conditioning can automatically spring to the forefront of our awareness.

Slipping further and further off balance, conditioned patterns can cause us to disconnect from our alignment with the Source that beats our heart, which is the vital energy of divine love that many people call God. As the familiar yet painful patterns of our past direct our reaction to the environment, we feel broken and completely disconnected from our True Self. This disempowering cycle reinforces our conditioned beliefs, causing us to stay stuck in misalignment.

When we meditate or practice mindfulness, we attempt to train ourselves to nourish our connection with our essence. When we seek psychotherapy or energy work, we look to the teacher to facilitate our return to our True Self. When we attend workshops, groups, or spiritual communities, we are wanting to reconnect with and embody our True Self in the presence of others. And when we long to make love and join with another in the most transcendent and spiritual union, we are wanting to amplify our essence through the vibration of bliss.

Living in alignment with Source and embodying the wholeness of our essence is possible for all of us. Since all are born aligned, transformation and healing brings us back to this sacred place within. As the only constant and true part of our inner world, our spiritual wholeness is vast, unbreakable and inexhaustible. Our vital force is inherently connected to the Source of all creation. When this vital energy is inhibited by pain and conflict, our essence is distorted; subsequently, we feel powerless, trapped, and alone. Conversely, when this vitality moves through our systems with ease, the boundless and enduring presence of our essence aligns with the essence of all life. This is where we feel a sense of belonging to the world where we are free, creative, and empowered.

Align is a loving reminder and a gentle guide to come back to who we really are. To access our deeper wisdom and find the seat of our True Self is possible in any moment. Restoring connection with ourselves, we can deeply connect with others. We can experience a deep repair in our systems and show our authentic selves to the world. As we consciously repattern how we experience ourselves and others, we begin to take up space in the world that holds the vibration of our expansive, powerful self.

As a psychotherapist and professor of transpersonal Gestalt Therapy, I believe there is nothing about ourselves that needs to be fixed; we are already whole. Because there is so much noise in the world telling us otherwise, living from that wholeness takes practice and guidance. I developed a psychotherapeutic framework called Spiritual Alignment Technique (SAT) to teach therapists and coaches how to facilitate this deep work.

In the pages of this book, I lay out the foundation and practices of living and loving from alignment to support you in opening the channel of boundless life force to move through you in all areas of life. I've also created a companion journal and a unique alignment map for you to use in conjunction with this book. Visit my website to download both today.

The practice of staying aligned and seated in ourselves throughout all the terrain of life is a courageous act of unconditional self-love and self-trust. It's a humbling journey of being a life-long learner, knowing that the only place to get is more in touch with what's right here within ourselves. As we come deeper into contact with our alignment, we can touch deeper layers of our healing and transformation. Discovering how we want to be with ourselves and how we want to engage with life nurtures our dignity on this sacred journey.

May we all experience the beauty of meeting life from the most integrated, updated, and authentic version of ourselves.

And may we all find that resonant vibration in the world around us, where our relationships are reflections of our wholeness.

Love,

Harmony

Part 1:

The Developing Sense of Self

Chapter 1

The Conditioned Self

Differentiating from Our Conditioning

Our conditioned sense of self develops quietly, in the privacy of our own mind. We use this sense of self to navigate the world, and yet it continues to guide us from a cloaked position of obscurity and dominance all at once. Both incessant in its beliefs about who we are and anonymous in its voice, our conditioned self can govern both our inner world and our movements in the outer world instinctively and impulsively, without conscious choice.

Our conditioned self was created during relational interactions with others and is rooted in the meaning we made from the way other people expressed themselves in our presence. The way others treated us and the way we observed them treating one another informed the way we learned to be in the world. At the time that our psychological identity was formed, we were young and dependent on our caregivers for safety and belonging. The conditioned thoughts and behaviors we developed were adaptive and came from a deep wisdom. We found safety, security, and a sense of power through our conditioned ideas and strategies. However, continuing to use the learned patterns that were created in the past keeps us from experiencing the life we long for in the present.

The conditioned self lives within the mind as an intangible and pervasive set of misbeliefs that we unconsciously use as we move through the world. Any moment that we are not actively choosing how we want to show up for ourselves, our relationship, and life itself we are relying on outdated ways of being. The false stories we hold about ourselves and the world become habitual narratives that seem true because we've been thinking them and acting from them for so long.

To discern our conditioned sense of self from the truth of who we are is the revolutionary act of claiming ourselves as whole, sovereign beings. To be sovereign means that we are autonomous and we have self-authority, where we are not acting or thinking from antiquated patterns and schema that we acquired from other people.

Awareness of our conditioned self makes it possible for us to be in choice about how we relate to ourselves and the world. When we are aware and in choice, we are able to respond to life from our sovereignty. Because the patterns of our conditioned self have been with us for many years, we unconsciously rely on them to navigate the world. Day in and day out, we stay asleep to the True Self when we follow the messages and patterns of our conditioned self around as if it is who we are. We must cultivate practices to increase awareness of our thoughts, mindfulness of our emotions, and consciousness of our words and actions.

This deep level of attentiveness to how we are makes it possible to see the imprint of our conditioned self with more clarity. This clarity is necessary to differentiate from our conditioned self, making it possible to distinguish our conditioning from our essence. Becoming aware of our learned patterns allows us to get distance from them. This space gives us the opportunity to be in choice. And to be in choice is what makes room for transformation and healing.

Until we can clearly distinguish our conditioned self from our True Self, every movement, every word, every response, every reaction that we express is influenced by our conditioning. Since these familiar ways of relating to ourselves and others were at one time adaptive, they "seem" to work. For example, if we created an adaptive strategy to keep stability in a family where one or both parents were emotionally volatile, we might have a very strong impulse to be a perfectionist. At the time we were dependent on our caregivers for safety, being perfect for them gave us a sense of power when we were powerless.

It made it so we could exist in an unstable and unpredictable environment.

As we grow up, if we continue to use our perfectionistic strategies habitually, the strategy becomes fixed. We continue to try to be perfect in all things, even when the threat of volatility is not present. Because we get a sense of control from the perfectionist's voice, we feel more powerful allowing it to guide us, even when beneath this voice is a fear of not being enough driving its patterning.

Since our conditioned self is rooted in experiences that happened long ago, habitually following the patterns of our conditioning and believing the distorted narratives is easy; it's the path of least resistance. It seems normal to believe the messages of our conditioning because we've been doing it for most of our lives. However, although easy to follow, it is this aspect of our inner world that is the cause of our limiting beliefs, relationship challenges, emotional pain, dissociation, and reactions. Continuing in this manner prevents us from living in alignment with our true potential.

The Role of Our Caregivers

We don't come into this life with a sense of self or an identity. Having just come from Source, the vital energy of divine love that many people call God, we are deeply rooted in the universal bliss of loving awareness when we are first born. More in the spirit realm than the physical realm, we are born in a state of oneness or confluence, where there are no boundaries between ourselves and others. Confluence means that our sense of self literally comes from others, that we are merged with them.

Boundaryless by nature, children only know they exist because they are seen, and what we are seen for matters greatly to our developing sense of self. Merged with those around us, we are dependent on our caregivers to teach us about who we are, both directly and indirectly. In the first few years of our life, what people say about us, how they treat us, how they seem to relate to the world, how they represent their gender, and how they relate to their own mind/body/spirit becomes our map for how to navigate the world. We either mirror it, or react against it, trying to find a way to fit in this world based on what we observe.

Walking around with an invisible umbilical cord that keeps us tethered to our biological mother, we begin to explore who we are as a separate being from her around the age of 18 months. Even in the case of early maternal death, adoption, or surrogacy, the energetic cords that tie us to our biological mother persist in the unconscious development of self, especially as it relates to our emotional and spiritual sense of self.

Finding our all-powerful will, discovering the word "no," and building competency is our task at this time, and the way that our caregivers relate to us in this process impacts the way we relate to our own sense of self and our power and will.

Wanting to find a sense of belonging and safety, we instinctively pick up on social cues and undeclared agreements about how to relate to the environment. And as we do this, we begin to make up stories about ourselves and others. We develop misbeliefs about who we are, and we start to identify with those thoughts. Our conditioned self informs our identity, causing our sense of reality to be seated in past experiences. From our learned sense of self, we collect evidence of where our worth comes from, and we cultivate habitual patterned ways of being based on our sense of worthiness.

Our nervous system is affected by these experiences, and we intuitively control our internal experience in order to find inner and outer stability. When the field around us doesn't support our health and wholeness, it's common to feel unsafe in our bodies; this is where dissociative patterns and denial of our somatic intelligence begin.

In the developing of these patterns, we begin to cloak our

vulnerability and hide our authentic expressions with a wall around our hearts. The cloak and the wall are invisible defenses against the pain of conditional love, coercion, and shame. Having come into this world with an open heart, ready to give and receive love unconditionally, hiding our vulnerability is antithetical to our true nature. Although painful, building walls around our heart seems like the safest thing to do in an environment that neither sees us for our fullness nor supports the wholeness of our true expression.

The Ego

From 18 months to 4 years of age, ego development takes place. This is when we implicitly develop a sense of self. Discreetly, in the privacy of our own mind, our psychological identity forms. Significant events that happen during this time have a clear impact on the way we self-identify. In Latin, the word "ego" literally translates to the word "I." The psychological meaning of ego is about our identity, who we think we are.

We need an identity to navigate the world. The ego is not bad. It's not something to rid ourselves of. It's simply important to know that in an effort to create an identity that gives us a sense of esteem and worth, the developing ego clings to information that gives us the most sense of power, security, and control. No matter how maladaptive the ego-identity seems, it is rooted in an attempt at helping us find our place in this world.

For example, when I was 4 years old, my parents divorced and my sister came in and told me that it was my fault that Dad left. My developing sense of self was influenced significantly by this experience. I became self-identified with the idea that there is something inherently wrong with me and that I make people go away. The way this sense of self caused me to relate to the world was through the lens of shame, hiding parts of myself to try to earn love and safety. Because I had a general sense of control utilizing this strategy, it "seemed" to work.

It became such an integral part of my inner landscape that I didn't even know it was present within me. I instinctively quieted my truth and hid my pain, protecting myself from more loss and heartache. Never really showing myself to anyone, I moved through the world trying to be as small and agreeable as possible.

We come to believe that *who we are* is the idea of ourselves that we created during events that happened when we were first developing an identity. Our sense of self isn't stagnant. It's an ever evolving and changing process that happens in relationship throughout our lifespan. However, when we stay fixed in patterns that are seated in our most formative years, our ego identity is very young and prevents us from experiencing the rich, deep relationships we know we're capable of co-creating.

From 5 to 7 years of age, we develop our superego, which is the acquired values of social standards that live as the self-critical voice within. For example, a superego may value being self-sacrificing, being "good" and virtuous, thinking of one's self first, or making our own way in the world. A superego may put a value on saving money, achieving success, or finding security in social groups.

The age of 7 is the phase of individuation where we know that we are separate from others. Developmentally, this is a very important milestone as we cultivate the capacity to think about how to approach a problem of our own volition.

And by the age of 10, our ego and superego are developed, and we build off of the messages of these constructs to guide our thinking and behavior. This becomes our patterned way of being in the world, which is called our personality or character structure. The root word for "personality" is "persona," and in Latin "persona" literally translates to the word "mask." The mask of our personality conceals our brilliant essence and the authentic expression of our vital force. From the age of 10 onwards, until we choose differently, this mask is the aspect that we use to interact with the environment.

As we identify with our conditioned self and use behaviors that mask our essence, we interact with the world from the most limiting, small version of ourselves. Hiding our heart and behaving as if we are disconnected from Source, we trap ourselves in learned behaviors. Knowing that there is more to who we are, we seek a way out of our conditioned ways of being. Even when we cannot feel the presence of our truest self, we are always connected to Source. This bond is unbreakable. However, we can easily forget how to be aligned within ourselves when our identity is rooted in a *false* aspect of who we are.

Our ego can distort much of our experience of ourselves and the world. For example, if we have perfectionistic tendencies, our ego created a delusion of perfection that gives us a sense of control and separateness. This delusion was formed as an adaptable way to find safety in the world; however, as a fixed delusion we follow our misbeliefs of our ego around as if they are true, as if there is some perfection to attain.

Unfinished Business from the Past
When any aspect of our life feels incomplete, it lives within us unfinished. Each one of us has several incomplete, undigested experiences that influence the way we relate to ourselves and the world. The culmination of the unfinished business from the past is what drives the impulses we have in the present. In an unconscious attempt to complete the unfinished business, we project the experience onto current realty and relate to the environment from our past pain and hurt. The thoughts we had during the original event and the meaning we made of the experience influences our current reality and prevents us from contacting this moment with presence and awareness.

The event that remains unfinished matters less than our relationship to the event and how it lives within us. An extremely painful event, like the loss of a parent during childhood, could be an event that feels mostly complete to a person if they had space and connection to feel the pain and fully experience the loss while held in love and compassion. Although the pain may surface from time to time, the relationship to the loss may be one of peace and acceptance. Reconnecting with the spirit of the loved one may be useful in saying anything that has been left unsaid, but the loss will not override the experience of the present when the person has had room to fully feel and metabolize the grief.

On the other hand, an event like being ghosted or stood up by friends in high school could have a more extreme influence over a person's way of relating to the world if they were never able to process the event. If they shoved their pain to the side, put on a face of indifference, and covered up their authentic experience, this could have a huge influence over the person's adult relationships. Perhaps the person has built a wall up to keep connection out so that they won't be hurt again, and they may even treat others as disposable if they never let themselves feel the hurt of being treated as if they didn't matter. They would do this, of course, not to purposefully hurt others, but in an unconscious attempt at resolving the past.

When the events that contributed to our sense of self live within us unfinished and unexplored, we develop strategies based on the incompleteness of the experience. In an unconscious attempt to make sense of our past, we utilize the strategies we developed during those events in an effort to complete the experience. The unresolved past influences how we engage in relationships or withdraw from them. It guides how we assert ourselves or collapse around our will, how we honor ourselves or betray our own boundaries, how we receive attention or deflect it, how we acknowledge our own needs or ignore them, and how we accomplish tasks or procrastinate them.

The impulse that precedes these strategies comes from the unhealed and unprocessed pain that lives within our felt experience and prevents us from making contact with ourselves and the world. It's a protective mechanism, a defense of sorts, which is unconsciously intended to secure our place in our family and social structures. However, these strategies disrupt our access to our wholeness and to intimacy, and by using them, we prevent ourselves from experiencing deep contact with our True Self as well as with the world.

When we try to create a new experience of ourselves and of relationships, yet keep finding ourselves in familiar emotional and mental patterns, we are being called to connect with the place in us that carries the pain from the past. Even if the mind thinks we're over the experience, the familiarity of the pattern tells the truth of what is incomplete. When we relate to the world embodying our unfinished business, we feel powerless to create any real change.

The story of the unfinished business is not as important as the felt sense of ourselves. By accessing the emotional expression and the misbeliefs, we can begin to metabolize the past. For example, if we withdraw from relationships because we were neglected in childhood, contacting the felt experience of withdrawal is an entry point to moving through the experience. As you'll see in Chapter 10, working with our inner young one is essential in fully moving through the past to completion.

To be present and open to life and relationship without the influence of the unfinished past inhibiting our connections, we must feel what we previously were unable to feel. And as we feel and metabolize all that our system is holding, we must be patient and compassionate with ourselves. There is no rush to complete the unfinished business. There's no urgency to be fully updated. We can only metabolize that which we are aware of, and our awareness will only see that which we are ready to look at.

The conditioned self developed as a means of self-regulation. In moments of stress and trauma, we instinctively developed thoughts and behavioral patterns in an attempt to soothe our dysregulation. We continue to use the conditioned patterns when we feel the activation of stress in our systems. The patterns themselves give us a sense of power, control, and safety. When we consciously stop using our conditioned patterns, we are choosing to feel and process the stress and trauma response that lives beneath the patterns.

The Role of Trauma

The word trauma can evoke different reactions in different people. With the continuum of trauma being so vast, it can be challenging for some of us to recognize our own trauma. Through the transpersonal lens, all trauma has us feel split from our connection from our alignment with Source. This split could happen at birth, when we were left in our crib to cry it out, when our experience was discounted, when we were neglected, when someone violated our boundaries, and so on.

When we have a generally "good" relationship with our parents, it can be challenging to identify any trauma that would cause us to feel disconnected from our alignment. With no obvious traumatic events to point to as the moment our limiting misbeliefs and patterned behaviors were created, it might seem like our conditioned self is normal or functional or just who we are.

Many of us do not realize that we are walking around with trauma until we dedicate our attention to looking within. Our habitual patterns are an attempt at regulating our nervous system, which is an indicator of the stress and trauma that was present when our conditioned patterns first began. Looking at the underlying cause of our habitual patterns, we might begin to see that we felt unsafe in life from a young age. Even if we can't recall the traumatic events from our explicit memory, the experience of not feeling safe is enough to create a movement into full identification with our conditioning.

Traumatic events are often not easily recalled because they seemed normal to the child who experienced them. Being accommodating and accepting of the unsafe, neglectful, or misattuned environment was the adaptive strategy that kept us safe. When our parents lacked emotional maturity, discounted our experience, and/or walked around in a state of stress, our response was an attempt at creating balance in a system that was not designed for our health and well-being.

For those of us with a chronic and complex history of trauma, we have more awareness about the events that shaped us. As a young child dependent on others for safety, the shock of trauma teaches us that we need to be vigilant in order to find our way in the world. This vigilance gives our conditioned self more power, leaving less attention and energy available to nurture our higher-level needs.

When we are in a trauma response, we don't have access to our alignment with Source as safety. Physical cruelty, sexual violations, extreme neglect, and near-death accidents can make it seem as if there is not a presence of divine love within or without. Emotionally immature caregivers, dissociated alcoholic caregivers, and abandonment or death of a caregiver can also contribute to the traumatic wound of being discarded or rejected from Source. In its place, darkness and loneliness can dim any perceived potential or hope for a different experience of life.

All patterns exist to ensure our survival. When we have experienced chronic trauma, we cling to our patterns in an attempt to keep us safe and alive. However, in using these patterns we are keeping ourselves fixed in the past, which prevents us from feeling truly alive.

When we contract around our pain and create our identity in response to other people's shadows, the imprint of darkness can seem too large to overcome. The influence of darkness and trauma on our sense of self is the first place that needs our attention. Because we were not given the space or guidance to move through the traumas, we integrated them as part of our self-concept as a way to make sense of the experiences.

Trauma that lives within us unfinished will find ways to get our attention, whether through panic attacks, rage, paranoia, insomnia, dissociation, social anxiety, physical ailments, lack of self-trust, and so on. These symptoms are an invitation to touch the places in us that were violated in the past and bring the loving awareness we needed back then into our being in the present.

Our ability to explore and move through our unfinished business shifts our relationship to our conditioned self. Metabolizing past experiences increases our awareness of how we cloak our essence and keep ourselves out of alignment. This awareness affords us the choice to honor our tender vulnerability, authentic truth, and essential wholeness. People from our past may have treated us in ways that made it wholly unsafe to stay in contact with these true and pure places within us; however, these places are still there. Beneath the layers of trauma and conditioning, our essence and alignment await.

To be in choice about where we live from, we take our power back from those who misused their power. We show up to life, fully expressed and whole. Knowing that there is so much more to us than what the world has taught us about ourselves, we get to create the life we want to live. Slowly, over time, as we unravel the web of learned misbeliefs, we discover that we have always been free.

Harmony's Story

I was alone in my room putting a puzzle together, my favorite pastime. My dad walked in and said, "I'm not going to be around as much. I'll be living in a different house."

Shock ran through my body. I was 4 years old and my family was breaking apart. He picked up his bags, and I watched through the front window as he walked to his truck and drove away.

I stood there alone for a few minutes, feeling the emptiness of my abandonment. Then I walked back to my bedroom and resumed solving my puzzle. As I tried to put the pieces back together, my sister ran in and yelled, "It's all your fault! Dad left because of you! I wish you had never been born!"

Since she was older than me and knew how to do everything better than me, I believed her. I went to check on my mom, and she lay on her bed weeping, "I can't believe he would do this to us."

I recoiled within myself, trying to hide my presence. If my being born caused this pain, I unconsciously reasoned that I needed to be as small, quiet, and as perfect as possible. My conditioned self became accommodating, trying to please those around me to earn my existence. My habitual thoughts became centered on my unlovability, and my habitual patterns were designed to try to find safety and love.

Because everyone else's pain was so great, I hid my pain and my truth. The mask I presented to the world was one of perfection. Part of being perfect included needing nothing and feeling unaffected by those who hurt me.

Exercise: Identify the Mask

Our conditioning will always be our conditioning. Living from this place is the path of least resistance. We find a sense of safety and control when we live from our conditioning. The conditioned self loops on in certain themes. Getting to know the themes of our conditioned self is what makes it more possible to differentiate from it. And differentiating from it makes it more possible to metabolize the experiences from the past and discover a new, more generative way of expressing our energy.

Knowing the mask of the conditioned self is essential in differentiating from it. When we can look at our mask with curiosity and clarity, we are no longer identified with it. We get space and distance from it, and in that space we are embodying a truer aspect of ourselves—our witness mind.

21

To begin the journey back to the True Self, we must first get really clear on the conditioned ways we move in the world. Take a few moments to consider what pulls the attention of your mind most of the time. What are the main themes of what you think about throughout the day? What impulses lie beneath those themes? For example, maybe work pulls the attention of your mind most of the day, or your appearance, or intimate relationships. What is the theme beneath those thoughts? Look deep within the matrix of your mind to discover how your conditioned values guide the way you currently interact with the world. Make a list.

Next, take a few moments to consider how you interact in relationships with those closest to you. Separate from what you think about all day, consider the way you show up during conversation and connection with others. Maybe you listen to others and hide your opinion, maybe you talk about yourself a lot, or maybe you talk about other people and gossip. What are the underlying motivations of the way you interact as you relate to others? Make a list.

Walkaway with Wisdom

The main concepts of this chapter focus on how we develop limiting patterns that become fixed ways of being in the world.

In early development, children only know they exist because they are seen by others. When a child is only seen for their roles, personality, and behaviors, they mature into an adult who identifies with those attributes. In the absence of an attuned, safe connection with their caregivers, a person's sense of self is limited to learned behaviors and survival strategies they developed in an attempt to self-regulate during childhood. Although these behaviors and strategies were once adaptive, when they become fixed patterns of relating to one's self and others, inner peace and deep connection are inhibited.

When an event feels stressful or traumatic, it tends to have a greater influence over our conditioned self. Because the ego wants safety and control, conditioned patterns persist to ensure our existence. When we identify with the conditioned self, we believe that who we are is what others taught us about ourselves. With an identity wrapped up in learned ideas and behaviors from the past, we live from the smallest aspect of ourselves.

In an unconscious attempt to complete the unfinished business, we project the experience onto current realty and relate to the environment from our past pain and hurt. To be present and open to life and relationship without the influence of the unfinished past inhibiting our connections, we must feel what we previously were unable to feel.

Chapter 2

The True Self

If the mind were silent and the constant thoughts about ourselves, our relationships, and our work were to cease, what would be left? Who would we be if we were to strip away the mask of our personality and all the things the world taught us about ourselves? Once we moved through any fear of not having a sense of control or safety by using the movements of our conditioned patterns, what would we find beneath the fear?

When our ego was first developing, our identity was created around experiences that we had in the third dimension, where we see ourselves as separate from other people and the universe. The higher dimensions of ourselves live in the fourth and fifth dimensions, where consciousness and spiritual states are held. These were ignored by others and overlooked in our developing sense of self. Mistakenly, we believed that *who* we are was decided by our roles, our bodies, and the way other people treated us. Our identity was formed to the exclusion of our spirit, subtle energy, or deeper wisdom.

Because we were not seen for these more mysterious and boundless aspects of who we are, our essence was not integrated as part of our identity or learned ways of navigating this world. Instead of learning to self-identify as the embodiment of Source expressed through us, our identity got entangled with other people's trauma, pain, and misbeliefs about what it means to be human. Even if we knew that they were not seeing the most important aspect of who we are, the imprint of the interactions with the people around us became our navigational tool that directed how we move through the terrain of life.

We are all born with the capacity to embody the most infinite, pure, and loving wisdom. And yet we are all also part of the greater field around us. To hold the vibration of the True Self when the field around us is imbued with shadow and distortion would take a grounding in sovereignty that young children do not yet have. The people around us were asleep to their own essence so, in an effort to find safety and a sense of belonging, we eventually forgot ours, too.

Beneath all of the lessons that informed our conditioned self, beyond our personality, there is a True Self that is untouched by the experiences we have in life. Sometimes called the essential self, spirit, or divine energy, this is the truest part of who we are. Omnipresent, our powerful and expansive essence is the part of us that remains whole, luminous, and aligned with Source always. It's the part of us that is never wounded or broken, even when the conditioned self generates messages that we are beyond repair, destined for a life of loneliness and pain.

When we have a high degree of trauma or cling to the conditioned self, it may seem like our True Self is a fictitious construct that is unimportant or not of value in this world. Similarly, if we have been around "spiritual people" who espouse beliefs about pain and ego not being real, we might resist the idea of a "True Self" because it brings up trauma around spiritual bypassing. The message of spiritual bypassing states "If we were truly present, we would have no pain or reaction."

To reconnect and identify with our essence and alignment is not to ignore or override our pain, stories, or history. When we embody our essence, we come to a place where we can be with our pain, stories, and history consciously. We can hold ourselves in all of our human experience in such a way that we can be in contact with the experience with intention rather than have the pain take over our existence.

The persistent and prevalent nature of the conditioned self makes it easy to identify with. It's loud in the forefront of our mind. The messages of the conditioned self offer strategies for how to find our place in this dimension. However, when we believe these messages and follow these impulses, we habitually get pulled off center. Stuck in old patterns while trying to find our way to a new experience of life, it takes tremendous courage and self-trust to set down our old map and discover how to navigate the terrain of life in a way that honors ourselves.

Discovering the True Self

We all have glimpsed the essence of the True Self at some point in our lives. When all pretenses and efforts subside, our essence emerges with ease. This can happen in nature, at a workshop, during therapy, sitting in meditation, while making love, while creating art, during yoga or childbirth or an extreme sport. The Great Mystery of the Universe is within us all, and when the field around us reflects the energy of the essence of life we are more likely to remember that same energy within us.

Discovering how to live from this place and bring our essence into all areas of our life is a task that takes more awareness. Because the conditioned patterns are habitually utilized in all areas of life, not doing those patterns day to day and discovering what wants to happen through us instead is an ongoing practice. This seems particularly challenging during relational interactions, which we will dive into more deeply later in the book.

When we stop enacting the familiar, habitual patterns of our conditioning, it's common not to know what to do instead. We may look to a teacher or a healer to tell us how to live from the True Self. We may ask trusted friends to advise us on other ways to handle a situation. We may journal or make lists to try to see what we have done and what we can do differently.

While feedback and self-inquiry is valuable and necessary, there is no "right" way to be when we are allowing the essence of our True Self to express through us. Wanting security of knowing how to be or different ways to show up for life is a drive of our conditioning.

There is no script to the True Self. The True Self is, by nature, calm, aware, and healthy. When we embody the essential aspects of our true nature, we are able to respond to life from our most regulated, aware self with clarity of choice.

Our vital force, the dynamic power that animates us all, does not have a blueprint for its expression. When we meet the world from our True Self, we surrender the illusion of control. We cease any attempt to manage, manipulate, or contort our inner world to get a desired outcome when we allow life to express through us. We remember that all beings have sovereignty and we stop trying to control the people around us, too.

When the old map becomes too limiting and small, we are ready to explore the world from our vast essential self. To be in continual discovery of what is true for us, moment by moment, we seat our trust in our Self. Spacious curiosity opens the mind to experience ourselves and the world with a new lens. And as we see the world with fresh eyes, we see that there are infinite possibilities for how we might show up.

As we unearth our True Self, we explore the terrain of life without a map. Calling on our deeper knowing, our wisdom, and intuition, we are fully present with ourselves and our environment in a way that supports the unfolding of life. With a high degree of awareness and presence, our witness becomes our identity. When pain and conflict arise, we allow ourselves to feel the experience. This, too, is an expression of life. Without clinging to the pain or wrapping our identity in it, we make room for the experience to move through us to completion.

Knowing that we are so much more than the roles, habits, and misbeliefs of our conditioning, we remember that we are an expression of the vital energy of the Source of Creation. Once we disrupt the habitual patterns of our conditioning, we can discover who we truly are.

The Family Story

Before birth, our spirit easefully rested in the universal bliss of oneness and unconditional love. In an instant, at the moment of conception, we came into this dimension and received the DNA of our family lineage. Along with the brilliance, resilience and talent of our ancestors, their unhealed pain and trauma was passed down in that DNA. Conditioned ways of being, energetic patterns, emotional tendencies, and predispositions to certain mental and physical illness all commenced their initiation into our human experience.

The emotional expression of the feminine presence in our life (frequently our mother or our most feminine caregiver) had a great influence on our learned way of relating to our own emotions, body, and our metaphysical heart. The vocational expression of the masculine presence in our life (frequently our father or our most masculine caregiver) had a great influence on our conditioned way we take initiative, direct attention, and have integrity with the intersection of our purpose and values.

As newly embodied spiritual beings learning how to navigate this dimension, we innocently looked to our own caregivers to provide us with the same depth of comfort and love as the divine presence of Source. However, instead of offering a consistent, attuned and safe environment, they were working through their expression of ancestral pain, human conditioning, and emotional and energetic patterns.

Since they were unable to consistently meet our emotional, spiritual, and psychological needs, we developed our conditioned self in an effort to get our needs met. In this way, our conditioned self was designed to give us a sense of power, even though we feel disempowered and disconnected using these strategies as adults. Awareness of the way we were shaped by our primary caregivers is important for our own healing; however, this awareness does not mean that we blame them for how we are.

Our inherent wisdom guided us to keep a sense of balance in the family and find a sense of safety and belonging. Any energy in the family that was disowned influenced the conditioned expression of each child born into the system. In an effort to bring wholeness and balance to the system, children are the reflection of what is needed in the family. For example, if anger was disowned, the firstborn child might embody that energy and express anger regularly. Then if sensitivity was disowned, the next child would come in and embody the sensitivity needed in the system. This is all in service of integration, which we will dive deeper into later.

The degree to which our caregivers became our reference point for our okayness and lovability is the degree to which we saw them as "God." Since they were the source of our life's existence, we looked to them as the "Source" of life. As such, our conditioned patterns became an unconscious way to get God's (i.e., our parents') attention and love.

For example, when our conditioned self thinks we're not good enough, the question then becomes, "who are we not good enough for?" The mind puts it onto other people, as if we're not good enough to deserve love from them. This misbelief is seated in our early childhood experiences with our caregivers. The conditioned self believes that being perfect for our parents would have validated our existence. If we were enough, we would have received the love, attention, and safety that we wanted and needed. Even though our conditioning puts the misbeliefs onto our relationships, unconsciously it is God who we want to be good enough for. The reason this compulsion continues to exist is because we have forgotten that we, ourselves, are an expression of the Source of life.

Believing that we are our conditioned patterns keeps us in a loop where we look to the "world out there" to decide our worth and value. As we do this, we get further and further away from the place within us that is inherently worthy and lovable.

We engage with the world from our barriers to love, wanting others to affirm our significance.

While some of us look to please our caregivers, others allow ourselves to feel our anger towards them. The anger directed at our caregivers is in actuality anger at God. The anger is projected onto relationships and the world at large, resentful for being born into a life that is painful. Where the child who pleases wants to change themselves to earn love, the angry child wants everyone else to be different so they don't have to experience the pain of this life. Still, the child who expresses rage is screaming out to be loved unconditionally.

If there were siblings and other adults in the home as children, this adds nuanced layers to the experiences we had that influenced our relationship with our True Self. When many siblings are present in a family system, each child finds their niche to fill. And there can be a competition for love with a belief that there is not enough love to go around.

On a human level, not having our needs met, feeling unsafe, and competing for love is stressful and painful. Experiencing our family of origin's patterning, DNA expression, and relational dynamics can feel agonizing. Though the pain, grief, and learned patterns of our human experience can feel like endless suffering, through a transpersonal lens this is all part of the soul's journey. The soul's contract is an agreement our soul made to come back to the third dimension and experience this particular life in order to learn the lessons our soul needs to evolve. On a soul level, we are always whole and we welcome the pain of the lived experience of our humanity as part of our curriculum. Although the experience is painful, the pain itself and how to heal, integrate, and transcend it is the program of study.

To use our human resources, which include breath, awareness, movement, touch, voice, and bodily sensations, we can contact the deepest wounds and patterns within us. We can metabolize and transcend the trauma and conditioning of this life. As we do this for ourselves, we up-level our DNA for future generations and we shift the dynamic in our family of origin. Bringing the consciousness of the True Self into our familial system can seem like a huge mountain to climb. And yet, when we are called to the deep work of transformation, this is what we are doing. As we emerge beyond the conditioned ways of being and complete our unfinished business, we bring the generous and boundless nature of our essence to everything we touch.

Given our unique family stories, honoring our ancestors and caregivers is supportive of healing our lineage. Because those who came before us carry the birthplace of many of our conditioned ways of being, we can acknowledge them for their ability to survive without making them wrong for their adaptive strategies. This can support us in moving forward with greater autonomy and choice. Until we do this, we continue to play out antiquated patterns that were passed down to us.

Coming into alignment, we honor the past as we metabolize the way our bodies hold ancestral trauma. As we learn to embody our True Self, we up-level our DNA and heal transgenerational patterns. From our essential self, we get to bring more awareness to the conditioned patterns and offer love to the places in ourselves and our lineage where the True Self became inhibited in our expression. This love and this awareness bring more of the consciousness and expansiveness that we've needed in our lives since the beginning of time.

Leaving One's Self

Reaching out to our caregivers for consistent love and presence was, in a very unconscious way, an attempt at looking to them to be God. As we matured and continued to use those outdated strategies in other relationships, we started to look at others as God. This is what it means to "leave one's self." When our source of safety and worth is dependent on others, we leave our contact with our Self.

We can have access to the divinity of our True Self and still get pulled out of alignment by our human tendencies. Making other people the source of our inner peace and enoughness, we relate to our environment as if we have no agency or deeper wisdom. We treat ourselves as if we are powerless and betray ourselves to try to earn other people's approval and acceptance. We ignore our body's communication, and we look to others as a reference point. When that doesn't work, we react against this pattern and resent others for not being willing or able to meet our needs. We try to find a sense of power by blaming others and resenting them for being human.

Anytime our thoughts are consumed by what others have done or what we can do to get others to be different, we have left ourselves. When someone else becomes our reference point for peace, enoughness, and lovability, we are not in contact with our Self. This can be true on a daily basis when life seems normal, and it can also be true when we are emotionally activated and looping in stories about other people. The looping is an expression of the way we've left ourselves. Consumed by thoughts about other people, we go over to their world and leave our own. Forgetting that our home base is a safe place to stay, we look to them for safety and become emotionally upset when they are instead unaware, flawed humans. Instead, if we were to allow ourselves to feel what is beneath the thoughts, we can begin to come back to our bodies and contact our Self.

Traumatic experiences can also cause a movement away from one's Self. Oftentimes we leave contact with our body altogether because it seems like our body isn't a safe place for our soul to be seated. When we leave our bodies and dissociate, we are utilizing a strategy to find safety. Instead, turning toward ourselves and feeling into the dissociation, we can come back home to our Self.

When we believe that Source is outside of ourselves, a separate entity that is not also here within us in this dimension, the inclination to leave our bodies to get back to Source makes sense. Even though this happens unconsciously, the idea that we need to die to get back to the safety and presence of Source has many people engage in low vibrational, death urge behavior.

To stay in one's Self takes tremendous self-trust. Cultivating a high vibrational life urge through devotional practices, embodiment exercises, intentional eating, breathing, and nonviolent communication can shift the patterns of leaving one's self into patterns of staying seated in one's self. There will be more on this later.

Attachment Styles

Looking through the lens of our conditioned self, we are self-identified with the pain of our attachment wounds. Attachment wounds develop when we reached out to our biological parents and/or primary caregivers and they weren't able to meet us with the divine presence and unconditional love we were longing to receive.

Secure Attachment Style: When our primary caregivers were *consistent* with their love and presence, we develop a secure attachment style where we feel safe in relationships. A secure attachment style serves us to develop self-esteem that has us feeling good about ourselves, while also trusting others. Feeling positive about ourselves and relationships, we know that we can reach out to others with our authentic truth and desire. If those we reach out to aren't able to be there or reciprocate our desire, we know that we can land fully on our own two feet.

Insecure Attachment Style: When our parents or primary caregivers are *inconsistent* with their love and presence, sometimes attuned and sometimes volatile or absent, we develop an insecure attachment style (sometimes called anxious ambivalent). An insecure attachment style expresses itself as anxiety in relationship, where we really want connection but don't trust it when it's there. Thinking less of ourselves and more highly of others, we can only be soothed or think ourselves worthy when others want us. They can become addicted to intimacy and obsess over finding a person or being close to their person.

Avoidant Attachment Style: When our parents or primary caregivers are *neglectful* with their love and presence, we develop an avoidant attachment style. An avoidant attachment style expresses itself as someone thinking highly of themselves and less so of others. Not trusting others to meet their needs, they decidedly take care of themselves and expect others to do the same. They view emotions as "needy" and see those who express emotions or needs in a negative light, and they feel most comfortable when they are alone. They are wired for disconnection and have an aversion to intimacy.

Disorganized Attachment Style: When we experience *consistent and complex trauma* in relationship to our parents or primary caregivers, we develop a disorganized attachment style. This attachment style is sometimes secure and available for connection, sometimes insecure, and sometimes avoidant. Within one relationship, a person with a disorganized attachment style can show up fully attuned and available for connection in one moment, then get activated in trauma and leave in an avoidant episode, and then come back insecure and needing to be soothed by another person. The dysregulation and unresolved trauma that lives beneath the patterns can cause their actions to be harmful and emotionally abusive.

Unknowingly, we have a tendency to believe our identity is our attachment wounds. Our attachment style is part of our conditioned self as it is a learned way of being, and it can consume a large part of our identity, especially in intimate relationships. Forgetting that we are whole, we not only think we are fragmented, we think we are our wounds.

Knowing the patterns of our attachment style is an important key to knowing our way out of the box of our conditioning.

While there are many free attachment surveys and quizzes to take online, paying attention to ourselves when we are in an intimate moment with another person and/or when we are in conflict with someone close to us is the best way to discover our attachment style.

For example, when we are gazing into someone's eyes, what happens within our system? Do we feel safe and open (secure)? Do we want to please them (anxious-insecure)? Do we feel discomfort and want to deflect (avoidant-dismissive)? Or do we feel anxious sometimes, deflecting other times, and safe during other times (disorganized)?

Similarly, when we are in conflict with someone close to us, what is our experience of ourselves? Do we feel trusting of our ability to listen and be heard, while also giving the other person room for their experience and process (secure)? Do we feel anxious to amend the rupture and talk it through as soon as possible (anxious-insecure)? Do we close of and want to leave, never to talk about it again (avoidant-dismissive)? Do we feel trusting sometimes, anxious other times, and completely closed off at other times (disorganized)?

If we follow the patterns of our wounding as if they define who we are, we never allow ourselves to open to real love. We perpetually make other people the source of our love and worth, and we forget about the true Source of love that lives within our hearts. Forgetting our own true nature, our conditioning tells us that we are only lovable when others are loving us and that we are only safe to open when other people are a certain way. This is a trap of the conditioned self that keeps our hearts cloaked. The moment when the attachment wounds began, we cloaked our hearts to protect ourselves from being hurt. And although it is a well-intentioned strategy, continuing to cover our tender, wise heart inhibits real love and true intimacy.

If we know that *we have* attachment wounds, rather than thinking that *we are* our attachment wounds, we can bring more awareness and love to our wound. We can honor our original experience of pain and confusion. We can see the wisdom we had in creating self-protective strategies and can offer ourselves the very thing we needed at the time the wound was created. We can say to ourselves, "I will always love you and honor your truth." We can make a commitment to hold ourselves, to never leave our Self. And from here, we can honor other people's capacity to open to real love or not. Without needing others to be different so we can stay seated in our hearts, we can meet our relationships from our deeper wisdom as an expression of Source.

Because our nervous system response is also affected by the movements of our attachment system, our higher level of thinking can be impeded in our relational interactions. This makes it extra important to turn towards ourselves in this loving, compassionate way where we can validate the experience of our wounding. The experience of the pain is valid even though the stories about ourselves and others are likely not. Being with ourselves in a way that deepens our contact with our Self, we can update these old patterns and remember that they are not who we really are. There will be more on this later, but for now it's important to recognize that when we treat ourselves with this deep unconditional love, we are embodying our True Self. Our wounds do not need to go away or be fully healed in order for us to bring the vibration of our essence into our being.

The Fertile Void

The familiarity of our attachment wounds and the messages of our conditioned self offer a strange comfort. There's a fictitious box that we stay within that defines our sense of self. Anything outside of that box likely produces an unknown result. While the box feels safe and familiar, it also can feel like death. Containing the full expression of our vital force, we slowly kill parts of ourselves when we stay in the confines of our conditioning and wounding. Our identity is so small and limited here, yet making a different move can seem daunting.

As we increase our awareness around our conditioned patterns, we elevate our consciousness. Consciousness occurs when we create space around our thoughts and actions. The space we create around our conditioned self by seeing it with more clarity provides awareness. This awareness creates choice. And when we cease habitual patterns, choosing how we want to be can move us deeper into the great unknown.

Since there is no script for the True Self, there can be great uncertainty when we stop following the impulses and misbeliefs of our wounds and conditioning. It is a valid human response to feel fear when we experience uncertainty. In fact, when there is a great unknown, the human mind has a tendency to fill it in with "worst case scenario" stories. Making room for the sensation of fear that arises without listening to the stories of the mind is always good practice. Although counter-intuitive, turning toward our fear and welcoming it is what allows it space to move through us and heal.

In the moment we notice the mind looping in fear and apprehension, we can pause and become curious about how our experience is felt in our bodies. When we feel the sensations beneath our thoughts, we can notice our relationship to our experience. When the unknown causes the mind to become fearful, there can be an impulse to try to find a sense of control and safety outside of ourselves. If we are resisting our deeper experience, trying to figure a way out of our discomfort, and/or turning away from our experience, we perpetuate it. The mind continues to loop in limiting narratives and our discomfort persists.

Instead, we can breathe around our fear and validate our experience. "It makes sense to me that you are scared," we can say to ourselves with tender compassion. Wrapping our physical experience of fear with awareness and love, we can make more room for it. Not all emotions need more space; however, fear needs room to move. Where chronic depression needs the ignition of life beneath it to mobilize its watery, overwhelming expression, fear needs space. Where anger needs to be mobilized by moving the body, fear needs breath.

As we differentiate from our attachment wounds, knowing that *we have* wounds and that *we are not* our wounds, and metabolize any fear that may arise, we create spaciousness to explore our True Self. When our wounds and conditioned beliefs are no longer in the forefront of our minds dictating how we think, feel, and act, we have the opportunity to drop deeper into the experience of our uninhibited life force. And from this free expression, we get to discover how we want to be.

These moments of expansive discovery are called the *fertile void*. With infinite possibilities of how to move through the world, being in discovery of how life wants to express through us is the ultimate experience of vitality. With no walls or barriers of self-protection, the universe flows through us as we flow with the universe.

Harmony's Story

I sat alone in my bedroom with my eyes closed as I repeated my mantra. I was 6 years old and was new to transcendental meditation. My mom had taken me to see a guru the day before, although I was still unclear on why.

My parents were progressive healers, and they had access to powerful healing modalities. They were well-loved in the community and were amazing humans; however, they lacked parental guidance and a mature, attuned presence. As a self-disciplined child, I willingly took on the role of the responsible one.

Keeping myself accountable to follow through with my new practice, I sat on the floor breathing in and out, repeating my chant. Suddenly, I heard a voice from within, "All of this pain has a purpose." The voice was deep and masculine, unlike my feminine 6-year-old voice. Although surprised, the voice felt familiar, like an old friend who was here to reassure me.

I continued with my mantra as I was shown an image of the world, with humanity moving around in certain ways so that goodness could prevail. I was raised without religion, so I wasn't taught about a personified "God" as a Father. However, in this image it seemed as though all of the people of the world were players in a game so God could win.

"All of this pain has a purpose," I heard once again. "You have a purpose."

The comfort of these words from deep within felt incredibly profound. I wasn't sure if this was a typical experience of meditation, so I didn't tell anyone. However, hearing the wisdom of my True Self at such a young age gave me reassurance that all of the pain I experience in this life does, indeed, have a purpose. I stayed committed to my meditation practice, and to this day I sit in silence twice daily. Sometimes I easily access my essence, and other times I don't.

This experience and the practice give me a place to train my mind to identify with my True Self. Although I sometimes fall asleep to this vital essence, my practices keep me anchored in the intention of living a sacred life. Reminding myself that this is who I really am, my expanded, essential self is always within me, awaiting my return.

Exercise: Describe the Indescribable

Think back on the moments in your life you felt most like yourself. Remember moments when you felt connected to your innate wisdom, to your essence, and to the whole of the universe. Maybe you were alone in nature, meditating, creating art, or at a workshop that guided deep transformation. Capture that memory in your mind as if it were happening right now. Feel in your body how you felt in those moments. Tap into the cellular memory of being in a flow state, and then jot down a few words that remind you about how you feel when you are in contact with your True Self. Remind yourself, "This is who I really am."

Walkaway with Wisdom

Beneath the limiting thoughts and patterns of the conditioned self, we all have a deep knowing that there is more to ourselves. Since the conditioned patterns are a miniscule aspect of our humanity, learning to identify with our True Self helps us to unlearn what the world taught us about ourselves.

There are many ways we leave the True Self. The most common way we forget our essence is through the identification with our attachment wounds. When our attachment wounds are activated, we look to other people to fulfill our needs and complete us. By creating a secure attachment with our Self, we can use the pain of our attachment wounds as a way to return to ourselves.

Chapter 3

The Integrated Self

The conditioned self encompasses our ego, our personality, and our attachment wounds. It organizes all our learned beliefs, values, and behaviors into our identity and provides us a way to navigate the world.

The True Self is our expansive essence that is untouched by the experiences we've had in this life. It is the boundless energy of Source expressed through us. It is our portal to infinite wisdom and intuition. It is the expression of loving awareness that has been with us always.

The integrated self includes the whole of who we are, not in fragments or parts, but as one unified human being. While it's true that we have different aspects of who we are and our personality is made up of a composite of psychological features, the whole of who we are is greater than the sum of our parts. This becomes more tangible as we do the work of integration.

Attention Guides Our Identity

If we passively allow our attention to be seated in our ego, personality, and attachment wounds, we self-identify with our conditioned self. From this place, our attention can become consumed by thoughts of powerlessness, not enoughness, fear, and resentment. Limited by our identification with beliefs we created in childhood, we feel trapped by our identity and patterned behaviors.

If we consciously seat our attention in our alignment with Source, the True Self becomes our identity. We can see the world through our expansive, wise Self. We can be still and open enough to invite in transmissions from Source, where we can tap into the deep wisdom that is the voice of the True Self.

We can see infinite possibilities for ourselves and humanity. From this place, there is a tendency for the ego to sneak into our awareness and try to make this power and expansion personal, as if we are the only ones with this special relationship to divine presence. The nuanced awareness of where our attention is seated matters greatly in the practice of differentiating from the conditioned self.

If we expand our perspective to incorporate and unify all the aspects of our conditioning with all of the beauty of our divine essence, we can seat our attention in our integrated self. From the vantage point of our integrated self, we are both flawed and perfect as we are—mortal and divine.

When our attention has the capacity to encompass the both/and of our spiritual nature and human imperfections, we can see the fullness of who we are with greater acuity. If we can look within to map out our conditioned self, practice bringing more loving awareness to our attachment wounds, and remember that our alignment with Source is unbreakable, we develop the ability to encompass the full range of our whole Self.

Regulated, updated, and clear, we can meet the world with the fullest expression of ourselves, or we don't. Either way we are in choice about how we meet the world. Perhaps through our discernment we don't show ourselves to someone; this can be an indication of the integrated self when there isn't the compulsion to be "honest" and vulnerable all of the time. No longer unconsciously trying to complete unfinished business from the past, we can hold ourselves with tenderness no matter what experience we are having at any given moment.

When we are still in a state of fragmentation, we try to get energy from other people, give our energy away, or keep people out completely. Trying to get energy from other people, thinking that they have the energy source that we lack, shows we believe that we are incomplete. Giving energy away, trying to rescue others and playing God, shows we unconsciously think other people are incomplete. And when we isolate ourselves completely, containing our energy and keeping others out, shows we unconsciously think that everyone is fragmented and broken.

With subtle and overt strategies, we unconsciously try to integrate by manipulating the world outside of us. On some level, we already know that the outer world is a holographic expression of our inner world. When we try to exchange energy with others as a way to get a deeper need met, unknowingly we are really trying to integrate this part of ourselves that is being reflected by the world outside of us. For example, if I am trying to rescue someone who is sad and lonely rather than respecting them enough to carry their own burden, I am trying to integrate the place in me that is sad and lonely.

From an integrated state, we are in full contact with ourselves and all the aspects of us that were previously unfinished or disowned are welcomed with love and self-compassion. From this place, we can be present and compassionate with a person who is suffering while also trusting their ability to find their way through the pain. We can also trust their ability to ask for support when needed. Without caretaking others or needing them to take care of us, we can stay in contact with ourselves while also honoring the dignity of others.

In an integrated state, we are fully present with ourselves and others. We are in touch with our own agency while honoring others' power. Without being cold or resentful or desperate, we share our full experience from a regulated and whole place, not needing to be anything for anyone else and not needing them to be anything for us.

And when a younger part of us becomes activated, as it inevitably will, we maintain presence and love for that aspect of ourselves. Knowing that this emotional activation is part of our humanity that we get to heal and love, we also know that it is no one else's job to take our pain away for us.

Directing our attention throughout our whole system, our awareness nurtures our integration. This is a fluid state of presence and vital energy, where the full range of our divine humanity is encompassed and embodied.

The Alchemy of Integration

In a state of fragmentation, it may seem impossible to become integrated. When aspects of our conditioned self fight against one another, the inner conflict strengthens the fragmented state. There's often a dominant voice that lives within our ego that overpowers a quieter voice that lives within our unconscious mind. The dominant voice of the ego manages our identity as it relates to the world around us. The quieter voice of our unconscious is the unexpressed truth that we disowned when it wasn't safe to reveal it.

The split of the fragmented state is uncomfortable to endure. Following it around and allowing the dominant voice of the ego to dictate how we experience life gives it power over how we contact the world. Similarly, resisting this inner conflict only reinforces it. Alchemizing our inner divisiveness into an integrated, whole state is the portal back to our essence.

Everything that pulls the attention of the mind is important to notice. Bringing more attention to the dominant voice and really hearing what it wants for us, we can contact this one aspect of our fragmentation. It is essential to learn from this contact. We can fully embody the energy of this one part and give it all the space in the world to have a voice. As we contact it and give it a voice, we speak from the first person, "I want to fit in. I want to make sure that you don't mess up our life."

Once we fully hear the dominant voice, we can make our way over to the quieter voice that hasn't had much room to speak. What does this part of our fragmented state want? How do we feel in our body when we take on the energy of this aspect of our inner world that's been suppressed? Giving it all the room it needs to have a voice, its message may likely be quite simple, "I want to feel free."

As we contact the divisive aspects of our inner world, we begin to alchemize the energy of the fragmentation. And as we do this, we are embodying a true aspect of ourselves that has the vital energy to create such a transformation. In the presence of a skilled Gestalt therapist, we can surrender to the facilitation of the communication between different aspects of ourselves that have polarized against one another. Most of us have multiple polarities that contribute to our fragmentation, making this ongoing work of integration a process, not a destination.

The inner sense of self-compassion, collaboration, and empowerment is part of the movement towards integration. When we allow ourselves to feel everything that is stored in our somatic memory, we metabolize our feelings by really experiencing them. We must feel in order to integrate, for integration is not something that happens only in the mind. As we experience the felt sense of fragmentation, various qualities of our inner world, and eventually integration, we can fully land in our bodies. We honor our energetic body, which goes well beyond our physical body. When this happens, we find our seat within ourselves and we can remember our unbreakable alignment with Source.

One aspect of alchemizing our fragmentation is integrating our higher consciousness in with our human experience. Divine, mortal, and whole—we shift our focus from thinking we are the fragmented, miniscule aspects of our humanity and we see the Meta view of our full selves where we transcend any delusion of brokenness or powerlessness.

From this transcendent, expansive perspective, we again can discover what is true for us. Separate from what we've been taught by others and beyond what spiritual teachers say, we access our deeper truth from our integrated self. We deepen into our own core values and have a choice in what we believe, which is self-responsibility. Similarly, as one whole, self-aware being, we have the capacity to make room for different values and perspectives. Honoring the truth of our heart without casting others aside, we stay in ourselves and trust other people in their own agency to stay in themselves, too. And if they don't, we trust their inherent wisdom to find their way back.

The integrated self does not abolish others nor vanquish any aspect of ourselves. By staying in contact with all of who we are, we can contact the environment in a way that honors ourselves. This work is *not* about creating happier thoughts or healthier behaviors. It is *not* about bypassing anything. It's *not* about fixing or changing anything about us. Integration is about getting more in touch with what is right here within us and inviting these various expressions of our humanity to be held in love by our divinity.

This deep integration is made possible by the unwavering recognition that the conditioned self is not who we really are, it is simply the way we learned to navigate the world. Self-identifying with the True Self creates the vessel for integration to transpire. When our wounds, our misbeliefs, our pain, and our patterns are met with consciousness, we embody the medicine we've needed to alchemize them for our transformation.

Integrated Felt Sense

Our felt sense is our own internal bodily awareness. It's how we experience our physical self in any given moment. Frequently, we ignore our bodily sensations and place more value in our thoughts. However, contacting our felt sense allows us to be present with our somatic intelligence, which is the inherent wisdom held in our cellular memory. In contacting our felt sense, our consciousness touches the gateway to our essence. Regardless of what aspect of our inner world is activated in the current moment, contacting our felt sense will support the continual movement of the renewal of our vitality.

Self-inquiries, such as, "What is my experience of myself right now?" or "What do I feel in my body?" can guide us back into presence and help us build awareness about where we are moving from. And if we focus on sensations rather than names of emotions, we distill our experience down to the essence of the vibration that we are currently holding.

For example, if I am doing the dishes and look within myself to explore my current experience of myself, I might think, "I feel anxious." But what does anxious feel like? Without putting labels on my experience, what are the sensations I feel in my body? Perhaps I notice a sense of hurriedness or urgency. I stay with myself and explore what urgency feels like at the level of sensation. Perhaps my heart is racing and I'm clenching my jaw. Then perhaps I notice that there is a fluttering sensation all around my heart.

As we deepen into contact with our felt sense, we inherently move away from our conditioned self and experience the way that life is currently being experienced in our bodies. This quality of contact with our current experience brings in more awareness, which in turn brings in more choice.

The next question we can ask ourselves is, "How do I want to be with myself right now?" If we're feeling a fluttering sensation around our heart, we might want to move our hands in a fluttery motion to fully embody the sensation. Or perhaps we want to make a noise and give it a tone. Maybe the flutter has words it wants to speak. Or maybe we want to sit down and place a hand on our heart and breathe love and compassion all around the flutter.

Exploring Your Felt Sense

Ask yourself, "What is my experience of myself right now?"
Notice the sensations in your body.
Ask yourself, "How do I want to be with myself right now?"
Breathe, move, and vocalize in the way your body is wanting.

We instinctually developed strategies to look away from our felt sense. This strategy was a learned tactic to leave ourselves to try to find safety in others. Turning away from our experience of ourselves, we perpetuate the same old patterns. Allowing our felt sense to stay hidden, we keep ourselves fragmented. Keeping our focus on the outside world, what we say and what we do is the priority. Looking within and choosing how we want to be with ourselves, honoring our whole being becomes the priority.

This level of curiosity disrupts the patterns of our conditioned self and opens the mind to access our own deeper wisdom. This opening becomes the initiation of our continual practice of integration.

"Integrated" is not a stagnant state. By doing this work we are not guaranteeing that we will always meet life from our integrated self or that life will always be easy. Transforming our fragmentation shifts our relationship to ourselves, and thus our relationship to the world changes. The places within us that hold the energy of our pain and wounding don't magically go away. While they don't rule our inner world as much, they can still become activated when the environment around us resembles the experience we had when the wounding first occurred. In these moments, it can take more time to come back to our sense of wholeness and integration. However, because we have done the work, we can find our way back there more quickly and we can integrate more fully with each and every activation of our wounding.

Returning to our contact with ourselves, we can soften into the sweetness of our own secure connection with our Self. Over time, we cultivate enough sovereignty to feel safe enough within ourselves to make deep contact with others.

The integrated felt sense has a quality of feeling solid in ourselves—like we are fully embodied or like there's a flag pole down our midline that roots us within ourselves. We no longer leave ourselves in the same way we did when we were identified with our conditioning, and we are able to return to this solid felt sense as our baseline. It also has a quality of expansion from the heart, where we are in love with humanity in all of its quirks and imperfections.

To meet the world from our integrated self, we show up from our most authentic expression. The loudest experience in our inner world is honored, and we don't try to hide it or disown it. If we're feeling insecure, we contact that insecurity and have choice about how we want to meet that experience. If we feel peaceful and wise, we embody the wisdom of our True Self without playing small. No matter what arises in the forefront of our awareness, we continually practice integrating all that is within us.

Harmony's Story

With a conditioned self that believes that I need to be accommodating, agreeable, and quiet in order to find safety, speaking my truth and embodying my essence in the presence of others can evoke a deep sense of fear in my whole system. Given the opportunity to stay quiet and disappear, my conditioned self would choose that every single time. Integrating my fear into my wholeness has been vital to me embodying my fullest expression, especially as a teacher and speaker.

When I was an undergraduate, I worked at a yoga studio. Eventually, I became a certified yoga instructor and I was terrified to teach my first class. I tried to disown my fear and find my courage, but the fear could not be contained. Every attempt at overriding my body's trembling caused the trembling to amplify. I pushed passed my terror and realized quickly that when the participants' eyes were closed, I felt more regulated. When people were looking within, I felt room as a leader to look within rather than perform.

For many years I began every event I led with a meditation

49

so the participants' eyes were closed and I could try to regulate. I tried to bypass my fear and manipulate myself into being courageous. Each time, when people would open their eyes and look to me as a teacher, I would tremble, my mind would go blank, and when I tried to talk, I would stutter. As a pleaser, my conditioned self was overwhelmed by not knowing how to get a room full of people to like me.

Rejecting my fear proved ineffective, as did manipulating the situation by having people close their eyes. Eventually, I decided to practice experiencing my fear with a room full of workshop participants looking to me to teach them what they came to learn. One evening, I was leading a couple's workshop to a large group of people. As I sat in my chair and looked at the room full of people, I took a deep breath and scanned my body with my inner eye. I was frightened and frozen.

"I'm feeling really nervous, so I want to take a moment to breathe and let the nervousness move," I said as I shook my arms and sighed with my exhale. Everyone watched as I felt afraid, and my conditioned self became even more afraid of being judged as incompetent. As my fear amplified, I tried to speed up to make it move more quickly. When that didn't work, I just started talking with a tremble in my throat.

Over time, I learned how to stay in contact with my body, my fear, and my Self. Making room for the full range of my experience, I welcome my fear with gratitude. Knowing that my conditioned self is looking for potential threats to my safety, I bring love and acceptance to my fear. Before I lead any lecture or workshop, I fully go into the experience of fear. I close my eyes, I tremble, and I say, "I'm so scared. I'm scared I'm not enough. I'm scared they're not going to like me. I'm so scared I want to just disappear." I tremble and give voice to my fear and I fully contact the felt sense of my experience.

As I turn toward myself and say, "I see that you're scared," I offer love and acceptance to the fear. This helps to integrate my felt experience, which allows me to be more solidly seated in myself. Then when I arrive in front of the room full of people, I stay in contact with myself as I begin to contact them. With my present moment awareness, I notice how my body feels in the presence of this particular group of beings.

"Being here with you all right now, I notice that I'm feeling (*whatever sensation I feel in my body as I am speaking*)." Then I ask others to share their felt sense, too. As we go around the room and I hear how other people are feeling in their bodies, my system settles more and more. As my system settles, my True Self feels free to take up space and I sit more solidly in my seat of power.

Exercise: Encompassing Multitudes

In this exercise you will build on the last two exercises where you identified your conditioned self and then anchored into a cellular memory of being in an expanded flow state. As you begin to identify with the True Self of who you really are, integrating the fragmented aspects of your humanity is essential to healing. We do not want to bypass pain with spiritual notions. We want to bring the loving awareness of the True Self deeper into all aspects of our humanity.

For now, choose one conditioned value or way of being that you are ready to transform and integrate. Look back at your list and choose the most prevalent theme of your conditioned self. Now, imagine what this aspect of your inner world looks like energetically. If this aspect was represented visually, what would it look like? Maybe it's a blob, or it's frail, or it might be giant and angry. Maybe it looks like you, or your parent, or darkness.

Sketch a visual representation of this aspect of your conditioning and give it a name. It could be a person's name or it can be a name like a label (i.e., "Mortimer" or "Sadness"). All that matters is that the name has a resonance with the energetic expression of this conditioned aspect of yourself.

Now look at your drawing, and really see how this aspect of yourself is feeling and validate it. "It makes sense to me that you feel (fill in emotion). I see you. I see that you feel (emotion), and I love you."

Now you're tapping into your True Self, bringing loving awareness to this aspect of your conditioned self. Keep loving this aspect as you breathe into your heart. And then ask it what it needs from you.

Shifting your relationship with your conditioning from one of being unconsciously driven by it to one of being in conscious, loving relationship with it is what allows for integration to transpire.

Walkaway with Wisdom

Our attention guides our identity. When we keep our attention seated on the incessant thoughts of the conditioned self, our identity is wrapped up in conditioned ideas. If we shift our attention to our True Self, our identity is seated in our essence. If we build the capacity to encompass our wholeness with our attention, we are able to integrate the fragmented aspects of ourselves.

The more integrated we become, the more our wholeness becomes our identity. Learning to access our felt sense is key in our own integration—this is where we contact our inherent wisdom.

As you walk through your day, stay in contact with your felt sense:

Ask yourself, "What is my experience of myself right now?"
Notice the sensations in your body.
Ask yourself, "How do I want to be with myself right now?"
Breath, move, and vocalize in the way your body is wanting.

Chapter 4

The Emerging Self

The conditioned self develops in childhood, and thus it is fairly unchangeable. The True Self is untouched by experiences of life, and thus is always present. The integrated self occurs from deep healing and self-development, encompassing all of who we are. The emerging self is constantly evolving as we step more fully into who we really are and includes future versions of ourselves.

Life force energy is not stagnant, it's generative. The energy of life is continually creating, discovering, and evolving.

When we step out of our box of conditioning and metabolize the past, we free up our life force energy to once again become generative. As children express this boundless vitality, so can we. Once we stop suppressing and fighting against our own inner constructs, our integrated self has room for life to move through us in the way we were originally designed to develop.

Like our life force energy, our developing sense of self is generative. In every encounter we have, we are developing our sense of self. And the more new experiences we have, the more we grow our capacity to develop more range for our sense of self. When we express ourselves differently with a loved one, trying something our conditioned self would never try, our developing sense of self emerges within that interaction.

For example, when I teach to one class of students, my developing sense of self is influenced by the combined energy of those particular students. I experience myself differently when I'm with them than I did before I met them. If I then go and sit in on another class and take the seat of student, my developing sense of self feels completely different.

We are part of the field around us. The field is not separate from us. We both influence and are influenced by the field, and the emergence of what transpires is seated in the energetic vibration of all the people present, even those who are silent. Every situation we step into becomes a new opportunity for our developing sense of self to emerge even more.

Life Urge

We all have within us both a life urge and a death urge. To fully embody our essence requires us to be more in our life urge than our death urge.

When we are following the habitual patterns of our conditioned self, we contain and distort our life force energy, this feeds our death urge. Our death urge includes any behavior that keeps us disembodied and less expressed in the world. Shallow breathing, withholding our authentic truth, or staying at a job we don't like are some examples of how our death urge could manifest. Staying in an unhealthy relationship, smoking cigarettes, drinking alcohol regularly, suppressive medication, eating mostly processed foods, large amounts of screen time, and anything else that has us feeling low vitality, insignificant, or dims the light of consciousness supports our death urge.

Unconsciously, we think we need to die to get back to Source. The death urge is seated in the belief that we were abandoned by God simply by being born into this life. And the more we indulge the behaviors of the death urge, the more this belief seems true. We dim our own light and keep ourselves from experiencing the true glory of being embodied.

Our Life urge is ignited by consciously bringing more divine energy into this dimension through our presence here on the planet. Our life urge includes any behavior that has us feel more embodied, clear, and alive. Sharing our vulnerable truth, speaking in front of a large audience or choosing work we feel passionate about are all ways our life urge could be expressed. We can nudge our life force with high quality food, breathwork, clean relationships, time in nature, plant medicine, homeopathy, dance, and anything else that brings the quality of vitality into our being.

When we are in our life urge, we can discover meaningful ways to be with ourselves that are also beneficial to the world. Becoming more fully expressed, we discover aspects of ourselves that we always knew were within us but hadn't yet revealed to the world. Our creativity shines through us. Inspiration flows. When we make a mistake or stumble on our journey, we open to learn and grow from the experience. Continually in our evolving sense of self, we're willing to feel the full range of our emotions and allow them to move through us.

Emerging in Relationships

Deepening our contact with our Self, as we emerge, we stay seated in our source of love and our source of power. We're able to hold ourselves in our experience while also staying curious to another person's contrary experience. We can see the thread of truth in all perspectives while also holding our own perspective with dignity.

The developing sense of self can be influenced in numerous ways as we interact with other people. For example, if I am with my children and I feel playful and happy, my developing sense of self includes my inner child. My life urge flows freely, and my uninhibited expression feels more alive and free.

Later that same day, if I encounter someone at the grocery store who is yelling at me and projecting their pain onto me, my developing sense of self has a completely different quality. Depending on how I respond to the situation, my sense of self will vary. If my conditioned self moves to the forefront and I judge, shame, or match the vibration of pain, I will likely leave the situation feeling small and powerless. If I stay in contact with myself and let myself feel the shock of being yelled at, I might stay in contact with my Self and extend compassion while honoring my boundaries, leaving me feeling aligned and solid in myself.

The words we choose and the actions we take matter less than the place within us from which we speak and move. The movement of the conditioned self is limiting and disruptive to contact. The movement of the emerging self is fluid and invites contact. Boundaries are an important part of contact, which we will discuss further later in the book.

Where the conditioned self is utilized because of the illusion of control the unconscious mind gets from indulging it, the emerging self leads the way because the essence of life is about contact and breath and freedom.

For example, if say "I love you" from my conditioned self, the words I speak hold a certain vibration that is more conditional and manipulative. They land in the other person as obligatory and needy. If I say the same words from my emerging sense of self, "I love you" resonates with the vibration of Source within the person who receives the words.

Emerging more fully into the True Self, the false self that we developed in our childhood simply becomes a map to use to find our way home to ourselves. Knowing our own values, desires, beliefs and essence, while still acknowledging the interconnectedness of life, we grow into the version of ourselves that we have always been intended to be. We become a reflection of the Source of all life, and that reflection is mirrored outside of us in our relationships and in planetary restoration.

Harmony's Story

I was overweight throughout most of my childhood. The head trauma I endured along with my early exposure to cannabis caused me to become dissociated and detached from my body. My mom was overweight, and overeating was an expected way of dining in my home.

I was depressed as an adolescent and young adult, self-medicating with cannabis, alcohol, nicotine, and casual sex. I didn't try to do well in school, and I never did any afterschool activates that were life-affirming. My intimate relationships were abusive, and I thought I deserved to be treated poorly. Since I believed that I was unlovable, I quieted my voice because I thought I didn't deserve to exist.

My death urge was so strong that all of my habits and ways of being were an unconscious attempt to kill myself and disappear. The suppression of my emotional pain suppressed my vital force. I was emotionally stunted and I was stuck. My growth, my well-being, my joy, and my intelligence were stalled in the fog of death urge behaviors.

Since the slow death just prolonged the pain, I seriously considered ending my life. When I was in college, I filled the bathtub in my apartment with water and placed a knife on the edge of the tub.

I lay down in the tub with my clothes on—I didn't want to be found naked. My vanity cared too much about my overweight body. I sunk down deeper into the water, and I took the knife to my wrist. I sat there, silently suffering, wishing I had the will to take my own life.

After about 10 minutes, I drained the tub and put the knife down. Soaking wet, I sat hunched over trying to figure out how to get out of the prison of my pain.

This rock bottom changed me. I immediately stopped all of my destructive behaviors: no more alcohol, drugs, abusive relationships, or playing small. I started eating healthily, exercising, applying myself to my studies. I started practicing yoga, and I reignited my meditation practice. I gave away my television, and I started teaching yoga and meditation. All of my attention was given to life-affirming behaviors.

One day, when I was finished teaching a yoga class, all of the participants had left and I was overcome with emotional pain. Alone in the studio, I lay on the cold wood floor of the yoga room and sobbed. "Why?" I screamed, "Why do I still hurt so badly? When will this pain ever go away?"

I cried for at least an hour, and then I peeled myself up off the floor and drove home. When I got home, I sat in meditation. I turned towards myself and sat with my pain. I became curious about my pain. I felt it in my body. I breathed around it with total acceptance, and that's when I saw my own light.

Bright, warm, and soothing, my light shined on every cell of my body. My life urge nudged my vital force to grow, and putting my attention on it nurtured its presence within me. Wisdom began to flow from the depths of my soul, and I cried in gratitude for the presence of this light.

Emerging and becoming, when I stopped killing parts of myself, I began to embody the True Self.

Exercise: Ignite Your Becoming

As you continue on your path of transformation, you are continually becoming more and more of who you really are. There is no destination to reach, no stagnant way that expresses your integrated self. There is no script for the True Self, and when you fully embody who you really are you are fully alive. And since it is our breath that keeps us in our body, that keeps us in our life urge, to stay in your emergent sense of self, the breath is the energy that precedes this experience.

This practice is called 20 Connected Breaths, and it comes from the lineage of breathwork called Kiyra Yoga Breathwork, first brought to the United States from India by Leonard Orr (1988). To do this practice, make sure you are sitting down and free of distractions. You'll breathe in and out of your nose only—if your nose is stuffed, you can breathe in and out of your mouth, but do not go back and forth between your nose and mouth. This is what makes it a "connected" breath.

To begin, take three long inhales through your nose like you're sniffing a flower. Really pull the breath in. Then when you exhale, completely drop the breath like you're dropping a pencil—not pushing it out, just surrendering it from your lungs out of your nose.

Now take 4 short breaths just like that—inhaling like you're sniffing a flower, exhaling like you're dropping a pencil.

Then take one long breath.

Repeat 5 times, making it 20 connected breaths. Breathing in 4 short breaths and one long.

When you're done, simply breathe naturally and notice what it feels like to intentionally pull new life, new energy, new breath into your body while completely surrendering on the exhale.

Walkaway with Wisdom

We all have a life urge and a death urge. In our death urge, we engage in behaviors that keep us dissociated and we limit our expression as we play small. Unconsciously, we think we need to die to get back to Source, which keeps our death urge behaviors in place. In our life urge, we embody Source here in this dimension. We engage in life afforming behaviors, we speak our truth, and we nurture our evolution as we are becoming.

When we are able to get our life urge higher than our death urge, the inertia of our life urge supports our emerging sense of self. When we are in relationships with others, it's important that we learn to embody our True Self. If we don't, there is a tendency to kill parts of ourselves in an attempt to keep the relationship. Being in our full expression as we emerge more fully into who we really are, we can embody our full potential.

Part 2:

Finding Our Alignment

Chapter 5

The Shadow

When we read all of the self-help books, try to speak our truth, and put effort into finding our connection with our True Self yet nothing seems to work, we are likely moving from a place that is out of alignment with the core of who we are. It can take a clean mirror of human reflection for us to see when we're out of alignment. This is because the familiarity of being off center requires contrast for us to see ourselves more clearly.

"I'm trying everything and I still feel like this" or "I spoke my truth and it didn't change anything" are common complaints from people who are attempting to create a new way but are still embodying the old way.

When we sit in the presence of someone who maps out the way we leave our alignment in real time, our awareness increases to the degree that we can see ourselves more clearly. This degree of awareness is needed to find our way back to the midline of our being so that we can move from our core.

Before we explore the experience of being in alignment, we must first discover with rigorous honesty how we move when we are out of alignment. When we map out the way our conditioned self navigates the world, we are looking at the light side of our personality, our mask that we present to the public world. To fully know the way we leave our alignment, we must also do shadow work, where we look at the darker side of our personality.

Disowned Parts

When we are identified with our conditioned self, that mask casts a shadow on the parts of us that we disown. In childhood, we repress or hide aspects of ourselves that the field around us claims to be unacceptable. We push these unacceptable parts down into the unconscious mind, and we actively try to rid ourselves of them when they bubble to the surface. If we grew up in a home where anger was unexpressed, resentment and rage live in the shadow. If sexuality was shamed or misused, a healthy expression of sexuality wasn't permitted and so the darker expression lives in the shadow. If we didn't have space to express our needs and wants, our access to our desire is hidden in the shadow.

Any and all aspects of ourselves that we were told, either explicitly or covertly, were not a welcome part of ourselves, we repressed in order to fit into our family system. Although hidden or only acknowledged in private, our shadow drives our deep unconscious motives, thoughts, urges, and emotional state of being all throughout our life. The nature of the shadow is that it is hard to see. It exists in our blind spots and guides us from a mysterious position of darkness.

We've disowned these aspects of ourselves for so long we can no longer recognize them as a part of us. Any aspect of our inner world that we are not fully ready to look at and experience sits in the shadow of our awareness like sediment at the bottom of a pond. This sediment gets stirred up in certain relational dynamics, events, or situations where we don't "seem" like ourselves.

"I'm not usually an angry person," one might say when they've just discharged an aspect of their shadow.

Any emotion, thought, or memory left unexplored and disowned in the recesses of our unconscious mind will come out sideways in dysfunctional and misguided ways. There are some common ways that rejected and repressed aspects of our inner world can be expressed in relationships:

- Disowned desire can be expressed as manipulation, criticism, control, betrayal, or resentment.
- Disowned fear can be expressed as control, jealousy, anger, deceit, indecision, or greed.

- Disowned anger can be expressed as rage, blame, volatility, helplessness, or collapse.
- Disowned grief can be expressed as depression, desperation, brooding, coldness, guilt, or hysteria.
- Disowned power can be expressed as betrayal, deceit, seduction, or victimhood.

Even joy disowned may be expressed as mania; and love disowned can turn into obsession. Because the word shadow evokes a sense of darkness, it's common to think only the disowned ugly parts live there. And it's true that we as human beings tend to disown the parts that we would rather not have other people see, like manipulation, control, or sexual deviancy. However, we can also be shaped to disown goodness and functional parts, too. We disown love when our conditioned self loops on anger. We disown pleasure when our conditioned self loops on achievement. We disown receptivity and softness when our conditioned self loops on earning worth and caretaking.

- When the conditioned self loops on criticism, the disowned experience is desire.
- When the conditioned self loops on control, the disowned experience is fear.
- When the conditioned self loops on anger, the disowned experience is power or boundaries.
- When the conditioned self loops on blame or resentment, the disowned experience is self-awareness or hurt.
- When the conditioned self loops on achievement, the disowned experience is pleasure.
- When the conditioned self loops on indecision, the disowned experience is intuition and deeper knowing.
- When the conditioned self loops on self-judgment, the disowned experience is agency.

- When the conditioned self loops on criticism, the disowned experience is desire.
- When the conditioned self loops on judgment of others, the disowned experience is insecurity.
- When the conditioned self loops on getting one's needs met, the disowned experience is love.

Looking within and being open to the reflection of the way others see us, we can be curious about the shadow our mask casts on our darker truths. If shadow work is new to us, making guesses about what we keep hidden in our shadow is the beginning of claiming what we were never given the space to claim.

The Role of Shame

When our caregiver in childhood is unable to meet our needs, we create a narrative where we are responsible for our caregiver's actions. This happens at an unconscious level to serve us in finding a point of empowerment in a situation that is beyond our control. Shame begins to grow, causing us to reject the qualities we believe caused our caregiver to treat us the way they did. We believe that if we didn't have certain qualities, we would receive unconditional love. This shame causes an internal split in our identity.

As the conditioned self develops, the egoic self, which holds the messages that dictate the voice inside our head, is shaped with the aspects that we feel good about. The ego is interested in those aspects that earn us acceptance and approval. Any part of our human experience that we believe makes us unworthy of love or connection, we reject and keep it in the shadow.

Our ego-based identifications produce the mask of our personality that we show the world. Our shadow-based identifications drive our unconscious impulses, behaviors, and emotional expressions. Where our ego is the driving force of our personality, shame is the driving force of self-rejection.

Feeling shame causes us to disown aspects of our inner world because we don't fully understand that all of our feelings are valid. We push unacceptable feelings aside, rejecting our authentic expression. As we create an identity around what is acceptable, we are learning to manipulate ourselves and the environment to try to earn love. The payoff of this split might be a sense of acceptance, but the cost is the interruption of our own life force energy.

Because our shadow is seated in shame, it is common to feel shame about having a shadow. We are not "bad" for having a shadow. It is a protective design of the psyche that allows us to find a sense of safety and belonging. However, continuing to disown aspects of ourselves gives our power over to shame. By ignoring what lurks in our own shadow, we deny important truths about ourselves.

If we stay more committed to fitting in then honoring the full truth of who we are, eventually our shadow will come out in a destructive way. We cannot see the darkest aspects of our personality because they are out of sight—until they're not. Once activated, the disowned shadow can take over and cause us to act in ways that are antithetical to our conditioned values and beliefs. When this happens, we can see the way our shadow contributes to the distortion of our life force energy.

If shame is the reason we rejected aspects of ourselves, why do we continue to disown our shadow as adults? We continue to hide and disown these aspects of ourselves for several reasons: 1) we have never had an example of a healthy, integrated adult, 2) we're scared of them because they are so intense, 3) we aren't ready to feel them or look at them, 4) we can't see them because they are in our blind spots, 5) we were blatantly told that these thoughts, feelings, and behaviors were not acceptable and/or 6) we haven't yet learned how to validate our own feelings.

Some people fully embody their shadow and create an identity around their darkness. In doing so, they disown the aspects of themselves that would be seen as acceptable to society. This typically occurs as a reaction against the norm, as an attempt to be different or special. The work is similar, though, in that there is something that needs to be claimed in order to be fully integrated and orient toward wholeness.

Making contact with our deepest darkest shadow, we touch the place within us that we feel the most shame about. We think that if we allow our shadow to be seen, we will be viewed as bad or unworthy of love. In this way, it makes sense that we reject this part of ourselves. However, continuing to disown any aspect of ourselves keeps us stuck in the unfinished business of the past.

Trying to be someone who is acceptable rather than someone who is authentic and real and true is painful. We allow shame to keep us locked in a cage of conditioned beliefs and limit our true expression. Owning our shadow is vulnerable. Trying to protect ourselves from rejection and annihilation is a young strategy that prevents us from opening to the possibilities that emerge when we are in alignment with our truest expression.

Projective Identification

When we ignore our own inner experience, we reject our feelings and will eventually sabotage our relationships. We see ourselves through our relationships, and the way we treat others is an expression of what is happening within us. When our shadow drives our interactions in relationships, we communicate our disowned feelings through the subliminal language of *projective identification*, where we unconsciously induce what we are unwilling to feel within ourselves in those around us (Ogden, 1977). These subliminal triggers occur when we don't have the inner awareness, ability, or maturity to give voice to our inner experience.

Projective identification is the main behavioral language of children who are not given the space to be in their authentic expression. For example, when a child feels powerless, like they don't have choice, they dig their heels in and refuse to be obedient. As they do this, they are subliminally inducing the feeling of powerlessness into their caretaker. Because the parent is attempting to control the child, the child's power lives in the shadow. The induction of the feeling of powerlessness into the parent gives the child a sense of power.

All humans communicate their shadow subliminally through projective identification in relationship. For example, if I feel hurt in a relational interaction and I keep my pain in my shadow, I am doing this because as a child I felt shame for being "too sensitive." My ego-based identification created an identity around being okay with everything, and my shame-based identifications told me to hide my pain. By disowning my hurt, I will subliminally induce my hurt in the person I am in relationship with. Rather than simply saying, "I feel hurt," I treat them in a way I know will cause them hurt in an unconscious, shadowy attempt to communicate my deeper truth.

We find ourselves behaving in ways that are unconsciously designed to evoke our feelings in the person we are relating with. When the shadow takes over, a person might say, "That's not me. I would never do something like that. I don't even recognize myself." However, the shadow always finds a way to express itself.

When we put our attention on the way someone else seems and what they did (i.e., trying to point out their shadow), we are inevitably keeping our own feelings, behavior, desire, and truth in the shadow. When we don't actively look within ourselves to see what is causing us to relate to the world in a certain way, we leave ourselves by being indignant about other people's blind-spots. It is in these moments when we induce our shadow into others or search for the expression of their shadow that we are called to look within and to the hard work of claiming that which we have worked so hard to disown.

Claiming Our Shadow

Disowning the parts of ourselves that we believe are unacceptable is what gives these aspects power over us. Claiming them is what gives us power over them. In bringing our shadow to the awareness field, we can integrate our darkness in such a way that we feel more whole and aligned.

If our shadow is in our blind spots, it can be challenging to know what to claim. When we have a challenging time knowing what's in our shadow, we must look to the people in our life who we feel the most intense emotional reaction towards. Our children, our partner, our sibling, our parent, our boss, our coworker all hold the mirror for us to see ourselves more clearly. Any activation of a disowned emotion that is ignited in a connection with another is bringing our shadow to the surface so we can see it more clearly.

There are several clues as to what lurks in our shadow:

When something irritates us about someone else, they are likely an expression of a part of us that we reject.

When we get angry at the people closest to us—our partner, children, parents, boss—our shadow is likely being ignited in relationship with them.

When we feel insecure around certain people, we have an opportunity to see where our shadow lives in that insecurity.

When we judge other people, the thing we judge about them is likely also in our shadow.

When we have intrusive thoughts, our shadow is trying to be seen.

When we have nightmares, something we have repressed is trying to be integrated.

When we have insomnia, something that we have rejected is trying to be seen.

When someone says something about us that we are convinced is not true, we might be avoiding our shadow.

When we are trying to convince someone of their own

shadow, we might be pointing to something in them that also lives in us.

When we want someone to be different, we are likely avoiding something in our shadow that we don't like feeling.

When we claim our shadow, we become less shadowy. For example, if I were to claim that I was trying to manipulate someone or control them, I instantly become less manipulative and less controlling. Owning the shadow takes the charge away from it, and all of the people in our lives can feel the difference.

Owning our shadow is an act of individuating from our past. We become more empowered and more integrated when we claim the parts of us that shame caused us to reject. Invigorated by the integrity of being congruent, our vitality can move through our system with more ease when we claim our shadow. When we own our shadow, we embody an aspect of us that is essential to our wholeness, and in doing so we allow Source to move freely through us.

Harmony's Story

Early on in life, I rejected my pain, my truth, my desire, and my power. Hiding essential aspects of myself, I was conditioned to believe that other people were more important than myself. What I didn't realize was that by keeping parts of myself in the shadow I was manipulating the environment to try to get my needs met.

After the light of consciousness was ignited within me, I graduated college and went on a walkabout, where I gave myself time to discover what I wanted to do moving forward. As I explored my emerging self, I still wanted to find a person to love and live life with. Dating seemed to be the place where I hid my shadow the most, and it would always come out sideways in a destructive and harmful manner.

I felt tremendous shame about myself, and I thought that *being wanted* was more important than being in touch with what

I wanted. Since I was taking such good care of myself, my body was a healthy weight and I received a lot of attention from people who were attracted to me. In order to fulfill my ego, I would soak up the attention from who I was dating while hiding my truth about how I felt about them, what I wanted, or if I felt hurt by the way they treated me.

Scared to be hurt, rejected, or humiliated, I would lure suitors in with my manipulative and seductive ways, and once I knew they liked me I would tell them I wasn't interested in them. Because I was unwilling or unable to feel my own fear of rejection and not enoughness, I would induce that into them via projective identification. I would hurt them in the way I was afraid of being hurt. Unknowingly, I wanted them to feel my pain for me.

Because I could see the harm that I was causing and was unsure how to be less shadowy, I stopped dating all together for a couple of years. I wanted to learn how to be with myself in a way that would allow me to be with another in a kind, healthy way.

Exercise: Claim Your Darkness

While it can be challenging to claim the very thing you've been taught to disown, shadow work can be the most potent way to take your power back from your conditioned self.

For this exercise, think about the last time you felt intensely emotionally activated in relationship to something happening in your world. It can be something that happened with a person you know, it can be about something you read, it can be something you saw on television, or maybe it's something related to a comment someone posted on social media. There are many options, but choose one that had you feeling at a level 4 of being dysregulated (on a scale of 1–10, 10 being the most and 1 being the least).

Now, write a list of qualities that you were perceiving that had you feeling emotionally activated. Maybe the person you were interacting with seemed self-centered, self-righteous, or manipulative and deceitful.

Once your list is complete, consider where these qualities might exist in your own blind spots. Journal about the times when you were unconsciously moving from your shadow, and internally amend that place in you by considering what you could have done or said that was more true and honest and clean. Bringing the shadow to light makes it so that it no longer lurks in the deep unconscious motives.

The moment we claim that we have a shadowy tendency in the moment it arises is the very moment we become less shadowy.

Walkaway with Wisdom

When we are identified with our conditioned self, that mask casts a shadow on the parts of us that we disown. We hide aspects of ourselves that we feel shame about, and these aspects live in the unconscious and come out sideways in our relationships.

These are some of the most common aspects people disown: Disowned desire comes out as criticism or control; disowned anger comes out as resentment or blame; and disowned power comes out as victimhood or collapse.

When we suppress our experience and shove it into the shadow, we unconsciously induce our experience into those around us. If we feel hurt and hide that truth, we unconsciously try to cause hurt into others. When we feel scared and are unable to say that, we unconsciously try to scare those we are relating with.

The way to become less shadowy is to claim our darkness. Owning the aspects of ourselves that we have previously rejected, our relationship with our shadow shifts.

Chapter 6

Distorted Life Force

Subtle Energy Body

Within and around us, there is a seemingly invisible energy that is our life force. With five layers of energy around us, and seven main energy centers within us, our subtle energy body is a large part of our experience of ourselves and others (Dale, C., 2013). When we are born, the pure vibrational quality of our untainted life force moves through our subtle energy body like a perfectly tuned instrument. A flowing river of energy, we can feel the bliss of creation in our bodies when there are no obstructions to the channel that our vitality flows through.

As we are developing our conditioned self, our subtle energy body is affected. When the environment around us is unsafe and we create adaptive patterns to find safety, our subtle energy body begins to harden and distort. Like a finely crafted instrument that has been jostled and mistuned, the vibrations of our subtle energy body become mistuned by life and blockages in our energy centers form. These blocks hold the unprocessed emotional, physical, and psychological pain of our past and prevent the open channel of our energy from moving freely.

When we start to identify with our conditioned self and push our unacceptable shame-based aspects into our shadow, our subtle energy body contorts to fit the inauthentic expression of our life force. Similarly, the imprint we acquire of the distorted life force in people around us also causes our own subtle energy to harden and fragment. For example, if our caregiver holds the distorted vibration of victimhood, that vibration imprints to a degree into our system. We might react against that imprint or identify with it; however, the imprint is still there nonetheless. Like a twisted rope, our alignment with Source remains warped by the delusions we hold in our psyche.

Because painful life experiences cause the hardening of our energy body, the ego orients towards these hardened places within us and develops an identity around them. The ego does this in an attempt to keep us safe and alive, but the impact is the prolonging of our distorted life force. These wounds become the filters we see the world through, and all of our actions arise from this distortion.

Relating to the world from our distorted life force never feels satisfying. Even when we think we're doing all of the right things to create a better experience of life, the impact of our actions feels wonky. When we meet the world from our distortion, the thing we want the most never comes to be. Everything feels off center and unsettled because we are out of alignment from life itself, trying to influence life from this place creates more results that are out of alignment.

We all have access to feeling our own subtle energy movements. However, it can be hard to see something within ourselves that no one else has ever acknowledged. This is why the presence of an attuned therapist or healer can feel so affirming. To be witnessed for more than our conditioned self, our subtle energy body begins to be returned to its true vibration.

Not only do we all have the ability to attune to our subtle energy body, we all have the capacity to see other people's subtle self. Since most people focus on third-dimension tangible energy matter, we rarely speak to the subtle Self. And because we rarely talk about the subtle Self, we move through life ignoring the most authentic aspect of ourselves and others.

The subtle body tells us more about a person than their words. Children are very skilled at seeing the subtle, but since adults rarely talk to children about their subtle Self, we are conditioned to ignore this important aspect of who we are. As we learn to pay more attention to our own essence and life force, we learn to pay more attention to other people's subtle self.

Exploration: Attune to the Subtle Self

To develop the sensitivity to attune to subtle energy, we must quiet the mind and focus on the vast energy field around us. We are habituated to look at the physical realm, and it takes conscious intention to focus on the subtle realm.

For our own subtle energy, it can be easier to begin by feeling the subtle movements and shifts in the sensations of our bodies. Slowing down and looking within, we can practice noticing our experience of subtle energy body: the pace, the weight, the size, the density, and the fluidity. Let's take a moment to pause and notice the sensations in our body as well as the space around our body. Does our energy move up, down, or out? Do we feel expansive, contracted, or in between? Do we feel contained, open, lost, or something else? Simply noticing and tracking our own subtle self gives us a lot of information about ourselves and about what we need to come back to our alignment. With practice, we can ignite the current of our energy to flow in health and expansion.

For example, if we are feeling grief and sadness, we may feel energetically slow, heavy, and dense. If we can attune to the way our energy body holds our grief, we can contact our subtle self and mobilize the energy in a loving and self-supportive way.

To attune to other people's subtle energy, we must practice cultivating the sensitivities of our metaphysical eyes as well as the feedback we feel in our own bodies in the other person's presence. When we have a baseline of what we feel like separate from another person, we can feel how our subtle energy is affected in their presence. Learning to differentiate from our own subtle energy movement when we are around others and our sensitivity to other people's energy takes a lot of practice, especially if we are an empath or highly sensitive person. The more anchored we become in our own alignment, the more obvious it becomes if what we are feeling is ours or someone else's.

Slowing down and feeling into our own bodies, we can use our metaphysical eyes to observe how the other person's energy body appears through our lens. It's important that we do not hold ourselves as the expert of the other person's energy, we are simply a witness and mirror. Holding our perception loosely and checking out what we are seeing/ sensing is the way to honor another person's agency. As we open our ability to see subtle energy in others, we can notice the pace, the weight, the size, the density, and the fluidity of their energy body. Do they seem sped up, expansive, contained, or something else?

One of the best ways to cultivate our own ability to see subtle energy is naming what we're seeing and then asking if the other person is experiencing that. For example, "You seem expansive and light right now. Does that fit for you?" or "You seem closed off and down. I'm wondering if that's true." The more attuned we become to tracking subtle energy, the more skilled we become and seeing the nuances of where a person's energy is blocked, contracted, open, or expansive.

The Line of Distortion

The stress and trauma that occur during misattunement, neglect, and abuse caused a split or fracture in our developing sense of self. In these experiences where fragmentations occur, we polarize between our ego and our shadow. The identification with our ego gives us a sense of having control and belonging in the world, and it drives the mask of our conditioned self.

In contrast, the identification with our shame forms our shadow, and we reject any part of our inner experience that we think might cause others to reject us. We developed these because somehow we felt responsible for what was happening, and unconsciously we decided that if we were different, our caregivers would show up for us differently.

The split between these two constructs, our conditioned self (which includes our ego) and our shadow (which includes our shame), cause our life force energy to come off balance, making the "Line of Distortion."

We can think of our distortion as a collection of conditioned ideas and values that live in our personality in the forefront of our mind, so forthcoming that we identify with them and believe that we are them. Within our conditioned self, we have subpersonalities that are functional constructs we use to navigate our environment, certain ways we present ourselves and think about ourselves.

From the conditioned self, there is an energetic line down to our shadow where anything unacceptable lives. Within our shadow exists repressed memories, unconscious drives and impulses, as well as unprocessed and unacceptable emotions.

For example, if my conditioned self says that I need to give other people what they want so that I can earn love, my desires stay seated in my shadow. This means that I move from my distortion when I relate from my conditioned mask of trying to earn love, which is polarized against disowned desire. The shame that causes this distortion is the belief that I'm not lovable, and the ego identification that reinforces it has me feeling prideful that I can give others what they want. This becomes a well-worn path, and it causes my relationships to be built on a distorted foundation of incongruence and inauthenticity.

The image below illustrates the line of distortion created by distorted life force energy. The person in the image thinks and acts from their conditioned self. They are identified with their personality, roles, and misbeliefs, and they are consciously and unconsciously disowning aspects of their inner world.

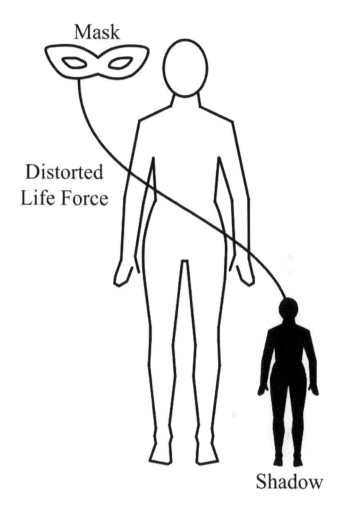

Mask

Distorted
Life Force

Shadow

The inner divisiveness we experience with two polarizing inner constructs working against one another causes us to feel off center. Out of alignment with the True Self, what we see, what we say, and what we do is filtered through our distortion. Twisting our perception of objective reality, the line of distortion warps our reality to fit the template of our wounding. When we are identified with this warped reality, we collect evidence to affirm our distorted perspectives. The way we experience ourselves and the world affirms our wounding and ultimately keep us cycling in outdated relationship dynamics.

Our distortion is the effect of our energy body and our inherent wholeness being mistuned or altered by the painful and chronic interactions we had with those closest to us in childhood. It is not the expression that we are meant to embody. It is the expression that we endure when we don't know how to make our way back to our essential self.

Most people live from their distortion, even those with very little trauma in their history. It takes very conscious parents who embody their wholeness to parent to their child's truest self. To engage with a child in a way that fully supports their emerging essential self and not react in ways that imprint projections and emotions onto them is nearly impossible. The level of God consciousness needed to be this type of parent is extremely high and unique.

The Polarity of Distortion

Rejecting any aspect of ourselves causes us to polarize against it, and we inevitably fall out of balance. For example, if we believe that it's selfish to ask something of another person, we disown our desire. When we reject what we want, we defer to other people's desire and give our will away to them. Although we have desire hidden in our shadow, we interact with others through our conditioned mask of being accommodating. Polarized between our shadow and our mask, this distortion perpetuates an inner discord and divisiveness.

If we think that anger is an unacceptable emotion, we disown our need for boundaries and change. Instead, we stay identified with our conditioned mask of being a victim to others and we hold onto blame and resentment. Anger stays in the shadow, resentment moves to the forefront of our awareness, polarized against one another and keeping us off balance.

If we believe that we need to play small in order to belong, we disown our power. When power lives in the shadow, we present a conditioned mask of needing other people's power to provide us with our worth. We might misuse our power, overpower others, or try to control our environment when we reject our own power. Our own power is polarized against our own conditioned ways of playing small, perpetuating our distorted patterns.

If we believe our voice doesn't matter, we disown our truth. When we hide our truth, we are being deceitful and manipulative. Our own truth is polarized against our own conditioned ways of being manipulative to get what we think we want.

If we believe that we are not enough, we disown our worth. When our worth lives in the shadow, we present a mask to the world of being "together" or superior. Polarized against our own fear of not enoughness, we try to find our worth by thinking and acting in inauthentic ways.

Any polarity distortions can be experienced as their opposite. For example, if we think that what we want matters more than others, we disown the part of us that is accommodating, and so on. How a polarity is expressed through our own distorted life force is unique to our own internal constructs.

Our polarity distortion occurs when our pride and shame are in conflict with one another. Any belief that gives us a sense of control lives in the ego, and any belief that gives us a sense of humiliation lives in the shadow.

We tend to prefer ego identifications because they seem to keep us functional, and we tend to dislike the shadow identifications because they feel dreadful to experience. Nonetheless, the inner polarity perpetuates our distortion and keeps us off center.

When we keep our essential self hidden beneath the distorted behavior of our patterned way of being in the world, we keep ourselves feeling small and looping in familiar yet outdated constructs. Interacting with the world from the line of distortion, life feels hard and painful. Any attempts we have to change ourselves from our distortion are futile if they don't include working with our polarity distortion.

Examples of common polarities:

- If we believe that asking for what we want is selfish, we disown our desire. When we reject what we want, we defer to other people's desire, giving our will away. Although we have desire hidden in our shadow, we interact with others from our mask of being accommodating and pleasing. This polarity perpetuates our inner discord and can create conflict in our relationships.
- If we believe anger is an unacceptable emotion, we disown our need for boundaries and/or change. Instead of creating clean boundaries or being in right use of power, we hold onto our conditioned mask of being a victim, holding onto blame and resentment. Anger stays in the shadow while victim moves to the forefront of our awareness, polarized against one another and keeping us off balance.
- If we believe that we need to play small in order to belong, we disown our power. When power lives in the shadow, we present a conditioned mask of needing other people's power to provide us with our worth and sense of belonging. We might try to power over others through control, or we might collapse around our power with manipulation. Our own power is polarized against our conditioned pattern of being inconsequential, causing our own life force to distort.
- If we believe that our voice doesn't matter, we disown our truth. When we hide our truth, we are being manipulative and deceitful. Our truth stays hidden in the shadow while our conditioned mask makes other people more important than ourselves. This common polarity creates a cyclical split between our own sense of worth and our desire to be loved.

- If we believe we are not enough, we disown our worth. When worth lives in the shadow, our conditioning tries to present a mask of being perfect. Polarized against our own fear of not enoughness, we try to find our sense of belonging by acting and thinking in inauthentic ways. In this polarity, it is common to want to know we are wanted, while simultaneously being scared of intimacy and connection.

Working with Polarities

To retune our energy body and undo our distorted life force, we need to embody the polarity between ego identifications and shadow identifications. We can move the energy of our distortion when we fully go into the split of the opposing energies.

Instead of working against one another, we can make deep contact with each aspect, taking the shape of the mask and the shadow. As we do this, we move back and forth between the polarization of our conditioned self and our shadow. We take the physical shape of our ego (for example, using our hands to show what control looks like). Then we take the shape of its opposite (for example, going into our body to take the shape of chaos or helplessness).

Mobilizing the polarity by going back and forth, using our words to say what we are embodying. "I have control over everything. I keep everything in its place," we say as we show that control with our hands. Then we move to its opposite and say, "Everything is chaos. I am helpless and have no control over anything," as we show that chaos and helplessness with our body. First we move back and forth quickly, and then we slow down and really contact each aspect of the polarity. Breathing and feeling into where the midline between the two might be. We sense into the shape of the space between the opposition and discover where trust lives within us.

It's important that we feel our way back to the midline and not think our way back here. The somatic intelligence of these movements offers more opportunity to move the pattern than analyzing ourselves.

There is an exercise below to guide us through this, and it's good practice to move these polarities any time we feel off balance. Looping in not enoughness, trying to make the shame go away, we can learn how to go into our experience fully, as well as its opposite. From the back and forth movement, we can find the midline, the place where we are in balance.

Embodying our polarities is what empowers us to stop following the impulses of our conditioned self. By contacting the familiar mental patterns in our bodies, we allow all of the shadow motives and urges to bubble up to the surface, which is extremely uncomfortable. It is exactly this level of discomfort that we need to get familiar with if we are to truly evolve and transform. Touching the places within that lurk in the shadow, we move the energy of the distortion and metabolize our unfinished business.

Harmony's Story

Ever since I was 6 years old and heard the voice of the True Self for the first time, I have been able to see subtle energy. As a child, I would choose a crystal and place it on a person's heart if I could see they were holding murky energy there.

As I opened up more fully to embody the True Self, I began to use the subtle energy cues that I was seeing in my clients in service of their healing and integration. As I began to trust my metaphysical eyes more, I learned that people love to be seen for more than their body. "How do you do that?" is a question my clients and students frequently ask.

Because in childhood we only know that we exist because we are seen, when we're not seen for our subtle energy, we think that part of us doesn't exist, even if we feel and know it ourselves. On my own healing journey, I sat across from a shaman who could see me with intensity and clarity. As he looked at me, I could see my own line of distortion. "What are you doing?!" I exclaimed, "I feel so distorted and deformed."

He hadn't yet spoken a word and he was clearly surprised that I could see what he was seeing, "I'm just looking. I've never sat with someone who can see that though. How are you doing that?"

This transpersonal experience changed me. Once I saw my distortion I couldn't un-see it. And once I was looking at my own distortion, I could see it in others too. The use of the subtle energy body in psychotherapy sessions became amplified once I could see my clients' distortion. And the more I noticed the polarity between the mask and the shadow, I started working with polarities in a way that brought people back to their midline.

The more aligned I became, the more I was able to support my clients in coming back into their alignment.

Exercise: Embody the Polarity

Begin by identifying an inner polarity. To do this, first consider one aspect of yourself that you really want to be seen for and known for. Then consider its opposite, the thing you really don't want to be seen or known for. These are two completely divergent extremes, one that you really want and the other you really don't want.

For example, maybe you want to be seen as competent, and the polar opposite is that you really don't want to be seen as incompetent.

Common polarities:

Polarized between wanting to be loved and afraid of being unlovable.

Polarized between wanting to be successful and afraid of being a failure.

Polarized between wanting to be perfect and afraid we are hideous.

Polarized between wanting to change the world and wanting to disappear.

Polarized between feeling worthless and prideful.

Polarized between feeling dependent and inaccessible.

Polarized between acting like we have it all together and afraid that we'll crumble into nothingness.

Polarized between hating our body and wanting to be more embodied.

Polarized between wanting to fit in and wanting to feel free.

Just choose one polarity to work with for now.

Think of the aspect that you really want and embody what it looks like. Use your hands and move your body in a way that really shows this aspect. As you do, say it aloud (ex: "I really want to be competent and good at what I do and appreciated and seen for how competent I am."). Whatever the words are for you, keep repeating them as you continue to embody what this expression looks like.

After a few minutes of embodying what you do want, move your body into the opposite. Use your hands and movement to express what you really don't want and find the words to accompany it (ex: "I really, really don't want to fail and be incompetent and do it wrong."). Keep saying the words as you embody this aspect of the polarity.

Then move back to what you do want and use your body and your words to express what you do want. Then quickly move back to your body and words expressing what you don't want.

Go back and forth, eventually just using your body and not your words. Then slow down and feel the connection between the two polarities. Slow way down until you find the midline: the place where both of these energies meet and there is balance.

Walkaway with Wisdom

The subtle energy body lives within and around us. This seemingly invisible energy that is our life force gets mistuned by the painful experiences we have in life. Like a twisted rope, our alignment with Source becomes warped by the delusions we hold in our psyche.

Our distorted life force energy can be seen as a polarity between our conditioned self and our shadow. When we're out of balance from our alignment with Source, we get stuck in our polarity distortion.

Differentiating from our conditioned self and claiming our shadow helps to bring us closer to our alignment. Contacting each pole of our distortion and moving through them consciously can also help us find our alignment.

Chapter 7

The Core of Our Being

The birthplace of our distortion lives in the painful moments of the past where we needed to be a certain way to find safety and acceptance. In trying to be a certain way for others, the flow of our vital force was impeded. Energetic containment, contortion, hardening, and other subtle energy movements that are not congruent with our true nature created the distortion. Along with the subtle incongruence, our thoughts became distorted in an attempt to make sense of the distorted environment around us.

When our life force energy is altered from its natural flow, we experience an internal polarization where opposing energies within us keep us internally split. This inner polarity keeps us off center from the core of our being.

When our human condition is such that we are meeting the world from our distortion, we are off center from our midline and not fully embodied. Vertically, up the midline of the body, lives the core of our being. The boundless energy of life that runs through our body, up past the crown of our head and rooted down into our connection with the earth. This is the midline of our being and it is our home base within ourselves. It's the place in us that we can always return to and feel the authentic truth of our whole being.

Sometimes called the kundalini channel, the core of our being can be an open conduit for higher frequency energy to move through our body. There are energy centers up the midline called chakras. As we metabolize our unfinished business and shift the energy of our distortion, the energy centers of our chakras are cleared of the emotional energy pollution that they've been holding.

Even though we may leave our alignment, it never leaves us. Always present, this rod of energy aligns us with our Source of unconditional love and healing. All of the work we do to metabolize our pain, look at our shadow, and map out our conditioned self is in service of finding our way back to our essence and aligning with the True Self. As we differentiate from our conditioned self while simultaneously claiming our shadow, we are on the journey of coming back to ourselves.

Finding Our Alignment

On our way back to our alignment, we will contact layers of stored emotional and psychological pain. It is not possible to fully embody our essence and come back into full alignment without first touching the places in us that have been distorted. Contacting our pain and misbeliefs allows us to see them with more awareness and clarity. Awareness and clarity are what make it possible for us to untangle them from our life force.

The subtle ways that we leave our alignment provide us with the most information about how to come back. For example, tension in our throat might precede the hiding of our truth or quieting of our own voice. Restriction in our stomach might precede the collapse around our own boundaries. Attuning to our own subtle emotional energy, we can learn the story of the patterns of distortion in our bodies.

When we cannot see ourselves clearly and consciously, the way we are is simply the way we are; it's our experience of being alive. Having a clear witness holding space, mapping out the way we leave our alignment, helps us to see ourselves when our patterns are hidden. Without trying to fix or change anything about ourselves, we simple elevate our awareness about how our life force moves and where it becomes hooked in a distorted pattern.

Each time we contact our pain with consciousness and love, we offer our wounds love and attention. This love and attention is in itself healing as it comes from the higher frequency of our True Self.

Inviting the pain to move, we can untwist the distorted narratives that we've created about ourselves and the world. As mentioned earlier, we map out our conditioned patterns to such a degree that we can differentiate from them, no longer believing that our identity is seated in the way other people treated us in the past. We integrate our disowned parts as we move through our polarity distortion, and we surrender to the way in which our inner split pulls us off center by going into it more fully. As we do this, we keep inviting our life force to mobilize. We support and guide the current of our vital energy to move in health, and we ignite the untainted expression of Source to flow through us. At first this may happen just a little bit. The next time we move through a layer of our distortion, more vital energy of Source might move with greater flow. And each time we open the channel of our true life expression, the more we untwist our energy center and come more fully into alignment.

In the image below, we see a person who is aligned with Source and whose vitality is moving through their system with ease. Their subtle energy body is supple and full, and their energy centers are clear and open.

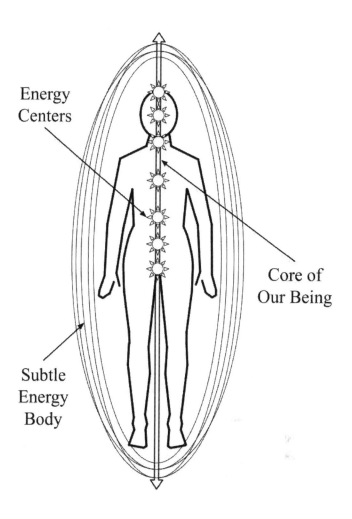

Energy Centers

Core of Our Being

Subtle Energy Body

When we find our alignment, we reconnect with our home base—aligned vertically up through the crown of the head and anchored down through the root to the earth. Solidly seated in ourselves, we maintain contact with the core of our being as we walk through life. When we come off center in a relational interaction, it becomes more obvious to us that we have left ourselves because we know what it feels like to be in ourselves.

The practice of moving through the layers of what gets ignited within us during an interaction is lifelong. And over time as we have more experiences where we are able to maintain contact with ourselves—seated in our bodies and aligned with Source—our life begins to change. When the way we interact with the environment is not a movement from our distorted life force energy, the world around us becomes less distorted. Moving from our alignment, the impact of our movements is more aligned. With our hearts and minds aligned, our will is an expression of Source through us.

Exercise: Opening Our Energy Centers

The energy that flows from Source comes into our body through the crown of our head when we open to receive that high vibrational energy. Bringing our awareness to the crown of our head with the intention of inviting the energy of Source into our human form is all that is needed to commence the opening of our energy centers.

Attention amplifies our alignment. Although our alignment is always there, when our attention is placed on our distorted thoughts and energy, our distortion is amplified. As we place our attention on the crown of our head, our attention amplifies the opening of our alignment with greater frequency. Our crown chakra, seated at the top of our head, is our bridge to the infinite. Beginning here, the vibration of Source can touch every energy center as we deepen into our alignment. As this energy comes more fully into our system, anything that is not of that frequency becomes more obvious.

Inviting life force energy from our crown to the space between our eyes, we can open and clear any blockages that provide access to our deeper knowing. The third eye is the seat of intuition. Often people furrow their brow here and block their intuition with worry and indecision. Bringing more presence and loving awareness into the space between our eyebrows, we can open to the infinite opportunities available to us when we are in flow with the universe. If this center is significantly blocked, we can take two fingers and gently place them on our third eye. Slowly and with great intention, we can move our fingers in a circular motion to open up more fully to our deeper wisdom.

From our third eye we invite the life force energy to flow into our throat. The throat is where many of us cap off our emotions, holding in our pain and quieting our voice. It is also where we prevent our system from receiving what is being offered to us if we don't feel safe. As we invite the presence and vibration of Source into our throat, we can open our throat and soften our jaw to move any energy that is blocking this energy center. Sometimes a vocalization can support the mobilization of the blockages. A tone or a scream can open the throat if it matches the tone of the vibration being held in the throat. If we choose to vocalize the tone of the blockage, it is helpful to stay with the sound for the entire duration of the exhale and to repeat this until the throat feels completely open. Opening our throat and continuing to clear our stored pain opens the energy centers that support deeper alignment.

From our throat we continue to invite the energy of Source down into our heart. Our wise, tender heart is the most vulnerable place within us. This is where we hold the purest love and compassion. As children, the purity of this love was easily accessible. When we experienced the pain that caused our attachment wounds, this openhearted purity became blocked off. To seat our attention in our heart while bringing in the pure essence of Source can activate a lot of stored sadness and grief. Letting ourselves feel that grief and allow the tears to flow will support the movement of all that our heart is holding. As this happens, we continue to invite in the presence of love. And we breathe.

From our heart down to our solar plexus, we continue to open the channel of the core of our being. The solar plexus is known for holding our sense of esteem; however, it also holds our polarities. When our life force energy remains distorted, we will feel this in our solar plexus. Like a tight band around our waist, the solar plexus gets the most twisted in its energy. By simply bringing more awareness and presence to the sensation in the solar plexus, we can wrap the twisted energy with pure love. Making more room for the solar plexus to release, breathing around the sensation, eventually we might find a softening or a surrender. As we do, continuing to breathe up through an open mouth with a soft jaw allows the channel of our alignment to flow more freely.

From our solar plexus down to our sacrum, we bring our attention to our center of creativity and sensuality. This is also where we experience our inner support and power. As we bring our attention to our sacrum, we might notice the ways in which we give our power away. We also might notice the ways in which we collapse around our own will and do not support ourselves. Continuing to breathe into our sacrum, we can gently engage our low belly to feel our power and inner support. Igniting our powerful energy in our body with the presence of Source guiding us, we can deepen into the embodiment of our sovereign self.

Lastly, from our sacrum down to our root, we can invite our soul to find its seat. Fully occupying our alignment, we land in our root, which holds our seat of safety and stability. Our root chakra lives at the base of our spine and can be felt in the area of our perineum, the pelvic floor.

Opening our root can feel vulnerable if we've experienced sexual violation and/or sexual shame. If we're unable to stay within our window of tolerance and regulate on our own, it is important to seek the support of a therapist who is well versed in trauma and somatic psychology. Any moment our emotions feel too big to experience, we need to slow down and orient to the space around us. Slowly looking at objects or colors around us can help us get present when we're flooded with emotions.

When we are contacting blockages in our root, it's important to slow down and contact what is being held in our energy body. Breathing love and compassion into this energy center, we can process and metabolize what is blocking the natural flow of our connection with the earth. Continuing to open our mouth and soften our jaw with the exhale, the open mouth exhale opens the root.

Continuing to breathe up and down the midline of the body, we open the flow of our alignment. We can move from side to side, remembering that the midline is fluid energy and not an actual rod.

There are 5 ways to move energy: 1) Awareness, 2) Breath, 3) Touch, 4) Movement, and 5) Tone/Vocalization. Using all 5 of these methods to open our energy centers supports the ongoing activation of our alignment.

Deepening our awareness around the way our physical body holds the subtle energy of our emotional and spiritual bodies, we can mobilize all of the subtle ways our energy has been distorted and open into deeper contact with the True Self. All of the layers of experience that we move through on our way to deeper contact with our alignment are welcome and valid. There is no enlightened state to achieve and maintain, only the continual devotion honoring the full expression of our lived experience as we continue to develop our sense of self as an emerging being.

Coming Back to Ourselves

It can be counterintuitive to mobilize our pain. Thinking that if we go into our pain we will amplify it, we develop suppressive techniques which prevent us from contacting lived experience. As we learn to mobilize and metabolize our old pain, we experience the fresh and light feeling of not holding in so much emotional energy pollution. Once we feel the goodness of being in alignment, it's common to want to stay there always. We might even be hard on ourselves when we slip into old patterns. Having grace for ourselves when we've left our alignment will certainly support the learning process of finding our way back to ourselves.

Our life force energy was mistuned in the past when our conditioned self was formed and when we experienced traumatic violations. When events occur that closely match the events that caused that original mistunement, we can become emotionally activated and come off center from the core of our being. Looking through the filter of our unfinished business, our perception of objective reality is distorted. As we see through a distorted filter, we create a distorted narrative about what just occurred that colludes with our unresolved pain.

For example, if we have a wound from a time when we were forgotten at school pickup as a child, this wound might filter our perception of how we see a situation when our partner is late coming home for dinner. The panic, anxiety, and uncertainty that we felt as a child wondering if our caregiver would ever arrive is ignited by these similar looking events. We might cry or have a panic attack as we wait to see if our partner has abandoned us. When they finally get home, we might express our pain in a disproportionate way to the actual events or contain our pain and try to hide it like we did as a child.

When we believe our distorted narrative, we either *express* the unresolved pain from the past onto the current situation or we try to *suppress* our reaction. This reaction is a reflection of our inner polarity distortion. Because we are not seeing the situation clearly (even if we are convinced that we are), we are unable to find the language of our True Self.

When we *express* our pain from our polarity distortion, we treat people and situations as we wish we could have when the original wound was created. We project our pain onto the person in front of us, and our expression is disproportionate to the actual current situation. Although the emotions are being felt, the unfinished business is not being metabolized because we are reinforcing our false, conditioned beliefs.

When we *suppress* our pain from this distortion, we tamp down our energy and contain our emotions. Our warped narrative stays hidden for the time being, yet we internally brood. Actively resisting or denying our own pain, *we also suppress our vital force*—we cannot pick and choose what we suppress. We cannot both suppress our energy and ignite our vital force at the same time. As we move away from our home base, we get entangled in our own warped thoughts and it can take time to find our way back to ourselves.

Because the misbeliefs and constructs we developed to protect ourselves from feeling hurt drive the energy of the distortion, it really takes tremendous awareness to not follow those patterns. Feeling unsafe in our body, our expressive and suppressive strategies are an attempt at keeping us safe. We learned to ignore our true experience and our powerful True Self.

We need to come back to our alignment with Source after a reactivated trauma response occurs by bringing loving awareness into our bodies. To come back to ourselves when we've come out of our alignment begins with a willingness to feel our emotions. Bringing our attention to the sensations in our bodies, we move away from the stories that our mind is looping in. As we experience our felt sense, we become more present with ourselves. Making contact with ourselves, we can wrap our pain with the love of Source. And as we care for our pain in this way, we can metabolize our emotions and continue to keep our energy centers clear with the techniques described above.

Slowing down, we can come back to our alignment.

The more experiences we have living from our alignment, the more we cultivate awareness of when we begin to come off balance. This awareness gives us a choice for how we want to be with ourselves in these moments, and over time we learn how to come back to ourselves with more ease and grace. The core of our being is always there within our bodies. When we move from our habitual patterns of our wounding and perceive the world through those filters, it may seem like our core is gone — but it's not.

By making greater contact with all of the layers of grief and pain and dissociation and disconnection and fear that become activated during relational conflict, we can make greater contact with our essential self. As we move our attention down the midline, we find our seat within ourselves in a deeper way. Inviting the movement and flow of energy, we can feel the bliss of being fully embodied and create a new map of how to navigate the world.

Harmony's Story

The first time I was aware of my own alignment was an empowering experience. I had become aware of my conditioned patterns in social situations where I was agreeable, without an opinion, and desperate to be liked. I was meditating 2 hours each day, and I was committed to my contemplative practices of yoga and dance.

My energy was becoming clearer, but I could not grasp how to be in relationships if I wasn't following my conditioned patterns. I wanted to learn how to bring my alignment into my relationships. I was still unaware of the dysregulation that lived beneath the patterns, and yet I wanted to take my power back from my ego.

In an effort to discover a way to stay aligned, I created an experiment for myself. I was going to a party for a kindergartener who was a friend of my daughter's. Parents were invited to stay, and I wasn't familiar with this group of parents. Before I left for the party, I looked at myself in the mirror and said, "Harmony, don't do it tonight. No matter what, do not try to earn anybody's approval."

Filled with anxiety, we drove to the party. As I walked in, I felt awkward and uncertain about myself. I spoke to a few of the caregivers who were there, and then I busied myself by looking about the kitchen, for what I was unsure. When I started to feel a bit crazy looking for something without needing to find anything, I went to the bathroom. I looked in the mirror and saw the panic on my face, so I sat down on the toilet and closed my eyes.

With my eyes closed, I realized I was anxious. My mind was racing with fearful thoughts, and I tried to calm down. The more I tried to get calm, the more my fear was activated. Instead of resisting the fear, I decided to welcome it. "It makes sense to me that this is scary to you," I said to myself with compassion. I placed a hand on my heart and repeated the words of validation as I felt my body begin to settle.

After some time, I realized I needed to check on my daughter. Before I left the bathroom, I looked at myself in the mirror again. "Do nothing, Harmony. It's okay to do nothing."

I walked out of the bathroom and found my daughter happily playing in the bouncy house. Then, I went and found a chair, sat down, and did nothing. I noticed the impulses of my mind, but I didn't follow them. In an open-eyed meditation, I breathed and increased my awareness. By not following my distortion, I learned how to stay seated in myself.

By practicing honoring myself, I increased my awareness of all of the little ways I harmed myself and betrayed myself. By stopping the patterns of self-betrayal and manipulation, I found my way home to the core of my being. In doing so, I learned to bring more of the vibrational qualities of the True Self into all of my relationships.

Although it was many years from this day that I felt the full flow of my alignment, this was the beginning of contacting my alignment. From this day forward, I showed up differently to all of my relationships. Subsequently, all of my relationships changed. People who liked being around me because I was accommodating and compliant no longer knew how to relate with me. These relationships dissolved, making room for aligned relationships, where my full self resonated with the person I was with.

Exercise: Activate Your Alignment

Close your eyes and sense into your body. Simply notice what it feels like to be you in this moment. Starting at the top of your head, bring in presence and awareness through the crown chakra. Empty your mind as you bring in more presence and spaciousness into your head. As you breathe, make any vocalizations that feel authentic and supportive of moving energy.

Slowly move your awareness down from the top of your head to the space between your eyes. Place your attention in your third eye chakra, opening into your seat of intuition and deeper knowing. Gently touch your third eye, moving your fingertips in a circular motion as you breathe.

Moving your awareness down to your throat, breathe in the full circumference of your throat. Opening your throat with presence and breath. As you notice the sensations of the throat, you can give the sensations a voice through a vocalization, supporting the movement of any energy blocking the throat chakra.

Now moving your awareness down to your heart, breathe into your heart like you are filling up a balloon; breathing into the back of the heart, the front of the heart, and the sides. Fully occupy your heart with breath and awareness. If you notice your heart holding any painful sensation or emotion, give it a tone to support the movement. If your heart had a voice, what would it sound like? Continue to vocalize with every exhale.

When you're ready, bring your attention to your solar

plexus, which is located near the diaphragm below the chest. As you contact your solar plexus chakra, notice how it feels. Is it tight? Soft? Or something else? Slow down as you bring more presence into your seat of esteem, will, and power. Direct your breath into your solar plexus, and if it feels tight give it a tone. Keep breathing and vocalizing as you make space for your solar plexus to soften.

Bring your presence down to your sacrum, which is located below the naval. As you drop into your seat of creativity and sexuality, notice how you feel. With your inner eye, look around the full circumference of your sacral chakra and notice if your energy body is holding anything here. Mobilize the energy of your sacral chakra with breath, movement, and sound. If your sex center had a voice, what would it sound like?

Now bring your presence and awareness down to your root chakra, located at the base of your spine. This is your seat of stability and security within yourself from which the foundation of your alignment is built upon. Relax down into your root with every exhale. As you bring more presence into your root, notice if anything is blocking your root from opening and softening down into the earth. Direct your exhales down as you vocalize, soften, and settle into your seat of security.

Once you feel anchored and grounded, bring your inhale up through the crown and exhale down through the root. Soften your jaw with each exhale. Stay with this breath pattern as you breathe up and align with Source, and exhale as you touch your sacred connection to the earth.

As you feel the anchor down and the alignment up vertically to Source, remind yourself, "This is me. This is who I really am."

Walkaway with Wisdom

When we stop following the patterns of our conditioned self, we differentiate from our ego and claim our shadow. As we practice this, we feel the stored emotional pain that lives beneath the patterns. Shame, fear, and anger may begin to bubble to the surface to be felt and mobilized.

Our alignment with Source is amplified by the movement of our own energy. There are 5 ways to move energy: 1) Awareness, 2) Breath, 3) Touch, 4) Movement, and 5) Tone/Vocalization. Using all 5 of these methods to open our energy centers supports the ongoing activation of our alignment.

When we open our energy centers up the midline of our body, we process and mobilize old emotional energy pollution. When we align with Source through the crown of our head, it's essential to anchor down to the earth. As we embody that high vibrational energy of Source, we must bring it to the third dimension in order for it to have any practical use in our lives.

To come back to ourselves each time we get pulled off center, we build the skill of staying aligned. The practices are like going to the spiritual gym, where we build the muscle to live in alignment with who we really are.

Part 3:

Contacting Our Essence

Chapter 8

Disrupting Contact

What Is Contact?

Contact is essential to human life. It's the place in which we touch our own essence, and it's the essence of all human relationships. Contact makes it possible for us to experience quality of connection, where our souls meet one another. When we experience direct contact with someone who is aligned and seated in themselves, the contact feels safe, healthy, and clean. When someone is in their distortion and identified with their conditioned self, the experience is lack of safety, lack of clarity, and lack of true contact.

Children thrive in the presence of quality attention and contact. We were born with an open system, ready to give and receive unconditional love. An emotionally mature caregiver who is integrated and aware can contact their child in a healthy way. When we grow up with such a caregiver, we develop a secure attachment style and feel safe to contact and be fully present with those around us.

When our caregivers are emotionally immature, misattuned, neglectful, inconsistent, and/or lacking boundaries, the relational field is distorted and we do not experience true contact. When we grew up in an environment such as this, we developed either an insecure, avoidant, or disorganized attachment style. Along with our core attachment wounds, we developed subtle strategies to regulate and make sense of the world—these strategies are called *contact boundary disturbances*.

These strategies were an attempt to find a sense of power when we felt confused, unsafe, or neglected. When our caregivers were not safe people to be open around, this was a wise and sophisticated strategy. Because we felt inherently unsafe in relationship with our caregivers, we didn't learn how to feel safe to make contact with others. The strategies that we developed to make sense of and feel safe in the environment we grew up in become habitual patterns that continue to cause us to disrupt contact with the environment. They endure as our own internal barriers against love and connection.

Contact can happen intrapsychically, where we contact our felt experience and stay seated in our alignment. When we are in contact with ourselves, we are aware of the sensations in our bodies. We can be with the felt sense of these sensations in a way that drops us deeper into our bodies. When we are regulated, attuned, and fully present with our alignment, we are in contact with our Self.

We can also experience contact interpersonally, where we contact the people and the environment around us. To experience quality contact with others, we must first cultivate quality contact within ourselves.

Contact Boundary Disturbances

Contact boundary disturbances are psychological and energetic habits that disrupt the flow of present-moment connection to self and the environment, perpetuating our distortion. Since we develop these habitual ways of disrupting contact with ourselves and others at a young age, they often seem like a normal part of our human experience. Even though the original circumstances are no longer present, we continue to disrupt contact with self and others for various reasons related to our unfinished business.

When we prevent quality contact with ourselves and others, we keep ourselves trapped by the patterns of our conditioned self. Contacting the vital flow of energy in our alignment on our own is part of deepening our internal contact. However, when we engage in intimate relationships, sit in large groups, or meet new people, the impulse to block contact can be almost automatic and completely unconscious.

Limited awareness around the habitual ways we disrupt contact interrupts our ability to feel fully present within ourselves and create fulfilling relationships. In the lineage of Gestalt Therapy (Perls, 1973), there are 5 *contact boundary disturbances*:

Introjection: When we accept other people's perspectives and values without evaluating them first, their ideas live in us as an introjection.

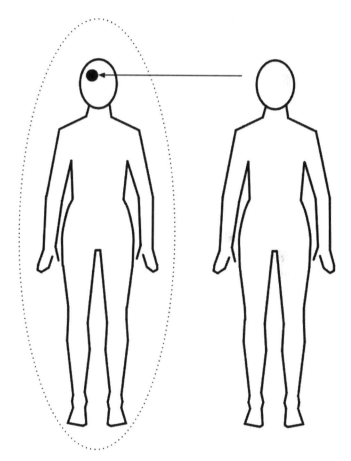

We all have numerous messages from childhood that we did not first evaluate before accepting as our own that continue to live within us unexamined. Acquired misbeliefs about ourselves and the world that are not part of our true nature are introjects. Learned beliefs about gender, monogamy, money, bodies, obedience, racial inequity, culture, privilege, and so on are also introjections. Allowing unexamined input from the environment to become a part of ourselves was an adaptable way to fit into a family structure.

When introjects live within us unprocessed, we unknowingly look at the world and ourselves through the lens of past ideas that belonged to other people. These ideas were absorbed at a time when we didn't have the cognitive abilities to question their veracity; however, continuing to leave them unexamined creates an internal landscape that is outdated and not aligned with our own truth. Continuing to hold these unexamined acquired beliefs as our own blocks our ability to experience quality contact with our Self and others.

Projection: When we place the responsibility of our experience onto the environment, even though it actually originates within ourselves, we are projecting.

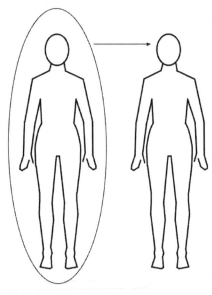

Seeing other people as problematic without looking at our own behavior is a projection. Evaluating someone else's personality as flawed when the same qualities are present in our own personality is a projection. Resenting someone for not being more present and vulnerable when we, ourselves, are not bringing presence and vulnerability is a projection.

Feeling the pain of our childhood wounding and blaming our partner for our pain is a projection. When we put an image of someone from the past (i.e., Mom, Dad, or caregiver) onto a current relationship, we think about and engage with that person from our introjections, we are projecting our own imprint onto our partner. This prevents us from experiencing quality contact with our partner as we relate to them from an unexamined place within ourselves.

Any time we look at others as the source of our problems and fail to look within and at what we are contributing, we are projecting. Any time we are not fully in contact with our own experience while also being openly curious about another's experience, we are projecting.

As we gain more self-awareness, projections can still be elusive. If we are emotionally regulated and curious about a person, we are not projecting. However, if we are dysregulated, want another person to be different, and blame another without genuine curiosity about what is happening with them, we can both be seeing the other person accurately and be in a projection. This means that we disrupt contact because of our emotional activation, blaming them for our own state rather than looking within to see what is alive within ourselves, which is an indicator of a projection.

Attempting to make sense of our own internal experience while placing the responsibility onto our environment, we project anything unfinished and unexamined within us onto others.

Confluence: When we feel no boundary at all between

ourselves and others, we are in a state of confluence.

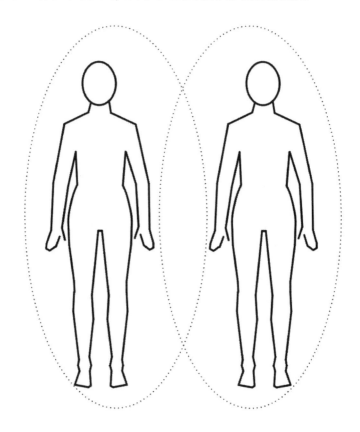

Because we cannot sense ourselves when we are in a state of confluence, we cannot contact ourselves or others. There is no separation between ourselves and the environment, and we merge into one.

We are born into a state of boundaryless confluence, where we have no sense of self as a separate person. What other people want, think, and feel become what we want, think and feel.

In adulthood, not having access to our own desires, beliefs, and emotions creates tremendous confusion intrapsychically and interpersonally. Confusion is sign of confluence, and it is also an indicator of an imprint of gaslighting in childhood, where our parents discounted our reality and misused their power. Not knowing where we end and another person begins, we are unclear on if what we want, feel, and think actually belongs to us, or them. Therefore, we tend to prefer being around people who are like us. Anyone who is too different from us can muddle our system and cause deep frustration.

Retroflection: Withholding our emotions, thoughts, and actions and putting them onto ourselves, doing to ourselves what we actually want to do to others, is retroflection.

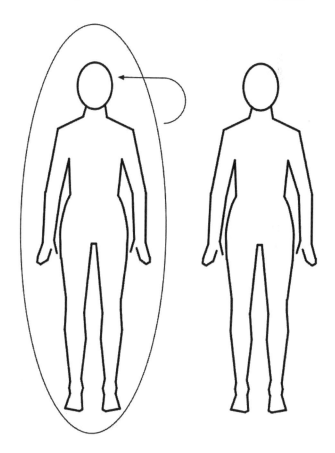

Instead of getting angry at our parents, we get angry at ourselves. Instead of feeling sad about the way we are treated, we get sad that we are not enough. Instead of asking our parents to be more competent, we become the competent parent. Instead of stating that we don't like what's happening, we stop liking ourselves.

Retroflection is experienced as an internal split between what we think we "should" do and what we want to do. The "should" thwarts our ability to fulfill our desire. Shame, guilt, and "shoulds" are retroflections that cause us to turn on ourselves and get absorbed in our flaws.

Having a perfectionistic attitude, an inner critic, struggling with indecision, not trusting ourselves, and so on are some of the inner expressions of retroflection. It causes us to move in the world as if we are unlovable or incompetent.

Deflection: When we prevent ourselves from feeling uncomfortable emotions by either blocking the discomfort or turning away from it, we are deflecting.

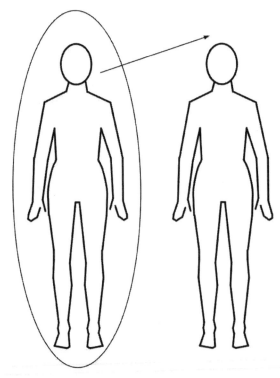

Avoiding direct contact, we stop the flow of energy in favor of a less satisfying, superficial contact. Putting up an energetic wall, turning away to avoid eye contact, or laughing when something is not funny are ways we deflect discomfort. Deflection is an unconscious attempt to ease tension within ourselves.

"Shouldisms" and "Aboutisms"

When we are identified with our conditioned self and believe that thoughts hold reality, we are prone to following thought patterns that keep us disconnected from our Self.

When we experience ourselves and the world primarily through our minds, we intellectualize ourselves, others, and situations, which keeps us removed from actually experiencing them. When we think *about* ourselves, we are not in contact with ourselves. When we think *about* another person, we are not in contact with them. When we think *about* an event, we are not in contact with the full experience of being in a particular situation or environment. *Aboutisms* that exist within our conditioned self can cause us to misuse our intellect in such a way that we avoid experiencing life and dim our light of awareness.

When our mind holds a message of how we *should* be, we are preventing ourselves from experiencing how we actually are. Similarly, when we believe that we know how other people *should* be, we are preventing ourselves from experiencing the other person's expression. And when we think we know how an event *should* take place, we prevent ourselves from experiencing what actually is. *Shouldisms* that exist within our conditioned self prevent us from shifting our habitual patterns by holding onto ideals of how we ought to be and how life ought to be.

Understanding ourselves and a situation on an intellectual level has value. However, when we identify with our conditioned self and cling to our *aboutisms* and *shouldisms,* we are attempting to manipulate ourselves and a situation to avoid the experience of what we are actually experiencing. We keep ourselves from being present with the full range of our experience and create a barrier to contact.

Making room for our mind to make sense of an experience is important, but not at the cost of contact. To notice what we think and then to deepen into our connection with what lies beneath the thoughts is to make room for our full experience. Cultivating the ability to be fully who we are, to encompass our authentic wholeness, the light of awareness is turned on to such a degree that we can be fully present with ourselves and others.

Creating Quality Contact

When we continue to subtly cloak our essence, we prevent ourselves from contacting the people in our lives with the quality of our True Self. These patterns become so habitual it can be challenging to notice them; however, noticing them is necessary to meet ourselves and our relationships in the way we have always longed to experience.

Given the insidious and subtle nature of boundaries and contact boundary disturbances, learning to recognize them within ourselves is important to experiencing quality contact with ourselves and others. To contact our essence, beyond the patterned ways we've learned to exist and interact, we begin to meet others from the depth of who we are. As we stay present to the experience of contact, we can experience transpersonal relationships that go well beyond our conditioned self.

When we are unaware of our disruptions to contact, we look to other people to provide us with quality contact, leaving ourselves even more. Bringing presence and awareness to our experience of ourselves will enhance our ability to notice the ways we block contact. When we are alone and bring more presence into our experience, there are less disruptions to contact the present. We might notice an introjection or retroflection consuming our minds when we are by ourselves. However, presence and awareness while we are relating with others will illuminate the multitude of ways we disrupt contact.

At the boundary between ourselves and the environment, we experience ourselves. Because relationships are our greatest mirror, when we are fully present and aware in relationship we can see ourselves more clearly.

Maintaining quality contact with ourselves, we give ourselves time and space to experience our felt sense. When someone speaks or acts and we notice our felt sense shift, we pay attention to what is occurring within us. The level of self-awareness we bring to our interactions guides the level of contact we experience. In the present moment, at the boundary point between ourselves and others, we can perceive any disruption causing a block in contact. The more awareness we place on the quality of our contact, the more clarity we will have about anything blocking it.

Simply noticing our experience of ourselves as we relate with others will guide us in finding ways to shift our unconscious patterns that block contact. The awareness we can cultivate by paying attention is what affords us the possibility of seeing other options for how to connect. Quality contact only happens in the present moment, and this is also true about our relationships. The more we metabolize our unfinished business and contact our alignment, the more able we are to be present for the quality of contact we desire for our relationships.

Harmony's Story

I had always longed for quality, clean contact in my relationships, but I couldn't see how I was preventing this from happening. *I was available for it,* I thought, *so why are all the people I attract and am attracted to unable to give it to me?*

When I finally admitted that I was the common denominator in my relationships, I started looking at my own dysfunctional patterns that limited my connections with others. I began to understand that the people in my life were reflecting to me the places within myself that needed attention and love. I had previously thought I needed to get that attention and love from others, but I was finally realizing that the person I needed attention and love from was myself for the outer world to shift.

The first time I became aware of this was when I was getting ready to end my first marriage. I had recently experimented with showing up differently at social engagements (as detailed in my story in Chapter 7), and I was also experimenting with being more congruent and authentic in my marriage.

At the time, it had been easy to focus on the controlling, criticizing, and contracted way my husband was in the world. Changing my own accommodating and pleasing conditioned patterns was a frightening idea; there was so much unknown around what would happen if I stopped colluding in this dysfunctional marriage. He was self-referenced and I was other-referenced, and I realized that if I didn't change this pattern I would die. Perhaps I wouldn't die a physical death, by my soul would certainly perish.

I started looking at how my projections shifted the boundary in my favor, making him wrong for the state of our marriage. In looking at this projection, I realized that I was projecting "older sibling" onto him, utilizing the same strategies I had used with my sibling, who was volatile, criticizing, and self-referenced. As a child, I was so scared of my sibling that I created an inner environment to try to stabilize the outer environment, cultivating codependent traits of being self-sacrificing, thinking that I was not enough, and working to earn approval.

Once I recognized my projection, I started to recognize my introjection from the time my sibling yelled at me when our dad left us, "It's all your fault. If you weren't born Dad would have never left!"

When I took my sibling's belief into my psyche, this became an introjection. Without examining the belief to see if I agreed with it or if it was true, it lived within me as part of my own self-concept. There was a part of me that wanted to hurt my sibling the way they hurt me, but instead I turned the hurt back on myself. This was a retroflection where my mind would put myself down and make me responsible for the pain of others.

I tried to find safety through confluence, making my then husband's values my values and making his criticism of me my own narrative about myself. I also deflected his words, keeping him out in an attempt to find safety with someone whom I felt unsafe being around.

All of these constructs lived within me and prevented me from contacting my Self. Engaging with the world from my contact boundary disturbances, I was preventing myself from experiencing the deep and beautiful intimacy that my soul longed for. Since I wasn't current with myself, I wasn't seeing my husband for who he was. Had I been in contact with myself, I probably wouldn't have married him. And soon after I learned how to stay in myself and cease the use of my contact boundary disturbances, I asked for a divorce.

Relationships that resonate with my soul manifest when I am in alignment with the True Self. I hadn't learned how to be in my alignment, and I hadn't learned how to be with myself in such a way that I wasn't driven by unresolved experiences. Updated and current, I can contact myself even when my contact boundary disturbances bubble up to the surface. I can see them for what they are and work with them in a loving and compassionate way.

My own awareness provides my wounds the space needed to be at choice. My own lack of awareness creates an inner environment where my wounds drive my actions. When I am in choice, I am responsible for myself and I am okay with the dissolution of relationships that do not resonate with my soul. As long as I am in contact with myself, my choice is neither a reaction nor a clinging. My choice is the self-responsibility that makes quality contact with self and others possible.

Exercise: Staying in Contact

One of the most important components of knowing your inner map is having a clear felt sense of being in contact with yourself so that you have a clear felt sense of when you leave contact with yourself. Contact with self is essential in order to be in contact with the environment; however, since leaving contact with self and disrupting contact with the environment is the path of least resistance, it takes a lot of practice to stay embodied in contact with self.

To begin, close your eyes and notice what it feels like to be you in this moment. Scan your inner world, and notice what's pulling the awareness of your mind. Notice the sensations in your body. Notice the quality of your breath. Notice what feels most alive within your body and where the quieter, less obvious places live.

Take a few sweet breaths, breathing in the breath of love. If you were to breathe in a way that was in service of self-care and self-love, how would you be breathing? Let that intention touch all the aspects of your inner world.

Now bring your attention to a place in your body that feels really supported and strong. Maybe it's your feet, your legs, or your seat. Maybe it's your belly, or your heart, or your mind. Wherever you feel the most supported inner strength in this moment, bring all of your awareness to this place in your body. Notice the quality of the sensation. Notice the shape and the color. Breathe all the way around it, and really seat your awareness into this inner strength and support.

Then, slowly you'll begin to open your eyes, but as you do keep your inner eye anchored into this area of your body. Moving slowly, as you continue to breathe, stay in contact with this sensation as you begin to take in visual information. If at any time you lose contact with this aspect of your body, you can simply close your eyes and come back to yourself.

Once your eyes are fully open and you can stay in contact

with this sensation in your body, continue to breathe, softening your jaw and settling into this contact with yourself as your eyes are open. Slowly look around the room. Pay attention to what it feels like to be in contact with yourself while also being present with the environment around you.

Anytime you meditate, contacting yourself with your eyes closed then slowly opening them to be present with the environment while maintaining contact with yourself, can serve you in staying seated in yourself in your relationships.

Walkaway with Wisdom

Contact is essential to human life. It's the place in which we touch our own essence, and it's the essence of all human relationships. Contact makes it possible for us to experience quality of connection, where our souls meet one another.

There are 5 ways we disrupt contact with the environment: 1) Introjections, 2) Projections, 3) Confluence, 4) Retroflections, and 5) Deflections. We all have learned strategies to disrupt contact with our environment. These patterns become so habitual it can be challenging to notice them; however, noticing them is necessary to meet ourselves and our relationships in the way we have always longed to experience.

To create quality contact, we need to recognize these strategies within. Bringing presence and awareness into our experience of ourselves will enhance our ability to notice the ways we block contact. And once we can see the ways we disrupt contact, we can begin to become more present and current with ourselves and others.

Chapter 9

We Are Already Whole

When the conditioned self believes that we are broken beyond repair, we work on ourselves to try to fix ourselves. We believe that if we figure out why we hurt so bad and experience the right treatment or take the right medication or read the right book we will be liberated from our pain. When we're in a tremendous amount of pain, our relationships are also likely wrought with conflict. We feel broken and that brokenness is reflected back to us in our relationship dynamics.

When we feel heavy with grief, limited by self-loathing, gripped with fear, entangled in painful relationships, lonely in a world full of people, contained by our inner critic, inadequate by our inner judge, or driven by our perfectionist, it makes sense that we'd want to try to change ourselves to make the symptoms go away.

But what if there was nothing to fix?

What if the design of how we are is the most adaptive way our system tried to find stability and health in an environment that didn't support our wholeness and well-being? What if instead of trying to make our experience and thoughts go away, we utilized that attention and energy to fully digest the trauma of our past so that we could be more fully who we are?

Our wholeness isn't something we create by working on ourselves. Our wholeness already exists. We try to fix our wounds because we're hurting and we want it to stop. The work of transformation, however, is less about the pain itself and more about our relationship to the pain.

Even though we want the pain to go away and try to find ways to stop experiencing suffering, we unconsciously perpetuate our own suffering by clinging to our painful emotions. We loop in our self-defeating thoughts because there is a familiarity and a comfort in the pain. It's been with us in some form or another for many, many years and it has become part of our identity.

Ultimately, we are trying to come back to our essence. All of the attempts at fixing and changing and learning a new way is our attempt at rediscovering our essential self. Remembering that our essence is already whole, we may have a shift in consciousness from resistance and self-loathing to compassion and love. This is where we can discover our own essence.

Blocks to Subtle Energy

When we are unaware of the blocks to our own subtle energy, we are unaware of our own distorted life force. From this state of being, we identify with our conditioned self, our misbeliefs, and our wounds. We orient towards these wounds because they were created when we felt unsafe or in pain. Unconsciously, we think the wounds hold the key to our safety, which we need to vigilantly watch in order to prevent further harm.

As we live our lives placing our attention on the fragmented, hardened energy of our wounds, we forget how to see through the lens of our wholeness. Cultivating the ability to see our distorted life force and our contact boundary disturbances, we can see and feel the places where our subtle energy has hardened with greater acuity.

Below is an image of a person's inner matrix that keeps them identified with their conditioned self. The person feels fragmented and broken because they are viewing the world through their constructs that have been acquired in this life that are not part of their true nature. Finding the way through this matrix is to find our way back to our inherent wholeness and essence.

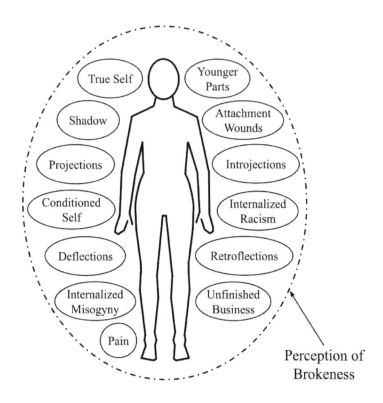

Perception of Brokeness

Once we can see the lens that we have been perceiving the world through, we can create space around it with our awareness and breath. Because the lens we see the world through has many filters, including our personal history, collective history, cultural influences, racialized trauma, and so on, it can be challenging to see our filter in any given moment. Gender, gender identity, sexual orientation, relationship status, socioeconomic status, physical ability, weight, age, ethnicity, and race all influence the location we occupy in the world, which influences the way we see the world.

The systemic power structures that influence the way we experience our location creates inherent biases that can live in our blind spots. Looking at the way society holds our personal location and the way we internalized collective narratives about our own power, worth, lovability, and beauty is part of elevating our awareness around the lens we see the world through.

Remembering that the work is not about fixing anything about ourselves or making our wounds go away, we increase our awareness in service of creating more spaciousness and choice about how we relate to ourselves and our environment. When we are able to welcome any fragmentation or hardened aspects of our subtle energy body, we create room to mobilize that which is not in alignment with our authentic truth.

Using the five techniques to mobilize energy as mentioned earlier in the book, we can use our awareness, breath, sound, movement, and touch to support our subtle energy body in surrendering into our inherent wholeness. With a natural movement towards health, we invite our pain, distortion, and disruptions to get back into contact with the wholeness of our essence.

Awareness, in and of itself, is extremely transformative. When we are aware of the lens we are looking through, we are able to differentiate from the lens. By seeing it with more clarity, it is given space. This space from the lens has us deepen into the seat of our True Self, allowing our subtle energy to begin to mobilize and the lens to shift.

Breath softens the subtle energy body in a few ways. In general, when we hold tension in our physical, emotional, and energetic bodies, our breath is stopped by the tension. We limit our capacity to feel when we limit our breath. When we are aware of the lens of our wounding, we can use the breath to make room around it—giving the subtle energy body space to move and soften. It's important to breathe around the wound and not try to breathe through it—trying to breathe through the hardness will only cause it to brace against the breath.

Sound and vocalizations give a voice to what we are holding. Once we contact the hardened subtle energy, we can often hear what it wants to say. It might be a suppressed, ancient scream.

It might be an old, unexpressed whimper. It might sound like a heavy groan or a high-pitched uproar. By matching the tone of the energetic holding with the tone of our voice, we can move the wound in profound and lasting ways.

Movement is an important element to softening the subtle energy body because we can become habituated to move in certain patterned ways. Through physical, emotional, and psychological trauma, our physical and emotional bodies can become rigid and stiff. When we are in the midst of moving a deep wound with our awareness, breath, and voice, we can support that movement by physically moving our bodies in a way that comes from deep within. By listening to our bodies, the movement that we need to unwind that pattern more fully becomes clear if that is what's needed.

Touch is a loving and tender way to increase awareness and mobility of what our energetic and physical bodies are holding. By touching our furrowed brow, placing a hand over our aching heart, or softly caressing our cheeks, we give ourselves what we need to feel held and loved. Safe and loving touch is an essential human need. To offer this to ourselves as we are moving stored energy and softening into our subtle selves is an act of self-love and self-care.

As our subtle energy softens, we can begin to orient towards the wholeness of our being. We can see ourselves more fully, and we can recognize that our pain is only the smallest fraction of our inner world.

Consciousness is awareness. The way that we elevate our consciousness is by putting more space around a thing. In meditation, we sit in the space between our thoughts, creating more awareness of our ego by wrapping it with presence. This is what makes mindfulness meditation so effective.

When we are working consciously with our subtle energy body, we bring awareness to the blocks of energy that are being held in our system. A block to our subtle energy might be challenging to find on our own because we are so accustomed to feeling the way we are; we are acclimated to the water that we swim in, making it challenging to distinguish. Any place we carry tension in our bodies is a place our subtle energy is blocked. This could be a tight jaw, a furrowed brow, pain in the heart, tension in the shoulders, and so on. Conversely, any place that we are unaware of sensation can also be a place our subtle energy is blocked. Not being able to feel our root, feeling disconnected from our bodies, feeling emptiness in our heart, and so on can be a sign of blocked subtle energy. If we are very disconnected from our bodies and subtle energy, a sign of blocked energy is the looping of our minds. Being fixated on an idea, desire, fear, blame, and so on is a sign that our subtle energy is blocked and we are looking through the lens of our wounding.

By slowing down and paying attention to our physical sensations and our subtle self, we can bring presence and breath around the places within that are blocked. If the mind is very active and looping in thoughts, this is a strategy of the conditioned self to keep us from contacting ourselves. Thinking about ourselves and others keeps us from accessing the deeper truth of why we are off balance. When this is happening, we can begin by noticing the theme of the loop, this gives us a bit of space from the looping itself.

Without trying to change any part of our experience or make anything go away, the presence of our awareness and welcoming breath begins to invite our system's innate knowing to gently move back to a state of balance and health.

Paradox of Change

Gestalt therapy has a theory called the "Paradoxical Theory of Change." What this theory tells us is that the more we resist something, the more it stays the same. The more able we are to welcome the thing that we don't like, the more possible it becomes to change that aspect of ourselves.

This might be the single most important thing to remember in our transformation. To wrap our pain with loving awareness, we bring the quality of presence and then can contact what's needed for transformation. To welcome the inner critic, we give love to the aspect of ourselves that needs it the most. To fully accept our bodies, we experience the very thing we want but think we need a different body to experience. To wholly and completely love our fear, we welcome the part of us that is trying to find safety.

Whatever is happening within us is the path to our transformation. Resisting it prevents our transformation. Welcoming our pain with loving awareness provides space to transmute it.

To validate these aspects of ourselves evokes the deepest feeling of integration. Instead of staying locked in a pattern that keeps us stuck, we can turn towards ourselves and see what's within us consciously. We can welcome all the aspects of our inner world and validate our emotional body. We can tell our fear, "It makes sense to me that you're scared." We can tell our perfectionist, "It makes sense to me that you want to get this right." We can tell our pain, "I see that you're hurting and your pain is valid."

The futile energy spent resisting any aspect of ourselves is a counterproductive impulse that only makes the thing we resist stay put. Resisting or suppressing our experience of ourselves, no matter how painful, keeps the pain living within us from reaching completion. Capping off our emotions in our throat, apologizing for our tears, and loathing any aspect of ourselves prevents us from evolving.

When we welcome our current experience, we can discover the life force energy beneath the resistance. This is where truth and authentic expression can emerge as a source of healing.

In the image below, we see a person who has integrated their wounds, differentiated from their conditioned self, claimed their shadow, and gotten clear on their projections. These aspects have not gone away; however, in the integration of self, the person embodies the wholeness of their being while bringing loving awareness to the aspects of their humanity that need it most. In this way, they meet the world from their wise, infinite, True Self.

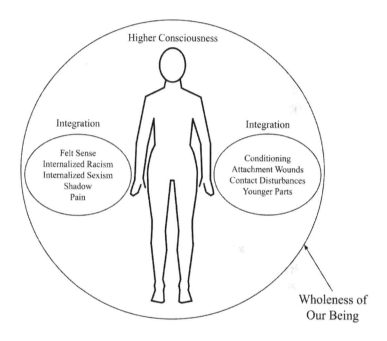

Harmony's Story

When I first learned that resisting my inner world kept my patterns locked in place, I was astonished. I had spent so much of my energy trying to become something that I was not, and I couldn't fathom being with myself in a more welcoming way. I couldn't understand how becoming more of myself would help me to change.

I learned about this concept when I was in graduate school, and I was so struck by the beauty of the theory that I wanted to try to love myself in such a way that I was empowered to shift my painful thought patterns. With an image conscious ego, my mind would criticize my appearance incessantly. And when I grew tired of that, my ego would internally judge other people's appearance incessantly.

One day as I was getting ready for class, I paused and looked in the mirror. I looked myself straight in the eyes and said, "I love you, Harmony."

Instantly my ego started negating this self-loving statement. My eyes assessed my appearance to decide if I was worthy of love. I stopped myself and did it again, "I love you, Harmony. You are amazing. You take good care of yourself, you're a good friend, and you are doing good work in the world."

I started to cry. Layers of shame started to mobilize and I wanted to look away from myself. Instead, I made myself look into my own eyes. "I love you exactly as you are," I said through my tears. And I started to sob from the depths of my heart.

This first experience was potent for me, and it has stayed with me throughout all of the work I do on myself and with my clients. When I am doing my own personal work, I wrap my pain in love. When I am sitting with clients, I ask them to do this, too. Unconditional love is the vibration of Source, and it is the key to healing. Self-development without self-love is not healing. Loving myself unconditionally, I can bring the quality of Source with me into all that I am and all that I do.

Exercise: Mapping the Patterns of the Conditioned Self

Using this wheel of wholeness below, map out the most common lenses through which you see the world. Draw from the exercises you've already done in this book, use this as an opportunity to see the water that you swim in with more clarity. The outer circle represents your wholeness; the inner circle represents your True Self. Each piece of the pie represents elements that we have covered thus far.

In the inner circle, write out the sensations you feel when you're in contact with your True Self. In each piece of pie, describe what the world has taught you about yourself and how you've used those lessons to make sense of yourself. In the chapters to come, we'll dive deeper into meeting the world from a truer place. But first we must get crystal clear on the places that are not authentically aligned with who we really are.

Walkaway with Wisdom

Our wholeness isn't something we create by working on ourselves. Our wholeness already exists. We try to fix our wounds because we're hurting and we want it to stop. The work of transformation, however, is less about the pain itself and more about our relationship to the pain.

Remembering that the work is not about fixing anything about ourselves or making our wounds go away, we can bring in more love to the places within that are hurting. When we are able to welcome any fragmentation or hardened aspects of our subtle energy body, we create room to mobilize that which is not in alignment with our authentic truth.

By becoming more of who we already are and loving ourselves unconditionally, we are empowered to be at choice. This is where change is possible.

Chapter 10

Returning to Innocence

The essence of who we are has been with us since before our conception. As we become conditioned to think, feel, and act in certain ways, our essence maintains the qualities of wholeness, presence, and wisdom. As children, we had greater access to our wholeness, presence, and wisdom because we were newly embodied. We had less suppressive techniques to hide and reject parts of ourselves, and life force energy had more space to guide our creative flow, compassionate heart, and deep wisdom.

In our human design, we are born with biological needs that are fundamental to our humanity. Along with the physiological needs of food, water, warmth, sleep, and safety, we have psychological needs that we look to our caregivers to provide: a sense of social belonging, a sense of trust in others, a sense of our own worth, space to connect with our own bodies, the experience of healthy touch, and the knowledge that we are seen and heard (Heller & LaPierre, 2012).

Our developing sense of self needs to trust our caregivers to provide a safe environment, to have appropriate boundaries, and to be attuned to our emotions. We are biologically designed to need to feel securely connected and attached to our caregivers for the health of our developing sense of self.

When these needs aren't met in a healthy and consistent way, we disconnect from our own needs and develop adaptive strategies that guide the distorted thinking and behavior of our conditioned self. These patterned ways of being create our inner polarity: *in the shadow of our unconscious, we feel a degree of shame about our own existence and we polarize against that shame in order for our ego development to find its place in the world.*

Our polarity distortion provides us with strategies to navigate our environment, and we continue to use them because we didn't develop the capacities needed to honor our wholeness. If our needs would have been met consistently, our developing sense of self would have learned to attune to our emotions, honor our somatic intelligence, make requests for what we need, trust other people, set boundaries, and receive sensual touch that honors us as sacred.

In using our adaptive strategies that made it so we could survive the painful experience of not having our psychological needs met, we create a life that is a reflection of our polarity distortion. In order to find a new way, we must first look to our inner young one and heal what was done to us.

The Relational Effects of Trauma

When there is a consistent disturbance to receiving our psychological core needs in childhood, we do not consistently feel safe and loved. This is relational trauma. Abandonment, enmeshment, and volatility from one or more of our caregivers causes relational trauma. Complex trauma, including blatant violations and abuse, are typically associated with the word trauma. While complex trauma has a huge impact on how we feel in relationships with other, the developmental trauma of not having our biologically encoded psychological needs met also influences our relationships.

When the experiences that caused our polarity distortion live within us unexamined and unfinished, we bring our once adaptive survival strategies from the past with us into our current relationships. As we use these outdated strategies, we are disrupting contact with ourselves and others, even though we use them in an effort to get connection. In order to develop the capacities we need to create healthy relationships, we need to tend to the trauma of not having those needs met in childhood.

The oldest part of the brain, called the reptilian brain, is where our reactivity comes from. When a relational interaction activates our reptilian brain, we might be surprised by our own reactivity. The only job of the reptilian brain is to keep us safe, and when we perceive an interaction as a compromise to our safety the reptilian brain takes over, many people call this being "triggered."

When our psychological safety is compromised in childhood, the reptilian brain may react in any of these four ways: *fight* (i.e., throwing a tantrum), *flight* (i.e., playing quietly by ourselves or going to a friend's house), *freeze* (i.e., containing our emotional expression and pretending nothing is happening), or *fawn* (i.e., trying to keep the adult stable by pleasing them and avoiding conflict).

When we are viewing our current circumstances through the filter of unfinished business, our reaction is seated in the past. This happens automatically when the current situation matches the historical experiences closely enough. We project the past onto the present, and the dysregulation of our old trauma becomes activated because it still lives in our bodies.

Even when our conscious mind knows that there is no real threat to our safety, an activated reptilian brain can still feel threatened. For example, when our partner is consumed by work and we want to connect, an old wound from childhood neglect can activate the reptilian brain. When this happens, we can loop in anger, indignation, and defensiveness.

If we've done the work of mapping out our conditioned self and have great understanding of the birthplace of our wounds, we can still react when a relational event touches those wounds. It is possible to be conscious of our patterns at play *and* hijacked by our reptilian brain simultaneously. We can have the ability to see that there is a solution available *and* be unable to regulate our nervous system at the same time.

We all want to know that we're safe to be in relationship. In childhood it was our caregivers' responsibility to provide us with that safety.

When they were able to meet our physiological and psychological needs consistently, we developed a sense of self based in neuropathways that reflect this relational safety. When we are raised in an environment that does not meet our core needs consistently, we develop a sense of self based in neuropathways that reflect this trauma. Our brain develops in relationship to our environment, and the more our needs aren't met the more our neural connections for relational trauma strengthen.

The beauty of the brain is that it is malleable. We can change our neuropathways through new and reparative experiences. A reparative relational interaction can fire a new neuropathway for safety in connection. Through the intrapsychic lens, this repair begins within ourselves and our relationship with our inner young one (which we will look at later in this chapter). Through the lens of interpersonal healing, this happens in couples and group counseling (which we will look at in Part 4).

Reactive patterns from our childhood most commonly get ignited with those closest to us, such as an intimate partner, our children, our parents, or even our coworkers or boss. Sometimes our old patterns get activated in an encounter with the facilitator of a workshop, a therapist, or some other person who is in a position of power.

Understanding that our reaction is seated in a younger part of us, we can cultivate the capacities to tend to ourselves in relationship. Rather than projecting our pain onto others, we can turn towards ourselves and offer ourselves what we've always needed: attunement and connection with our bodies while acknowledging our worth, trust, and autonomy.

The Role of Our Inner Young One

Any time we become reactive in our relationships, a younger part of us is activated. This statement can be challenging to really take in, especially when we are certain that the other person was in the wrong, that they treated us poorly, and that they are unconscious, shadowy, and distorted. This statement, however, is not saying that the other person holds no responsibility for what they contributed to the interaction. What it is pointing to is that our reactivity is seated in a younger part of ourselves.

From our mature, integrated self, we can stay in contact with our bodies, our truth, and our wisdom. We can regulate our emotions and stay connected to the present moment. We can hold ourselves in our experience and choose how to respond in relationship.

When a relational interaction transpires that confronts a core wound, the intensity of the emotional dysregulation is a signal that the pain precedes this moment.

If we think of our inner young one in terms of linear clock time, we might think that those events happened long ago and do not have the ability to influence the way we react to our current life circumstances. However, if we think in terms of our spiritual body, there is no linear time. The young one who existed in the past still lives on within us.

In the image below, we can see a person who is currently about 38 years old according to linear clock time. When we think in terms of linear time, this person might think back on their 4-year-old self and the events that happened back then. Then they might think about their future self and what they hope to be doing in 5 years from now. However, even as that person thinks about the past and the future, all of that exists right now in their spiritual body, in their essence.

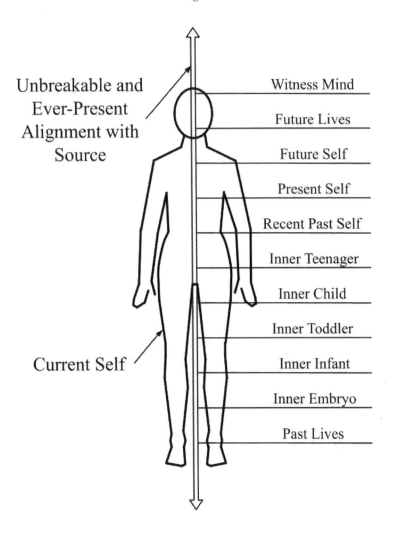

Unbreakable and
Ever-Present
Alignment with
Source

Witness Mind

Future Lives

Future Self

Present Self

Recent Past Self

Inner Teenager

Inner Child

Inner Toddler

Inner Infant

Inner Embryo

Past Lives

Current Self

Working with Younger Parts

Time is such a part of our context that by changing our
relationship to time we change our ability to heal. When we
work with a younger part, we are not thinking back in time
to access them. We're not even thinking about the events that
happened to shape them. We are looking within ourselves,
in our hearts where our purest love resides, to discover what
our inner young one is holding that isn't congruent with their

true nature.

Thinking about or knowing the events that happened in the past is not necessary to open the portal to our younger self. By putting our attention on our inner young one and seeing them for the patterns and misbeliefs they created is enough. This attention transports us to the spiritual time where this young one exists. And when we are with ourselves in this transpersonal way, we can commence the reparenting and healing of ourselves. We can transform the birthplace of our patterns and wounds, and we can integrate the places in us that split from our alignment so that we can come back to our Self.

Our younger parts get activated in relational interactions that confront our core wounds because our inner young one needs to be seen, validated, and loved. When we think the person we are relating with is to blame for our pain, our reaction has us wanting them to see us, validate us, and love us. However, the work of integration and alignment begins with us creating a secure connection within ourselves. Of course we want to experience that security with others, but we are the common denominator in all of our relationships. How we show up for ourselves matters more than how others show up for us.

By acknowledging that there is a younger aspect of ourselves present in our current experience, and not just as a past construct, we can contact our young one in this moment.

If this concept is new to us, it can be challenging to differentiate our inner young one from our actual current self. The familiarity of our patterning might seem like what is activated in us is just part of our personality because we have always been this way. If this is the case, we can ask ourselves, "When was the first time I remember feeling this way?" This question points to the truth that our reactive patterns are not part of our true nature, they are learned ways of being during times when our core needs weren't met.

We do not need to remember the exact age of when we

experienced the trauma that shaped this wound or pattern. We simply need to close our eyes, put all of our attention on our inner young one, and see them for their experience. Since our conditioned self develops early in life, focusing on the age of 4 can be helpful if we don't recall the exact moment. However, the imprint can be from prenatal development all the way to our teen years. We're simply looking at the youngest version of ourselves that we have access to in this moment.

Exploration

Take a few moments right now to think about an experience from childhood that contributed to the shaping of your conditioned self. Maybe it was being on a team sport and comparing yourself to the other athletes, believing that you weren't good enough. Or maybe it was something more traumatic, like having an alcoholic parent, your parents getting divorced, or being physically abused. Or perhaps it was the experience of neglect, where nothing specific happened to you but you weren't seen for your deeper experience. It can help to get a picture of yourself from that age so you can really see your inner young one.

If you have been able to identify a core wound, this is likely the crux of your attachment wound. Consider what this young one was needing from the adults around them, and take a moment to complete this sentence:

"When I'm emotionally activated, my young one needs _____ from me."

When the mind looks to someone else to fulfill what you want in order to feel regulated and okay, turn to your inner young one and give them the thing they want. Close your eyes or look at a photo of yourself as a child, and bring all of your attention to them. Attune to how they were/are feeling. Without trying to figure them out, change them, or rescue them, simply hold them in your awareness as they are.

"I see you. I see that you feel (state emotion)."

Breathing into your heart, see your inner young one for their deeper experience. Recognizing that this unfinished business from the past prevents quality contact with yourself and others, give yourself space to repair this experience now for yourself.

Once the inner young one has fully received your attention and attunement, make a commitment to give them what they wanted from their caregiver(s) and want from their current relationship experience.

For example, if you feel lonely and unwanted, and your young one was neglected, say to them, "I will always love you and I will always want you." Repeating the restorative statement allows your inner young one to feel the connection and safety that you've always wanted and looked to other people to fulfill. This is how you begin to build a secure attachment to Self as Source, where you honor yourself with attuned love and safety.

Disrupting the patterns of your attachment wounds when they are activated is important in coming into deeper alignment with your Self. Since your emotional triggers are seated in a younger part of yourself, learning how to be with your inner young one in a loving and healing way makes it possible to integrate what was fractured in the past in a deep and lasting way. The next time you are emotionally activated, remember what your inner young one needs and give that to them.

Harmony's Story

The young one within me that gets activated most frequently is preverbal. This has changed over the years. Healing happens from the most recent stress or trauma to the oldest. The more transformation I have experienced, the more my preverbal trauma becomes activated.

Whether I am giving a talk, teaching a class, or connecting deeply with my husband, when my young one feels insecure, she is frightened of being annihilated. The part of me that needed my caregivers to be there for me when I awoke on the top bunk of a bed and nearly died because they weren't there for me thinks that death will happen again. She thinks that she is not important enough for others to care about her existence, and she believes that she shouldn't reach out at all.

Because this inner young one is so precious to me, I spend time creating a secure connection with her any time she is scared. I close my eyes, I turn towards her, and I tell her, "I will always hold you. I will never set you down."

It is my job to hold myself. It isn't anybody else's job to be there for me one hundred percent of the time or respond to me positively at each encounter. It is the other people's job to be in their truth and hold themselves in their experience. This does not mean that I do not ask for co-regulation. This simply means that I attach to myself in service of healthy relationships with those around me.

Staying in contact with myself, I reveal what's happening within me. When I'm with my husband I might say, "I am noticing my heart racing and I'm having a hard time regulating. I think my young one is scared that you will leave her. I'm going to take a few breaths into my heart and let her know that I will hold her." If he is resourced, I might ask him if he is willing to hold me. This is a very different scenario from crying and begging for attention while I blame him for being so distracted, which is what happens when I speak *from* my young one rather than *on her behalf*.

If I am giving a talk or teaching, the work is similar but less intimate. I always reveal my sensations and take a few minutes to self-regulate before jumping in. Being in contact with myself is what makes my actions effective. Modeling this to others is a gift, showing them my humanity is what allows people to feel in contact with me.

Exercise: Reparenting Your Inner Young One

As you develop clarity on the habitual theme of your conditioned self and attachment wounds, working with that characteristic in a deeper way can offer the key to deeper healing and integration.

Common characteristics that are seated in wounds of a younger part include the following:

Believing you're not enough.

Feeling worthless.

Trying to earn love.

Feeling unsafe in relationships.

Feeling powerless.

Feeling scared to speak your truth.

Thinking you are responsible for other people's happiness.

Thinking you need to be perfect to be loved.

Thinking people will leave you if you set boundaries.

Thinking that you are too much.

Thinking that wanting something makes you needy or bossy.

For this exercise, choose one misbelief that underlies a characteristic of your conditioned patterns. Once you are clear on the misbelief you will be working with, consider at what age you first remember acquiring this misbelief or pattern.

In this example, we will use the pattern of *feeling powerless.*

Close your eyes and see the younger version of yourself who acquired this misbelief. Even if you don't know the age, open up your higher consciousness and see your inner young one in your mind's eye.

Breathe into your heart, and say to your inner young one, "I see you. I see you and I love you." Your presence and witness allow your inner young one to have space in a new way that honors the birthplace of your wounding with love and understanding.

As you see your young one, see them for their experience at the time the misbelief was created. "I see that you feel *powerless* (alone, angry, scared, sad, unlovable, etc.)." Continue to breathe and soften your jaw on the exhale as you repeat this statement to your young one. While the young one certainly experienced more than this, focusing on where the conditioned pattern is seated is important in increasing awareness of the conditioned habits.

Wrap your young one with love and awareness as you continue to breathe into your heart as you repeat these statements, "I see you. I see that you feel *powerless*. I see you and I love you." Repeat these statements until you can sense that the young one knows they are seen. Let yourself feel all of your emotions as you continue to breathe. Stay within your window of tolerance without bypassing anything. The presence of your awareness can bring forth a lot of emotions and allowing yourself to feel everything that arises is part of metabolizing our unfinished business.

From here, validate your inner young one. "It makes sense to me that you feel *powerless* (alone, scared, sad, etc.)." As you repeat this statement over and over, your young one can really take in the validation. See the field around them that was disempowering as you validate. As you validate, you're honoring your young one's wisdom and adaptability by creating this strategy. Validation has the ability to soften even the most rock-solid walls surrounding the heart. And since this young one lives on in your heart, your heart can open and expand in the presence of your own validation.

Looking at your younger self, see the strategies you created at the time the experience occurred. If you have this level of awareness about your own patterns, see your inner young one for the wisdom of their strategy, "I see that you needed to *give your power away to find safety* (stay quiet, be perfect, deceive, take care of everyone else, etc.). They weren't able to be there in the way you needed." Repeat this until it sinks in and your young one feels fully seen.

Tell your inner young one what is true. Since the misbelief is false, what truth are you ready to replace it with? *You are powerful, and your safety comes from you.* Or *You are safer honoring yourself.* (You are lovable; your voice matters; your truth matters; you are wise; you are wanted; etc.) This truth amends the violation.

If you are aware of the misbeliefs you acquired at this time, it is possible to cleanse your young one of introjections. For example, if your young one feels powerless, you might have a misbelief that being accommodating and hiding your truth and your pain is the only way to find safety and belonging. As an adult, you can help your young one clear this misbelief. Simply ask your young one "Are you ready to stop carrying this belief around?" If they are, an invitation to remove the introjection might be enough to clear it. You can also call on the cosmic realm for support, asking your ancestors, Buddha nature, Universe, or guides to help clear the energy you're holding that does not belong to you. If the young one is not ready to give it back, it is likely because they feel responsible. If this is the case, check in to see what you want to tell your young one about the misbelief.

Then, make a commitment to honor your young one in the way they need, *I will always honor your power.* (I will always love you; I will always honor your voice; I will always want you; etc.) Repeating this several times allows the young one to really take it in.

Once that feels complete, tell your young one how old you are now in order to fully update them and become more current with life. "I'm (current age) years old." And then take your young one's hand and show them your life now. Slowly show them the home you live in, the career you have, the lessons you're still learning, and the people you have relationships with. If this feels joyous and there's a sense of pride, let yourself feel that. If this feels painful and you see what you want to change in your life, let yourself feel that. Updating your inner young one is important because the conditioned patterns that filter your perspective of life have influenced the decisions you made. Seeing your life clearly with awareness of your patterns, you can be at choice for how you want to move forward.

After the young one orients to current time, affirm the truth you just said to your younger part from the first person, "I am ready to *claim my power*." (I am ready to speak my truth; I deserve to feel safe; I am safer honoring my boundaries; I am ready to love myself unconditionally; etc.) Claiming your truth is a powerful punctuation at the end of this process. Repeat the statement three times to really anchor it in.

Affirmation Process: Write down the true statement on a piece of paper. At some point, either now or in the next few days, work with this affirmation to continue to excavate the misbeliefs that lurk in the shadow and discount your truth. To do this, you will write the affirmation, and then you will write down all of the reasons why your conditioned self says this isn't true.

For example: The affirmation in this example would be, "I am safer honoring my power." Then the unconscious misbeliefs that get in the way of embodying this truth might be: "People don't like it when I'm powerful. I don't know what my power even is. I might die if I fully step into my power. The only way to stay safe is to play small. Etc."

Get all of the misbeliefs out, then write the affirmation again. Repeat this five times, even if the same misbeliefs are written and even if they don't make sense; then end with the affirmation.

Walkaway with Wisdom

Anytime we get triggered, a younger part is activated. Triggered in this sense is more than simply being angry: fear, obsession, mania, and resentment to name a few are expressions of unprocessed experiences from our childhood put onto our current environment.

When the experiences that caused our polarity distortion live within us unexamined and unfinished, we bring our once adaptive survival strategies from the past with us into our current relationships. As we use these outdated strategies, we are disrupting contact with ourselves and others, even though we use them in an effort to get connection. In order to develop the capacities we need to create healthy relationships, we need to tend to the trauma of not having those needs met in childhood.

When a relational interaction transpires that confronts a core wound, the intensity of the emotional dysregulation is a signal that the pain precedes this moment. Acknowledging that there is a younger aspect of ourselves present in our current experience, and not just as a past construct, we can contact our young one in this moment.

Learning to create a secure attachment with our inner young one by attuning to ourselves, honoring ourselves, and giving ourselves what we need, we stop looking to others to fulfill our unmet childhood needs.

Chapter 11

Deepening into Our Experience

Sensation is the experience of life. To ignore or resist our physical sensations is to ignore or resist life. To contact our sensations is to deepen into life itself. Once we stop using our conditioned patterns, we need to feel the dysregulation that lives beneath the patterns. Our habitual ways of being are an attempt at regulation. To deepen into our experience of ourselves in a full and mindful way, we begin to feel the places within that are holding the dysregulation of our past experiences.

Our bodies express our lived experience through sensation. Through sensation we have direct access to our inherent wisdom, which is called somatic intelligence. Welcoming our sensations and contacting all the layers of our lived experience provides us with insight into how to mobilize our unfinished business and bring more vital energy into our whole being.

When we develop our polarity distortions, we ignore and/or resist our lived experience. We tamp down the flow of energy in our systems, and we leave contact with ourselves. We move through life paying attention to our analytical minds while denying the inherent wisdom that resides within our bodies, which is called *cognitive bypassing*. The denial of our somatic experience becomes a habit, giving our power to our conditioned thoughts and behaviors.

Staying in our analytical minds not only moves us away from the inherent wisdom of our somatic intelligence, it also moves us away from feeling vulnerable. Deepening into our experience in our bodies, we can cultivate the capacity to honor our deeper wisdom and attune to our emotions. It is here, in the body, where we can elevate our awareness to include our essential self and bring our whole being with us as we contact the world.

From a dysregulated state, we might become anxious and speed up in an effort to control the world around us. Or we might slow down and disconnect from our bodies and our environment. This is the way our nervous system relates to stress, and this is adaptable. Speeding up with anxiety and slowing down with confusion and depression are two signs that our nervous system is dysregulated and we need to tend to our somatic experience before we do anything else.

As we scan the environment for psychological safety, our evolutionary strategy is to look for four things: physical threats, judgment, incongruence, and the unknown (Dion, 2018). When we perceive any of these four threats to our safety, our nervous system responds by either speeding up with urgency or slowing down into a collapse.

The purpose of regulation is not to become calm. As we regulate, the purpose is to feel and experience our nervous system's response to a perceived threat to our safety. Bringing more awareness into our emotional, physical, and energetic bodies, we can touch all the layers of dysregulation with compassion and tenderness. As we practice this, we are moving away from the stories or meaning making that we have about the events, and we are staying in contact with ourselves.

Somatic Curiosity

Healing happens in the present moment at a deeper level than our mind. When we become aware of the way our bodies hold our experience, we become present to our own healing potential. Contacting the emotional pain and subtle energy blockages stored in our bodies is necessary to metabolize our experience. However, because our unprocessed emotional and energetic blockages are linked to experiences when we felt unsafe, we might feel unsafe to experience the full range of our emotions in our bodies. Somatic curiosity is the beginning of feeling safe to move into sensation, transforming stored pain and trauma into new life and new energy.

Our vital force runs through our bodies as a channel through the core of our being. As we experience life, sensations in our bodies influence our vital force. The more blissful and joyful the experience, the more our vital force flows with ease. The more painful and traumatic the experience, the more our vital force becomes thwarted.

The full range of our life's experiences are felt in our bodies. As human beings, though, we have a propensity to analyze and ruminate on events that have occurred. Although we all have the capacity to experience the world through our minds, bodies, and hearts, we each have our own primary way that we experience the world.

When we are prone to experience life primarily through our mind, the lived experience of our bodies, including sensation, is quieter. When we have a propensity to experience life through our body, our lived experience is heightened. When we primarily experience life through our hearts, we can feel split between our mind and body.

Whether we can easily access our somatic sensations or if it's more effortful, curiosity about how our body holds an experience is important. By slowing down and paying attention to our somatic experience, we can discover what we need to move through the experience fully.

As we think about or talk about past experiences that were painful or traumatic, our body responds. It is important to deepen into this inner mind-body process as we increase our awareness about the events that shaped our distortion and caused us to disrupt contact. If we stay at the level of the mind without noticing the way our bodies respond to our thoughts, we keep ourselves in the loop of our conditioning.

The frontal lobe, also known as the creative brain, is the newest part of the brain. Whereas the reptilian brain reacts, the frontal lobe holds our ability for higher level thinking and communication. If we stay in our higher level of thinking as we process past events, we end up analyzing ourselves and others rather than contacting our lived experience in our bodies.

This same part of the brain, however, has great capacity for curiosity. If we choose to use our frontal lobe to turn towards our bodies with attentiveness, we can open ourselves to deeper levels of contact with Self. Once we bring curiosity into our bodies, our limbic system, the center of emotions and memories, can regulate our nervous system as we learn how to deepen into our inner mind-body process.

Using our brains to cultivate somatic curiosity is necessary for self-regulation. Self-regulation is the process by which we love ourselves in our experience and call on our breath to bring greater compassion to our lived experience. Sometimes we think we're self-regulating when in fact we are suppressing our emotions and capping them off. If we notice ourselves doing this, we can bring this same quality of love and compassion to the place in us that resists; and we can regulate the resistance.

Our somatic patterns are so familiar to our experience of ourselves that sometimes we cannot identify them on our own. Similarly, because habitual somatic patterns are a persistent part of our inner world, we can tend to resist them. Thinking that nothing good can come of looking at our physical discomfort, the tendency might be to look away from what we feel in our bodies. Alternatively, sometimes the constant nature of a sensation makes it seem as though it is not noteworthy. Just like everything that pulls the attention of our mind holds a key to what is pulling us off balance, every single thing we experience in our bodies holds the key to where we are storing unprocessed emotions.

Directing our breath into our bodies and around the sensation, not through it, begins to mobilize our blocked energy, making room to process and move through unfinished business. Our breath is the only part of our autonomic nervous system that we have conscious control over. Because of its contribution to self-regulation, the breath, combined with our curiosity, is the most effective way to move through out emotional experiences.

Throughout our bodies there is a cranial nerve called the vagus nerve (Porges, 2017). The vagus nerve is responsible for relaying information from our brains to our digestive system and organs. The vagus nerve responds to traumatic stress via the autonomic nervous system with a decrease in heart rate and blood pressure, as well as decreased blood flow to the brain.

As we breathe, we can soothe our vagus nerve with touch. Taking the fingertips of both hands to the top of our head with a firm but comfortable touch, we can slowly bring our fingers down the sides of our head, down around the ears, and down both sides of the neck. Slowly, we bring our fingertips towards our heart and then down towards our solar plexus. By repeating this several times, reminding ourselves that we're safe to be in our bodies, we can deepen into our full experience as we regulate.

Metabolizing Old Emotional Pain

When the stress of life has been complex and chronic, our regulatory system begins to shut down as a means of self-protection. Numbness, not being able to feel our bodies, is an indicator that this has occurred. Dissociation, where we feel disconnected from our mind and body, is a way to disconnect from the pain that lives within us.

The more time we spend not feeling our pain, the more our life is filtered through the lens of our stress and trauma. We need to become associated with our pain and trauma in order to metabolize it. We need to be willing to access what we're feeling right now without stopping our experience with our thoughts.

If the accumulation of our pain and trauma is backlogged, beginning to become associated with our experience can range from "challenging to feel anything" to "intense." As we deepen into our experience, we can stay in our window of tolerance by ensuring that we have the ability to continually regulate (Stanely, 2019). If we begin to panic and feel overwhelmed, we have moved into a state of *hyperarousal* (fight/flight). This is an indicator that we need to feel the fight/flight in our bodies and discover a way to let the energy move through us until completion. Hyperarousal has us feeling disembodied, so when we stay with the sensation in our system without cognitive bypassing we can become more embodied as we regulate.

If we begin to shut down and disconnect, we have moved into *hypoarousal* (freeze). This can be more challenging to work with as we might be dissociated, in a collapse, or in deep depression. When we find ourselves in this state, it's important that we honor our experience while also finding our inner spark— otherwise, our vital force can become cloaked by heaviness and our conditioned self can loop in there being no way out of the experience. Associating to our experience, validating what's happening in our bodies, and then finding an inner resource can begin to allow the heaviness to move. If we're in a state of dissociation, orienting to our surroundings can help us be present. Feeling what a freeze feels like in our bodies is also helpful. For example, what does numb really feel like? What does disconnection feel like?

There is wisdom in our nervous system response. By turning towards ourselves and our experience, we honor our body's inherent wisdom. Healing and transformation happen in the somatic phenomenology of our felt experience. Phenomenology means that we are conscious of our direct experience. Somatic phenomenology means that we are in direct contact with our bodily sensations, and we consciously experience our felt sense.

Many people brace against their somatic phenomenology. Since we hold our pain and trauma in our bodies, our bodies seem like they are not a safe place to reside. Even when the threat to our safety is no longer present, our bodies bear the burden of holding our pain. And as long as we continue to hold that burden in our bodies, we hold our bodies responsible for what was done to us—encumbered by our pain and trauma.

Beneath the resistance to attune to our bodies is the unknown answer to these questions:

"Am I safe in my body?"

"Does this body belong to me?"

"Is this sensation safe for me to feel/experience?"

During moments of stress and trauma, our bodies were not a safe place to be. Leaving our body was the wisest way to protect ourselves. Slowly, over time, we can learn to move toward our body's sensation and know that we are safe to do so. We are safer coming back into our bodies than we are staying dissociated. We are safer claiming our body and all that it's holding than believing that anyone who misused their power over us owns us.

As we metabolize old pain, each layer we touch within our bodies is the place that needs our awareness in that moment. Without pushing beyond what's present, we contact each layer of emotion and sensation with love and compassion. Reminding ourselves that we are already whole, we are not trying to fix or change anything about ourselves. We are simply bringing more loving awareness into our whole being so that we may embody more of our essence and align more fully.

Becoming more embodied, our soul relaxes deeper into its seat within ourselves. Our body becomes the safe place we've always wanted to experience, and our awareness becomes the loving caregiver of our wholeness. As we honor our somatic intelligence, we develop the capacity to attune to our needs with tenderness and love. In doing so, we create a secure connection with ourselves.

From a place of deep contact with our somatic sensations, we can become curious about what our bodies want to say. For example, if our chest is tight and we bring our attention to the sensation, we make more room to listen to our bodies. Perhaps our chest wants to speak in a tone that sounds like shaky fear or heavy sadness. Or perhaps our chest actually has words for us, like "pay attention to me" or "I'm holding too much." Attuning to our somatic experience provides us tremendous wisdom about our own needs that go deeper than the stories of our analytical minds.

The Role of Chronic Physical Pain

When we have chronic physical pain, being in our bodies can be excruciating. We detach from our bodies to detach from our pain, and this seems to be the only way life can be bearable. We resist our bodies and resist the pain, and at the same time we orient towards the pain. We stalk the pain, even, watching it vigilantly. As we do, we forget about the rest of ourselves.

When our bodies are screaming at us in pain, it's counterintuitive to turn towards our bodies and our sensations. Paying attention to our relationship to the pain is a key element in our personal transformation. Resistance exacerbates the pain.

Noticing how our ego creates an identity around our chronic pain, we can begin to work with the underlying reason why our identity is wrapped up in our pain. Noticing how the pain can be a wall to connection, we can begin to see how our pain is a barrier to love and nourishment. By seeing the ways we resist the pain, we can begin to bring awareness to the ways we keep the pain locked in place.

Bringing more awareness to our pain and our relationship to it, we can see and hear what our body is communicating to us. We can listen to our bodies with gentle curiosity. We can begin to create more space around the pain, which gives it room to move. With our attention, we can breathe all the way around our pain with awareness, love, and compassion. This, in and of itself, can be healing. As our inner suffering decreases in relationship to our pain, our pain begins to decrease. We bring in more essential qualities of the True Self into our bodies, and we allow our conditioned self to rest.

Slowly, over time and with practice, we become more and more embodied. And the more we fully occupy our bodies, the less we hurt.

Harmony's Story

Once I came though my chronic depression in my early 20s, my expression of trauma became one of being highly functional. In my perfectionistic tendencies, I tried to control my environment by being well-organized, looking composed, and being available for others at all times.

With so much attention outside of myself, I was completely unaware of how unprocessed experiences lived within my body. Instead of paying attention to my bodily cues, I bypassed them and functioned over them, treating myself like an object. Anytime I felt stuck or limited, I would use my strong psychological analyzer to think my way out of my experience.

After I started teaching yoga and awoke to my essential self (detailed in Chapter 4), I recognized the value in being with my somatic experience. From this point on, when I practiced yoga, I no longer paid attention to how I looked in an asana. My inner eye looked within to be in discovery of how I felt as I moved through my practice. When my mind started assessing my performance and comparing myself to others, I would redirect my attention into my body.

Spontaneously, old somatic patterns began to unwind. The twist in my spine from my old head trauma began to come back into balance. The grief stored in my lungs began to move and I could breathe the full expansion of my lung capacity. The protection over my heart began to shift as loving forgiveness grew.

Learning that somatic experience is the sensation of life, as

I continued to experience life, I needed to maintain curiosity of the layers of somatic intelligence within myself. As I deepened into my physical sensations, I deepened into contact with my Self.

As a psychotherapist, guiding my clients into deeper awareness of their inner mind-body process is the portal to guiding them into contact with themselves. People want to tell me about themselves and their lives, and everything they say is important. However, the way their somatic intelligence responds as they speak is even more important. The body doesn't lie. Associating to our somatic experience is where we contact the truth of our experience. Even if we feel numb in our bodies, associating to the numbness is vital to becoming more embodied.

If I stay more focused on what a client says than on a client's connection with the sensations in their body, I would be colluding with their defense strategies that keep them stuck. Staying in the psychological analyzing of oneself keeps one removed from their True Self. By becoming aware of the inner mind-body process, my clients become aware of the way they leave contact with themselves. This makes it possible to process unresolved pain. This awareness and processing is what makes choice possible. And when we are at choice, we are closer to embodying our True Self.

Exercise: Somatic Attunement

To deepen into our somatic experience, we need to be curious about what we're feeling on the level of sensation. Without analyzing why we feel a certain way, tuning into vibrational qualities within our bodies can help us metabolize our emotions and become more embodied and present.

Step 1: Ask yourself "What am I feeling?"

When you notice that your mind is latching onto a story about what happened or about a fear that you are holding, stop the stream of thought and inquire within yourself about what feeling underlies your story.

There are five basic human emotions: Anger, Fear, Sadness/ Grief, Joy, and Love. When you identify your feeling, make sure that you are truly coming to the feeling body and not staying stuck in your story. For example, "I'm feeling like you're attacking me" is not a feeling. "I'm feeling angry" is more in line with the level of clarity you're wanting to nurture with this practice, and you can add "My story is that you're attacking me" if that helps you to weed out story from emotion.

Step 2: Ask yourself "Where am I feeling this?"

After you identify your emotion, use your inner eye to check in with your body and experience the somatic sensations and textures of your emotion. If you're feeling angry, you may have a pounding heart, tight muscles, and a clenched jaw. Go looking around your body to discover the actual felt sense of your emotion.

Step 3: Allow yourself to experience your somatic sensations

Keep your inner eye anchored into the present-moment sensations within your body. You may find yourself wanting to breathe around the sensations, move with them, touch your body, vocalize the tone of the sensation, or something else. Stay with your body as you allow the emotions to discharge fully.

Step 4: Ask yourself "What does this feeling need from me?"

Once you've moved the energy your body was holding, inquire with the sensations about what they are needing from you. Perhaps they need love and compassion. Perhaps they need protection. Perhaps they need more attention. Simply inquiring within your body to see what your somatic intelligence is communicating to you is the bridge to becoming more embodied. This is where you build the capacity to show up for yourself in all areas of your life.

Step 5: Stay present with your body

Slowing down your breath, stay present with your body. You

may feel tingling throughout your body, you may feel more seated in your body, or you may feel lighter and more open. Whatever you discover on the other side of the emotions, stay with yourself. Keep breathing and allow yourself to surrender into your body, your sacred vessel.

Walkaway with Wisdom

Sensation is the experience of life. To ignore or resist our physical sensations is to ignore or resist life. To contact our sensations is to deepen into life itself. Healing happens in the present moment at a deeper level than our mind. When we become aware of the way our bodies hold our experience, we become present to our own healing potential. Contacting the emotional pain and subtle energy blockages housed in our bodies is necessary to metabolize our experience. This transforms stored pain and trauma into new life and new energy.

When we have chronic physical pain, being in our bodies can be excruciating. We detach from our bodies to detach from our pain, and this seems to be the only way life can be bearable. We resist our bodies and resist the pain, and at the same time we orient towards the pain.

The more time we spend not feeling our pain, the more our life is filtered through the lens of stress and trauma. We need to become associated with our pain and trauma in order to metabolize it. By becoming aware of the inner mind-body process, we become aware of the way we leave contact with ourselves. This makes it possible to process unresolved pain. This awareness and processing is what makes choice possible. And when we are at choice, we are closer to embodying our True Self.

Chapter 12

Systemic Inequity

Field Theory

In childhood, how we perceive and experience the environment around us shapes our conditioned self. Our family system is the primary environment we exist within, and we are greatly influenced by the energetic bubble created by our family as a whole. Each family member's state of being affects our state of being. On an energetic level, the strategies and misbeliefs that we created in childhood were an unconscious attempt at creating balance in our family system.

For example, if our primary caregivers had a conflictual relationship, we instinctively developed strategies to maintain balance in the system. We might have become accommodating as an attempt to not add to the stress, believing that there was too much pain in the field around us to bring any more disruption. Conversely, we might have become rambunctious or disruptive as an attempt to get attention and deflect the tension between our caregivers. Or maybe we spent a lot of time at social events or activities as a way to avoid being in the field of dysfunctional relationship.

Beyond our family system, we exist in a larger social context. Community, schools, government, law enforcement, economic systems, social structures, etc., are all part of the greater field around us that influenced our ancestors, our family, and ourselves. In deep and lasting ways, we are affected by the larger systems that we exist within beyond our own family system.

When the field around us is not designed to nurture our health and well-being, we adapt. We attempt to control our internal environment to ensure stability in our external environment, which is called *homeostasis* in Gestalt theory.

When the environment we exist within is built on systemic structures that are designed to keep us unwell, our internal environment becomes inflexible. Internally, our energetic, spiritual, and psychological states are restricted in an attempt to survive in an unhealthy environment. While homeostasis is typically known as a healthy balance point, in field theory we see that living in an unhealthy external environment generates an internal homeostasis that is off balance. Given that our ability in childhood to influence the larger systems is limited, adapting in this way is healthy, even though it is also the source of our internal imbalance.

The field around us influences us, just as we influence the field. This means that when we exist in an unhealthy field, it influences us in ways that are not in support of our health. This also means that as we cultivate more internal health, the environment around us begins to transform in kind. We are not only in the field; we are part of it. By disrupting the homeostasis we created in response to an unhealthy system, we can find our way back to health. As we all do this individually, the collective paradigm also shifts. The result is a disruption in the systemic inequity that exists in our society. As we become fully expressed, those systems must eventually change to find a new balance that reflects the health of the environment we are creating internally.

The Role of Power Structures

The power structures that exist within the greater field around us affect us all. Built on distortions of misused power, systemic biases distort the environment around us. These systems are constructed to disturb our interconnectedness and perpetuate ego delusions of exclusion.

Our collective internal polarities create an external polarity, where values and concepts are expressed in a binary model. Even our binary language represents the inner polarity of the majority population. On one end of the spectrum we have liberals, and on the other we have conservatives. These polarized values and perspectives keep society divided.

People tend to polarize and hold onto one way as the right way because it is too much for them to feel the discomfort of uncertainty. The comfort of the known, even if it's a false knowing, is something that people are driven to protect so they don't have to feel the discomfort of the unknown. Those who have the most fear are the ones who fervently cling to methods and patterns that feed the illusion of control.

All social issues held in a polarized division distort our societal power structures. Gender is not binary, nor is sexual orientation, race, or religion. As human beings, there are more than two options for us.

Because societal inequity keeps the collective field in a state of imbalance and unrest, each one of us responds to the field by creating an internal environment that will ensure our own survival. For example, people who hold locations of privilege denying their misuse of power is a survival strategy that perpetuates the distorted systems.

For those of us in white bodies, looking at the way we have benefited for centuries from systems that are built to ensure our position of power is essential, although often painfully confronting of our cognitive dissonance. If you are in a white male body, seeing the way that white men have been misusing power and causing harm can be excruciating. Even as a conscious, loving white man who is in right use of power, you still benefit from these systems. The power structures are so much the proverbial water that you've been swimming in for so long that looking at it for what it is can be daunting. It might even seem like since you didn't create the system it is not your job to change it. If you have inflexible views on societal power structures and/or are unwilling to look at the inequity in our society, you are likely addicted to the power that the larger systems of our society enable you to have.

It's important to acknowledge that there is a huge problem with the power imbalance in our society. White cisgender men who own property, are financially well-off, have neurotypical brain functioning, are able bodied, heterosexual, and educated have more power than the diverse body of human beings who occupy this planet. When men with power misuse their power and perpetuate systems of inequity, the field maintains imbalance. Meanwhile, the rest of society simultaneously adapts to an environment that is not designed to support their full health while also trying to change the system. Collective power, where large groups of people work together to change systems of inequity, influences the field, yet true balance and restoration requires people with power to be in right use of power.

It is not healthy for the men in power to have such a high degree of influence over the systems that govern our society. Because the environmental imbalance is a reflection of their internal imbalance, it is imperative for their own well-being and developing sense of self to take an honest look at how they affect the field and how they feel within that field is a reparative act that begins to shift the paradigm of power structures. Because of your position in the power structures of society, it is your duty to come into right use of power, where you become informed, compassionate, connected and more skillful (Barstow, 2017).

For those of us who are cisgender white women, heterosexual, educated, own property, are financially well-off, have neuro-typical brain functioning, and are able bodied and slim, we simultaneously hold a position of privilege and oppression. The way we have been influenced by societal inequity has been split between systems that have evolved to include us in its privilege and systems that exclude us and keep us disempowered. Laws that govern our bodies, sexual violence, and the proverbial "glass ceiling" are contrasted by the many privileges we are endowed by our whiteness and conformity to gender norms.

The conditioned patterns, misbeliefs about our worth, and relationship to our own power are affected by these power structures. The internal imbalance we have created in response to the field around us keeps that field imbalanced. By shifting our own relationship to our power and privilege in relationship with our environment, we change the field. This includes being an active ally for people in marginalized groups.

For those who are in Black or Brown bodies, the web of systems designed to disempower, violate, enslave, and annihilate you are inherent in the fabric of our society. Given that systems are structured against your well-being and in service of your demise, the current homeostasis of society is dependent on your struggle. This is a blatant violation of your humanity and reparations are due. The collective homeostasis is disrupted to a certain degree each time the truth of systemic inequity is highlighted to the masses. However, more must be done collectively to bring a much needed repair and equilibrium to the field as whole.

Indigenous peoples live within power structures that were formed to rob you of your peace. Systems were built to govern your stolen land, your heritage, and your health. While power structures persist that violate your sacred rights, you exist in an environment that is designed to keep you and your community unwell, disempowered, and isolated. Amending these violations is an integral component to the restoration of our planet, and this begins when people who have the most influence surrender the power structures that exist at the cost of your inherent privileges.

Undocumented and documented people from other countries move into power structures that govern your rights. Influenced by the environment of your homeland and your new country, the way you are affected by power structures varies depending on your ability to assimilate and/or pass as white. Living in a system that does not honor your culture, your language, or your homeland, your safety becomes dependent on the degree to which you conform to the ethos of people who have the most power.

Gender expressions that live outside of the norm as defined by people in positions of power are marginalized. Non-binary, transgender, and inter-sex individuals live in a society that doesn't welcome or take time to understand your gender expression. This power structure is not designed for you to be in your highest health and potential. Systems, laws, and societal norms that exclude you and oppress you are injurious. To stand in your true expression with dignity is a sacred presence that is more profound than those stuck in binary models can comprehend. If you also hold other marginalized locations, such as being in a Black or Brown body, being an undocumented citizen, being indigenous, and so on, the layers of systems designed to disempower you are interwoven. These systems affect your well-being in numerous ways, and by relating to your own body with unapologetic self-love is a revolutionary act of claiming your power.

Power structures also affect people whose sexual expressions live outside of the norm of those in positions of power. Pansexual, homosexual, bisexual, polyamorous, open marriage, and more are not perversions or distortions. The authentic expression of one's sexuality has been the target of prejudice, violence, and systemic oppression for centuries.

Conditioned values around physical appearance, race, ethnicity, culture, gender, gender expression, size, ability, and age that are acquired by our environment and reinforced through systemic power structures are the cornerstone of societal inequity and internal dis-ease. This is felt by all people, even those in power. Living within us as introjections and disrupting contact with the environment through projections and retroflections, power structures are part of all of our inner make up. Introjections of internalized misogyny and internalized racism can live within all people, causing unconscious misbeliefs about ourselves, others, and our community. When we turn in on ourselves and believe something is wrong with us, rather than expressing the truth of our anger in a healthy way that would change the systems, we experience retroflections that perpetuate self-harm.

From the way our caregivers misused their power to the way systemic racism and oppression inform who we are in the world, we are all in the field and are affected by the status quo. By accepting ourselves as we are, cleansing ourselves of acquired misbeliefs, and being in right use of power, we shift our internal environment. When we no longer engage with the world with our internalized oppression or misused privilege, we are empowered to change the systems that keep the true nature of humanity out of balance.

To have power means to have influence, and we all have our own personal power and ability to influence. Innate power that is aligned with Source empowers all beings. When this clean and expansive power that we all have access to flows through us with ease, our internal system comes into balance as does the field around us. Whereas ego power either "powers over" others or collapses around power, aligned power is generative and healing. Creating systems that are designed to keep all beings in a state of health is necessary for planetary restoration.

Bridging the divide between polarized power structures is just as important as working with our own inner polarities. When each one of us is dedicated to doing the work to come into our own alignment, the environment around us begins to shift. While returning to aligned power is good for all of us to do, those of us who occupy positions of privilege in society are accountable for how we use our power. It is our duty to look within and be in right relationship with how we influence the field around us.

If we're not actively trying to change the system we are in, we are part of the problem. Our presence contributes to the inequity of power structures simply by being silent and complicit. Right action and right speech is right use of power.

Ancestral Patterns

The lived experience of societal inequity is passed down in our DNA. We inherit ancestral patterns of racialized trauma, misogyny, and misused power. Before we develop awareness of the systems that are built on racial and gender inequity, we already embody the cellular memory of privilege and oppression. When our caregivers perpetuate the distorted patterns and narratives of misused power and oppression, our ancestral patterns are explicitly passed down to us.

Our most painful, dysfunctional, and seemingly unchangeable patterns are seated in our family lineage. Each generation has an opportunity to look within and discover the transgenerational pattern that is being expressed through them, asking to be healed.

Because our family system holds the values of our ancestral patterns in deep and unconscious ways, we can feel simultaneously overwhelmed and motivated to shift the patterns. The fear of our family system not understanding our own growth and not knowing how to relate to us when we change might keep us feeling even more stuck in the patterns that we desperately want to change. To do the work anyway is a courageous act of honoring ourselves. And while it may seem like we are dishonoring our family lineage, living in alignment with our own values, our own transformation heals the field around us in deep and lasting ways.

All family lineage has a history of racialized trauma and misogyny. While marginalized populations are well aware of their experience of racialized trauma and misogyny, those in positions of privilege can have a more challenging time identifying how racialized trauma and misogyny negatively influence their experience of life. The patterns and prejudices that are passed down in a family lineage must be looked at with clarity and experienced in the body in order to transform them.

While our genetics are fixed traits we inherit, *epigenetics* are inherited DNA sequences that have been added to our genes through experience and can be changed. Stress, trauma, diet, alcohol, tobacco, and environmental pollutants have been found to be the cause of this DNA modification (Waddington, 1942).

Since our ancestors have crossed over, they aren't physically here to tell us what events occurred that modified their DNA. They aren't able to tell us about their trauma and the patterns they developed that are similar to what we're experiencing. Nonetheless, when working with transgenerational trauma through a transpersonal lens, we are looking for the birthplace of pattern in the ancestral lineage.

Even if we do not have a conscious understanding of our ancestors' patterning, we can use our own sensitivities, intuition, and understanding of ourselves to get a sense of where the pattern was acquired. As we look within and do this work, we can also look to our ancestors for help. As we discussed in Chapter 10, on the level of spirit there is no linear time. Shifting our relationship to time helps us to shift our relationship to our healing potential. In the fourth dimension of timelessness, our ancestors still exist. By bringing our attention to them and asking for their support, they are given the opportunity to help us transmute the patterns that they were unable to shift when they were in their human form.

By doing this courageous work of looking within, processing ancestral unfinished business, and differentiating from values that were passed down to us, we can bring a higher level of health into our family lineage. We can talk about our transformation with our parents, caregivers, siblings, and children, even if they might not fully comprehend it. Shining light on our process allows us to fully embody our True Self. We don't transform only to hide our transformation from our family or society. Compartmentalizing our alignment is a distortion.

Distorted behavior in one relationship negatively affects all of our relationships. Learning how to hold the vibration of our truth is essential to bringing the collective field around us out of distortion and into alignment.

Decolonizing Psychotherapy

Therapy has the potential to be a sacred container where deep transformation can unfold. However, it can also be a disappointing experience for a variety of reasons. When a therapist isn't in contact with themselves or us, we can feel dissatisfied, invisible, confused, or even retraumatized. To be in contact with one's Self means to be in an integrated state where we are aware of our introjections, including internalized racism and misogyny which are colonized constructs, meaning they were brought by settlers for their own benefit and are not original to the indigenous peoples of this land.

The courage it takes to show up at a therapist's office and vulnerably show ourselves to them is profound, and to be missed by that therapist can feel devastating. While there are many factors that influence a therapist's capacity to hold a quality therapeutic container, their own awareness of the lens they see a client through hugely impacts their ability to actually see that client.

Since the foundation of the field of mental health is seated in ideas generated by psychologists who were cisgender white men, the earliest research was conducted through the lens of unchecked privilege. We can see this through some of the early psychological treatments provided to women, where medication and institutionalization were the cure for "hysteria" and "melancholia," or through pathologizing homosexuality and trying to cure the person with conversion therapy. While the concepts and ideas generated during psychology's nascency hold tremendous value to the field, the limitations they have are countless when considering people who are not cisgender, heterosexual white men.

With the fabric of our society founded in colonized systems of societal inequity, the field of mental health has various threads of power structures woven within it that must be deconstructed. While racial and gender biases are accounted for more now than ever, there continue to be many "best practices" that are largely built on research conducted in the colonialized education system by psychologists who may or may not be actively looking at their own privilege.

On a systemic level, having psychological research and diagnostic criteria that uses a definition of normal that describes one's ability to conform to the norm of society is oppressive. When the people conducting that research have historically been in white bodies, the lens of normal is skewed to a colonialized standard. This means that many evidence-based practices are exclusive to people in white bodies. While there is more diversity represented in the field of psychology than ever before, the standard of normal continues to be influenced by the field of systemic inequity.

On a personal level, the counselor or therapist has an ethical duty to actively look at the way they influence and are influenced by power structures. However, a person cannot see what they cannot see. If a counselor has been trained in best practices that are rooted in colonized research, their interventions may perpetuate societal inequity. Similarly, the therapist may not have the awareness to identify and investigate their own biases if they cannot see them.

Given the harm that has been caused by systemic racism, misogyny, transmisogyny, cissexism, ableism, classism, and weightism, a therapist, coach, or healer has a duty to repair that harm rather than cause further harm. To own their prejudices and investigate their blind spots is part of having the privilege of holding space for others. In doing so, a therapist can discover new ways to be with themselves, which allows them to be in discovery of how to truly make contact with others. Without the veil of introjections and projections clouding their ability to see, a counselor can be open to the mystery of humanity as they sit with a client.

A true healer embodies their wholeness and reminds others that they are already whole. Whereas colonolized psychotherapy wants to fix, change, or analyze, decolonized psychotherapy offers restitution. The great unlearning is a collective effort that brings us back to our original state.

Harmony's Story

Our first awareness around our own race and gender expression is powerful in our developing sense of self. I remember being a young child and looking at myself in the mirror, surprised that my skin was white. Since my family had white bodies, my surprise may have seemed strange; however, this was my first experience of knowing that I had a race.

Around that same age, I sat in my elementary school classroom learning about the Holocaust. I attended a Jewish school, although I was not considered Jewish because my mom had not converted. As we learned about the genocide and misuse of power against Jews, my teacher looked at me and said, "They wouldn't have killed you because you have blonde hair and blue eyes. The men would have kept you to be their wife." In this moment, I knew implicitly that my appearance and gender expression were simultaneously a key to privilege and oppression.

In that same year, a white man violated my body by touching my genitals. He was the stepfather of my best friend, and he was getting ready to put us in the bath. When he touched me, my body froze in fear. I stayed silent, looking at him to assess if anything more was going to happen to me. I then looked to my friend who was standing right there and she smiled, clearly accustomed to being violated. He then put us in the bath and groped both of us, and I pretended that it was fun in order to stabilize my internal world and find safety in the strange environment I was in.

While these experiences were mine, the more I learned about my family lineage, I could see that they were transgenerational patterns that were being expressed through and around me.

On my father's side of the family, I come from a lineage of white men who were in right use of power with their whiteness. My grandfather was a Jewish immigrant who came to the United States from Europe by himself at the age of 13 in the 1920s. His father was a Rabbi, and he left behind 12 siblings as he set out to make a life for himself. As an immigrant who assimilated quickly, my grandfather first became a pharmacist and was an early advocate of birth control. Eventually, he moved to Michigan and became a realtor. However, in his business he would only sell property to the Black community. Having known pain and oppression of misused power, he knew that land ownership would empower the Black community in a racist world.

On my mother's side, I come from a lineage of misogynistic white men who misused their power. My grandfather was a first-generation immigrant whose parents came from Italy. While still in Italy, my great-grandfather had an affair with his wife's sister and they fled to the U.S. together to make a new life for themselves. This same man sexually abused my mother throughout her childhood. My mother and my grandmother endured sexual violations from men who were supposed to care for them, and those patterns of misogyny were strong in my ancestral lineage.

These divergent patterns lived within me in conflicting ways. On the one hand, I was very aware of my own privilege of being born in a white body. I was aware that it was important to be in right use of my own power when it came to racial inequity, and that it was my duty to shift power structures. On the other hand, I was very unaware of my own internalized misogyny. With self-hatred dictated by my conditioned self, I was a misogynist and I colluded with men who were too.

Before I was aware of my own misogyny, I tolerated emotional and physical abuse from some of the men I dated. When the man I was dating was white, I buried my outrage that they would exert control over me in patterns of misused power while simultaneously giving my will over to them. When the man I was dating was from a marginalized population, I expressed my compassion and understanding while giving my will over to them.

As I learned to love myself, I also learned how to own my power. Once I felt the power of the True Self flowing through my body, I began the vulnerable practice of claiming my power in relationships. Self-betrayal was the way I gave my power away. Honoring myself was the way I owned my power. I was in disbelief at how simple yet revolutionary this practice was. The more I honored myself, the more the power of Source had influenced my life. Because the pattern of self-betrayal was conditioned, the power of self-honoring was essential to the fabric of my wholeness.

To be anti-racist and anti-gender-bias requires my continual looking at my own use of my power and privilege. Where I was once uncertain if my self-love and claiming of power would make a difference in the world, I now would literally use my own body as a shield to prevent racial and gender violence. All beings deserve to be honored, and now that I know how to honor myself, I stand in honor of humanity. Books that help me in my learning include *My Grandmother's Hands* (Menekem, 2017), *How to Be an Antiracist* (Kendi, 2020), *Your Body Is Not an Apology* (Taylor, 2021), *White Fragility* (DiAngelo, 2018), and *Stamped from the Beginning* (Kendi, 2017).

Exercise: Right Use of Power

This is an exercise designed to evoke more awareness of your relationship to your own power within the systemic power structures given your location in those systems. Remembering that you are part of the field and influence the field, consider the ways you are impacted by and influence the field around you with these questions.

Get a piece of paper and journal about the following questions:

Given my location in systemic inequity, how powerful do I feel in the world?

Where do I feel the most influential?

Given my location in systemic inequity, how disempowered do I feel?

Where do I feel most disempowered?

What do I think it's like to be a marginalized person in these systems?

What do I think it's like to be a privileged person in these systems?

What beliefs do I hold that keep me empowered?

What beliefs do I hold that keep me disempowered?

What actions do I take that are a misuse of my power?

What actions do I take that keep the systems imbalanced?

What actions do I take that are a right use of my power?

What actions do I take that create more equality in the field around me?

How do I feel in my body when I contemplate systemic inequity?

How do I feel in my body when I consider systems changing to a more balanced structured?

What actions am I committed to taking today to be in right use of my power?

Walkaway with Wisdom

We exist within a social context. The field around us influences us, just as we influence the field. This means that when we exist in an unhealthy field, it influences us in ways that are not in support of our health. This also means that as we cultivate more internal health, the environment around us begins to transform in kind. We are not only in the field; we are part of it.

The power structures that exist within the greater field around us affect us all. Built on distortions of misused power, systemic biases distort the environment that we exist within. Our collective internal polarity creates an external polarity, where values and concepts are expressed in a binary model.

The lived experience of societal inequity is passed down in our DNA. We inherit ancestral patterns of racialized trauma, misogyny, and misused power. Our most painful, dysfunctional, and seemingly unchangeable patterns are seated in our family lineage. Each generation has an opportunity to look within and discover the transgenerational pattern that is being expressed through them and asking to be healed.

Part 4:

Aligned Relationships

Chapter 13

Interconnection

Throughout Part 4, we will explore being in relationship with others. In the language used there is a focus on intimate partnership; however, all of the concepts and tools are relevant and useful in all of our relationships. The full spectrum of the human experience includes our individuality, where we are uniquely ourselves; it includes our group identity, where we share similarities to some people; and it includes our unity, where we are all one. These three dimensions of human identity acknowledge both our uniqueness and our interconnectedness.

The deep work we do to come into our alignment and embody our wholeness creates many different changes in how we experience ourselves. We may find that we prefer spending time with different groups of people once we are more aligned with our True Self. And as we increase our internal awareness and move deeper into our integration, our relationship with the world changes as well, where we treat others with the same compassion and love with which we have begun to treat ourselves.

When we see our own distorted life force with more clarity, we can start to see how relating to the world from this place has impacted our relationships and our work in the world. To see this is humbling. To recognize our own contribution to the demise of our relationships can leave us wondering if we will ever find a new way to be in clean, aligned relationships.

If we are not consciously choosing alignment, we are choosing distortion. If we are not consciously choosing the True Self, we are choosing the conditioned self. Because of our interconnectedness, the choice we make internally influences what we experience externally in the world around us.

As our conditioned strategies become more and more

outdated, discovering how we want to be in relationship with others is an undertaking that has no map. Because our sense of self continually develops in relationship to our environment, contacting our authentic experience as it emerges is an embodied practice where we honor our somatic intelligence.

Entangled Relationships

When our inner polarity distortion guides the way we interact with the world, we engage in relationships from a place that will eventually cause an entangled pattern of confusion and conflict. Unable to stay aligned with our Self, we see our relationships through the lens of our conditioned self, our wounds, and our polarity distortions. Our patterned ways of disrupting contact (projections, introjections, retroflections, deflections, and confluence) inhibit our ability to contact others.

The closer we get to a person, the more likely we are to engage with the relationship from our conditioned ways that we learned to disrupt contact. We do this unknowingly. What we truly long for is deep connection. However, the context of intimacy has the power to activate our deepest and oldest patterns: introjections guide our misbeliefs about ourselves and relationship; projections are put onto the people we connect with; confluence makes it hard to know where we end and another person begins; retroflections keep us feeling responsible for and obligated to others; and deflection keeps us from dropping into deep connection.

Because of the imprint we have in our conditioned self and our distorted life force, we attract and are attracted to people who fit the image of our imprint. This happens below the level of awareness, as we think that we are attracted to a person because of qualities that are not like our imprint and are often surprised when in their shadow lives a pattern that triggers our deepest wound.

Even when we're in a new relationship that we're excited about, contact boundary disturbances are already present: introjections about how relationships ought to be, projections onto our partner about who we think they are, retroflections of how we should act/look/feel, confluence where we merge together, and deflections where we prevent any feelings that cause discomfort can already be present. From the very beginning of a relationship, we are using conditioned patterns that we learned from our caregivers with our new partner. Although our wound was not caused by the other person, their conditioned patterns mirror the events around our wounding and ignite our pain—not to harm us but to help us heal.

As the relationship progresses and conflict arises, we might blame the other person for "making" us feel a certain way. Before we met this person, we didn't feel this way. When we're not around this person, we don't feel this way. Because we only feel this way when we're interacting with this person, it would make sense that our ego would believe that the conflict and entanglement is their fault. The mind reasons that if they would become more aware or seated in themselves, we could have a healthy relationship. When we blame someone else for our feelings, we are giving our power away to them while simultaneously ignoring the truth that we are responsible for our own emotional state.

All relationships are a mirror for us to see ourselves more clearly. However, when we look to relationships to fill a hole within ourselves or make us happy, we fail to see ourselves through the reflection of the people in our lives. When we engage in relationships from our distorted life force energy and unfinished business, we attract and are attracted to people who reflect what we have disowned and left unexamined.

Because we have aspects of our distortion that need our attention, we find the perfect partner to match that frequency. We might even feel at home when we first meet the person, which is a sign of the deep match to our distorted patterns.

Instead of looking at and feeling our own pain, we project our pain of our unmet needs onto our partner in an attempt to self-regulate. To really look at ourselves and discover what lives in our own shadow is too painful so we put it onto our partner. If we stay unwilling to look at ourselves, it is inevitable that our relationships will dissolve and we will stay engaged with our distorted patterns.

Projections happen on the subtle level, so paying attention to the subtle ways we move into our distortion cultivates the awareness we need to stay in contact with ourselves. Projections are so subtle, in fact, that even with the reflection of a trained therapist it can be challenging to see ourselves clearly. The subtle energy of the projection is simply the lens we look through; it's not obvious or concrete like the behaviors of our partner.

The image below illustrates two people who are interacting from their line of distortion. They are each identified with their mask of conditioning, and they are seeing the other as if they are their mask, too. They are looking to one another as the source of love, and they are each activating one another's disowned parts. As they do this, they become entangled in projections, and they communicate their deeper feelings through projective identification, where they unconsciously induce their deeper pain into one another. This, of course, leads to conflict and heartbreak.

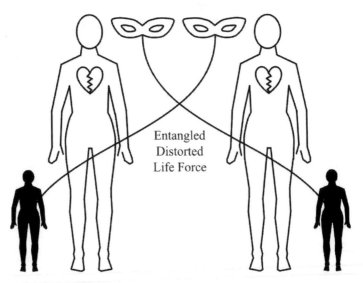

Entangled Distorted Life Force

There is a paradox that exists in relationship, where we are simultaneously sovereign and interconnected.

As a sovereign individual, we are responsible for everything that arises within us. Nobody makes us feel anything, we simply feel certain things in reaction or response to interactions with other people. But what arises within us is ours. It's ours to be with consciously. It's ours to own. And it's ours to learn from and heal. Our reaction and response is influenced by the way we perceive other people's words and actions. We may be seeing through the lens of an old wound or a projection. Knowing what's happening within us and where we are perceiving the relationship from is what cultivates the autonomy necessary to tend to the place of interconnection.

Autonomy is the quality of self-responsibility that we garner by working with our inner young one and being in choice about how we make contact with the environment. When we talk about sovereignty, we are talking about a state of autonomy where we are no longer driven by our conditioned self, where we have agency and choice around how we engage with the world.

Self-responsibility, however, does not mean that we are unaffected by others. It doesn't mean that other people don't have their contribution to the entangled conflict patterns. And it does not mean that we don't want connection. It simply means that we are securely attached to ourselves and we have the ability to self-regulate. We have clarity around what we want, what we need, and what we are available for in our relationships. And this clarity gives us choice. This choice is the foundation for self-responsibility and sovereignty. In its highest expression, sovereignty means that we can be fully our Self regardless of how another person behaves. This degree of sovereignty comes from completing our unfinished business, differentiating from our conditioned self, and staying in contact with our deeper somatic experience.

To tend to the point of connection in our relationship

where we affect and are affected by others takes tremendous awareness. To do this when we, ourselves and the other person, have our wounds activated takes even more capacity to stay in contact with ourselves.

The stress and trauma that influenced the development of our conditioned self occurred in relationship with the people who were supposed to love us and keep us safe. As we get closer to intimacy, this trauma gets activated with our partner because they match the imprint of our wound precisely, or close enough.

By design, our wounds fit together with our partner's like two pieces of a puzzle. It may seem like an enigma when this happens, but our unconscious psyche guides our attraction so that we can discover and heal all of the barriers that we have built against love.

As we contact the layers within ourselves that prevent us from experiencing deep connection, we touch deeper levels of our Self. We can stay in contact with ourselves and remember that we have our own energy Source within us up the midline of our body. We can stay seated in our alignment, and we stay with our somatic experience, away from stories and meaning making. Without blame, we can stay in contact while we untangle the distorted conflict that we co-created in our relationship.

Polarity Distortion in Relationships

When we unconsciously move from our distortion (identified with our conditioned self and disowning parts of ourselves), we attract and are attracted to partners who embody what is in our own shadow. Similar to our own inner polarities, our partner embodies a polarity that we, ourselves, have diverged from within ourselves.

For example, if I have polarized to being highly competent and have not yet integrated my own fear of incompetence, I might attract and be attracted to a partner who embodies incompetence, reinforcing my misbelief that I need to be competent in order for things to be done properly. A person who disowns their sexuality might attract and be attracted to a person who has heightened sexual desire. A person who has disowned their emotions might attract and be attracted to someone who is highly emotive. A person who rejects their own opinions might attract and be attracted to a partner who is highly opinionated.

On a conscious level, we are not actively aware that we are attracted to our partner because they embody our shadow. In fact, when we realize they mirror back an aspect of something within ourselves that we don't like, we become irritated by them. We reject the part of them that we have rejected within ourselves. However, there is a symbiotic relationship between polarities of partners where our unprocessed stress and trauma creates painful relationship patterns.

The unconscious reason that we are attracted to people who embody our shadow is that on a deep level we want integration. When we think that a person will complete us, we are being motivated by a desire for our own wholeness. And since we have not yet integrated our disowned parts, we unknowingly seek out a partner who has so that we can see ourselves more clearly through their reflection.

As depicted in the image below, you will see the most common pairing of couples who are meeting one another from their distortion. On one side of the continuum, a person who is self-sacrificing, lacks boundaries, and not in touch with their desire typically attracts and is attracted to someone on the other end of the spectrum who exploits others, has rigid boundaries, and is self-centered. (Note: Using labels can be both clarifying and limiting. In this chart, words used to describe tendencies of relating are not in service of diagnosing or pathologizing anyone.) Codependent traits typically exist in a person who is "other referenced"—where they look to other people as their point of reference. Narcissistic traits typically exit in a person who is "self-referenced," where they look to themselves as the point of reference and assume others will as well.

Relationship Polarity Continuum

Codependent Traits	Narcissistic Traits
• Self-sacrificing	• Sense of self-importance
• Compelled to help	• Need for admiration
• Self-critical	• Disregard for others' feelings
• Perfectionistic	• Inability to receive feedback
• Lack of boundaries	• Defensive
• Overly understanding	• Sense of entitlement
• Overly compassionate	• Exploits others
• "Other" referenced	• Demeaning & intimidating
• Subversively controlling	• "Self" referenced
• Anxious-insecure attachment	• Avoidant or disorganized attachment

Our codependent and narcissistic traits do not make us bad. They are simply an expression of our adaptive survival strategies that we developed in childhood when our pure vital energy was mistuned by the events taking place in the field around us. In the symbiosis of our patterns, we mutually agree to act in distorted ways from our unconscious desire to heal. The way a person with codependent traits betrays themselves fits together like a puzzle piece with the way a person with narcissistic traits misuses their power.

In the shadow of the codependent lives a young one who really wants attention. And in the shadow of the narcissist lives a young one who desperately wants everyone around them to be okay. These aspects were rejected in order to keep a sense of control in a system that was designed to have us distort our life force to fit in and keep balance. The degree to which a person is self-sacrificing is equal to the degree to which the person they are attracted to exhibits a sense of self-importance, and vice versa. These polarities can become more extreme when we are in a diminished state of awareness and psychological health.

When we do not have awareness of our own polarity distortion, we can easily get entangled in relational patterns that are seated in distorted narratives about ourselves and others. Because the birthplace of our own distortion occurred in childhood, we must continue to deepen our connection with our inner young one and create a secure attachment with our Self throughout the context of our relationships with others.

Confusion as to our own truth and reality is a sign that we experienced gaslighting in our childhood imprint. When a caregiver causes a child to question their own perception, reality, or memories, that adult is misusing their power and gaslighting the child. Anxiety, confusion, and an inability to trust oneself is the effect of gaslighting. People with narcissistic traits tend to gaslight, as this is how they learned to control their environment in childhood. People with codependent traits tend to have an inability to trust themselves, which has them give their power over to the person gaslighting.

If we are conditioned with narcissistic traits and tend to distort reality for our own gain, looking at the birthplace of this pattern within ourselves is vital for our own healing. Without defenses, looking at how we cloud reality with our own distortion is essential for us to gain the awareness necessary to make a different choice. Somewhere in our childhood, someone we trusted acted in ways that were unconscious and we were impacted. The imprint lives inside of us as the way to relate with others. Seeing our young one for their adaptive strategies and committing to holding them with truth begins to undo the patterns. Living daily with the intention to increase awareness of our patterns and alignment is where our transformation really unfolds.

If we are conditioned with co-dependent traits, we tend

to abandon ourselves and make others more important. The anxiety that underlies self-doubt makes us susceptible to become entangled with narcissistic strategies of gaslighting. Without blame directed at the other, looking within at our young one for their adaptive strategies and wisdom is the beginning of undoing this pattern. Living daily with self-trust and self-honoring is where our transformation really unfolds.

Regardless of which pole we hold, the conditioned thoughts and behaviors are an attempt at regulation when our nervous system perceives a threat. The threat our nervous system can be perceiving may very well be our partner's incongruence, judgment, or their potential rejection. How we respond to that is our responsibility, and tending to ourselves with love allows us to stay in contact with ourselves and metabolize our unfinished business.

As we work with our inner young one, we cultivate more and more awareness around the way we disrupt contact with the world and discover alternative expressions of how we want to be. One way we can identify how a younger part is activated in relationship is when we think we will only be okay when the other person becomes more aware, present, or different. Looking through the lens of our attachment wound, our conditioned self might unconsciously believe that we will only be whole and okay when we get what we want. Remembering that our wholeness is inherent and cannot be acquired through relationship, we can tend to our inner young one with care and love in the way we wish our partner would.

Because our attachment wounds and conditioned patterns have been present within us for a long time, they are well-worn paths on our inner map of how to navigate the world. Making our way through the matrix of conditioning towards clean, healthy relationships is impossible when we cannot see the patterns or alternative pathways. Our own dedication to looking at ourselves through the mirror of our relationships allows us to see the matrix with more clarity. By looking at ourselves through the lens of any relationship, the reflection we receive makes it possible to integrate more fully and emerge even more into who we really are. Eventually, as we do this deep work of transformation and coming back to our essence, we find regulation where we feel safe to discover our natural rhythm. Neither reacting with restlessness and anxiety, nor collapse and detachment, we find our way back to the core of our being. This makes it possible to be truly present for our relationships.

Anytime we look to the other and point out their blind spots we are actively not looking at our own blind spots. To look within, even when we can see all the things the other person isn't seeing, is our work. Cultivating our own awareness and integration is ours to do, just as our partner has their own integration to do.

If we are aware of our polarities, we can use the container of our relationship to be with them consciously and integrate more fully. When we are open to seeing ourselves through the reflection of our relationships, we can be with ourselves and others in a way that feels more aligned with who we truly are.

Exploration: Take a moment now to think of a relationship where you have felt emotionally activated or dysregulated. This may be with your partner, a former partner, parent, boss, coworker, or some other close relationship. Recall the incident and the intense emotions that arose within you. Look within and get curious about what you were reacting against. How did the other person seem, and how did you feel when you were with them? "The other person seemed_____, and I felt_____."

Once you are clear on how the other person seemed, look within to see where this quality lives inside of yourself. For example, if the other person seemed controlling, look within to see where you are controlling. See all the places in the relationship where you want to control the other person.

Once you're looking at your own shadow, you might choose to share this with a person close to you. Speak aloud how you, yourself, embody the same qualities that you dislike in the other person. Words are powerful. Claiming your relational polarity distortion will bring you more into alignment with the core of your being. Having a witness to your words amplifies their truth and resonates even more deeply in the body.

If you want to bring more intimacy into the relationship that you are looking at, you can tell the person who you felt a reaction against what you are seeing in yourself. When you can embody and own your own shadow in relationship with others, the world around you begins to change. We can feel vulnerable when we share or shadow with others, and this deep vulnerability is what cultivates deep intimacy.

The Polarity of Feminine and Masculine Energies

Within each one of us, we hold a range of energetic expressions. The polarity between the internal feminine and masculine energies holds a lot of charge. Because our conception requires a woman (egg and womb) and a man (sperm), the imprint of the DNA of our biological mother and father, as well as the ancestral patterns from each side of the lineage, hold a lot of energy within our systems.

Externally, we are seeing a bridge in the gap between the traditional binary gender polarity of men and women. Gender fluidity is an important expression of this, as is a broader expression of sexual orientation. However, cisgender women, or those with more feminine traits claiming their power and cisgender men, or those with more masculine traits becoming more in touch with their emotional interior is also an important part of this shift.

The external world is a reflection of our internal world. As we individually shift our relationship to our own internal polarity of feminine and masculine energies, we see the divide bridged in the world around us.

The quality of the healthy feminine energy is found in our physical body, in our metaphysical heart, and in our range of emotions. Our relationship to our bodies is an indication of how we relate to the feminine. Even if we are in a male body, trans body, or non-binary body, the contact we have with our bodies is an indicator of how we relate to our internal feminine energy. Our ability to stay seated in our heart center and to metabolize our emotions is also an expression of the health of our internal feminine energy.

The quality of the healthy masculine energy is presence, direction, and right use of power. Whether we are in a male body, female body, trans body, or non-binary body, our relationship to our quality of presence within ourselves, the way we direct attention, and how we are in right relationship with our power is an indicator of our healthy internal masculine energy.

When we are off balance with our internal feminine energy, we are detached from our bodies, closed to our hearts, and/or emotionally volatile. This is an indicator that we have disowned our internal masculine energy. When we bring presence into our bodies, direct our attention with clarity, and claim our power, our inner feminine feels safe and surrenders.

When we are off balance with internal masculine energy, we are restless, demanding, controlling, and/or deceiving. This is an indicator that we have disowned our internal feminine energy. When we contact our emotions, feel the sensations in our bodies, and connect with our hearts, our internal masculine settles into a balanced state.

In a monogamous relationship between a cisgender woman and man, there is a tendency for the woman to disown her inner masculine and the man to disown his inner feminine. Reflecting to one another what they each have disowned, the relationship can be an opportunity for each person to come back into an inner balance if they are each looking at themselves and doing their inner work.

Regardless of gender or relationship design, cultivating an inner balance between our own internal feminine and masculine energies allows us to integrate more fully and come into a deeper alignment with Source. Present with our emotions, hearts, and bodies, our own internal masculine touches our own internal feminine with divine love. Welcoming our power, desire, and truth, our internal masculine feels unconditionally loved by our own internal feminine.

Finding Resonance

For intimacy to occur, we need both resonance and polarity in our relationship dynamic. Resonance is the quality of similarity that gives two people a shared meeting place or vibration. Polarity is the opposing quality that creates a charge in two contradictory ways of meeting the world. Resonance brings a level of comfort to the relationship, and polarity brings a stimulating sense of excitement to the relationship.

If there is too much resonance, the relationship will likely feel boring and practical. If there is too much polarity, the relationship will likely feel triggering and volatile.

When we react rather than respond, we are charged by a polarity that is activating something within ourselves that we have disowned. In our polarity reaction, we are either looking to the other to complete us (looking to them as God), or we are looking to control or rescue others (playing God). We leave ourselves when we react, and in doing so we resist integrating an essential aspect of our own inner experience.

When we respond rather than react, we are resonating with the vibrational qualities of our own healthy, aware state. In our resonant response, we are aligned with Source, embodying God. We deepen into our somatic experience and maintain a loving connection with our Self. This makes it possible to be present and associated in our relationships with others.

When our relationships are overcome by our polarity reactions, we lose sight of our own essential vibrational qualities as well as the resonant qualities of our connection. Bringing attention to the vibrational qualities that we resonate with in our relationship will create an anchor for us to continue to deepen into our connection regardless of polarity reactions.

Resonance occurs within our bodies and allows us to regulate in the presence of another. As we deepen into our own somatic experience, our partner also deepens into theirs. When we practice this together consciously, we can find the resonant vibration of our essential energy through the regulation of our physical bodies. This creates space for the sweetness of our interconnection to come into the awareness field. Considering that in many relationships we focus on the painful places of interconnection, tending to our resonance is important for the health of our relationship.

Five steps to finding resonance with a partner:

Step 1: Ask the person you are with if they are willing to try a practice with you called *finding resonance.*

Step 2: Once they agree, you'll both close your eyes and deepen into your somatic experience.

Step 3: One person will begin by slowly sharing three sensations in their body that they are aware of.

As they do this, they will describe the sensation with depth and nuance, sharing where they feel it in their body, the textures, temperature, and quality of the sensations.

If any sensation is uncomfortable or ungrounded, the person will also share how they are going to move or breathe or adjust to create more grounding in their body as they are doing it.

The person listening will be tracking in their own body

how they resonate or respond to what is being said.

Step 4: The other person slowly shares three sensations in their body that they are aware of.

As they do this, they will describe the sensation with depth and nuance, sharing where they feel it in their body, the textures, temperature, and quality of the sensations.

If any sensation is uncomfortable or ungrounded, the person will also share how they are going to move or breathe or adjust to create more grounding in their body as they are doing it.

The person listening will be tracking in their own body how they resonate or respond to what is being said.

Step 5: Slowly alternate turns at least three times until resonance is found. You will know this has happened when both people feel regulated and embodied while also feeling more connected to one another.

As we integrate our disowned parts and learn how to hold our own vibration, our relationships change. The relationships we have been in can no longer exist as they were when we move from distortion to alignment. We might want to leave the context of the relationship all together if we cannot find a way to stop contorting and distorting to fit into the relational polarity distortion. To use our relationships as a container for personal growth means that we are more invested in who we are becoming than we are in staying in a relationship that does not resonate with our essence. Reacting from our distortion and leaving in blame and anger is different from staying seated in our Self and leaving from a place of love and compassion. The key is to make sure we are not avoiding looking at our own shadow or that we are not blaming others for our inability to hold our own vibration.

As we move more fully into our life urge where vital force

moves through us undistorted, we can be intentional about what feels aligned with our essence in terms of how we interact with others. From our sense of sovereignty, ending a relationship with someone who is unwilling to receive their reflection through us, not caring how they impact us, is an important way to honor ourselves. These types of relationships are karmic in that they are here to teach us important lessons about ourselves, rather than being lifelong partnerships.

Harmony's Story

My conditioned patterns were always confusing and elusive to me. Because my parents were such lovely people, it was hard to see the impact of their neglect. When friends would see the way I tolerated abuse in my relationships, they would ask me where this pattern came from. It was liberating to learn that our sibling relationships shape us just as much, if not more, as our relationships with our primary caregivers.

Because I looked up to my sibling, I would do anything for her. She was more expressive and demanding than me, and the whole family catered to her volatility. Walking on eggshells in an effort to keep her stable, my trauma response was one of fawn, where I was always acquiescing to her at the cost of my own well-being. I unknowingly brought this relational survival strategy with me into my intimate partnerships.

Conditioned to be caring and self-sacrificing, my patterns fit perfectly with those who were conditioned to lack empathy and needed a lot of attention. I thought I was unlovable, and I was attracted to and attracted partners who had a high degree of self-importance. My relationships were founded on and existed because of our relational polarity distortions.

Although my relationships were wrought with pain and abuse, the polarity created a charge that seemed necessary for sexual compatibility. The intensity of the sexual chemistry I had with my partners, combined with my lack of self-worth, hooked me into staying in relationships that existed because of my own self-harming.

Eventually I realized that these relationships were mirrors for me to see myself in. The way my partner treated me was a reflection of my own shadow. Instead of waiting for them to become loving, I practiced being self-loving. Instead of focusing on keeping the relationship, I focused on my own well-being. Instead of compulsively giving other people what they wanted, I started contemplating what I wanted. Instead of giving my power away, I started to see how I influenced my environment.

As I began to focus on myself, it became obvious when a relationship was dependent on my self-betrayal. In my first marriage, overcoming all of the conditioned values around marriage and divorce was challenging; however, I could not stay more committed to the construct of marriage than I was to myself. Risking poverty and social standing, I chose life, truth, and my own personal evolution. Unsure how to navigate the unknown of life beyond my conditioning, I set out to discover who I truly was.

Seeing my relationships as a playground for my own personal development, I started integrating my disowned parts. The more integrated I became, the more I found my seat within myself, where I stopped making other people God and attached to Self as Source.

I am now married to a man who I have a lot of resonance with. We are both healing patterns of codependency, and we both have a tendency to want to please one another. To have so much resonance means that we function well together, like one another, and have minimal conflict. However, without the charge of polarity, we can become inert in our connection. Intentionally creating experiences where we can explore our desires, needs, and dominance is important to keep the spark in our connection active.

Exercise: Connecting to Your Inner Young One

In Chapter 3, you started the practice of reparenting your inner young one. You completed the sentence, "When I am emotionally activated, my inner young one needs _____ from me." This practice becomes even more essential when it comes to our intimate relating. Attention that is healthy, attuned, and which has clean boundaries is what all children want, and it's what adults who are emotionally activated are trying to get from their partner. Instead, give this to yourself.

Remind yourself that what you require you can also provide. You are your own Source of pleasure, love, and security. You can listen to yourself, honor your own wisdom, and create a secure connection with your Self.

Turn towards your inner young one who still exists inside of your heart and tell them "I see you... I will always honor your wisdom and keep you safe." Give your inner young one attention, as you wrap them with love.

When you bring all of your presence to your young one, you are bringing the quality of your internal healthy masculine energy. So many of us feel betrayed and abandoned by the unhealthy masculine outside of ourselves. To integrate that quality within yourself, your young one feels seen, held, and wanted by you.

As you do this, notice what you feel in your body. Breathe and let your emotions move through you. Tap into the purity of your own heart. When we become more embodied and in touch with our emotions, our heart feels safe to open.

As you nurture your secure attachment with yourself, remind your young one that the person you are with is not the same one who originally caused you harm. Remind them how old you are now and that you are not trapped like you were as a child.

This practice, in and of itself, stops the entanglement patterns where we look to our partner for the thing we always longed for. We become our own secure base when we tend to our inner young one. We become more sovereign when we take responsibility for what is being activated within our inner world.

Once we come back into connection with our Self, we can then be in choice about how we want to come back into connection with others.

Walkaway with Wisdom

As our conditioned strategies become more and more outdated, discovering how we want to be in relationship with others is an undertaking that has no map. The more disconnected we are from our Self, the more we look to others to fulfill us. Our inner disconnect is seated in unresolved trauma and unprocessed experiences from the past.

The more disconnected we are from our Self, the more we look to others to fulfill us. Our inner disconnect is seated in unresolved trauma and unprocessed experiences from the past. As we work on transforming our relationship with ourselves, our relationships with others transform.

When our inner polarity distortion guides the way we interact with the world, we engage in relationships from a place that will eventually cause an entangled pattern of confusion and conflict. Unable to stay aligned with our Self, we see our relationships through the lens of our conditioned self, our wounds, and our polarity distortions.

As a sovereign individual, we are responsible for everything that arises within us. Nobody makes us feel anything. We simply feel certain things in reaction or response to interactions with other people. But what arises within us is ours. It's ours to be with consciously, it's ours to own, and it's ours to learn from and heal. Our reaction and response is influenced by the way we perceive other people's words and actions. We may be seeing through the lens of an old wound or a projection. Knowing what's happening within us and where we are perceiving the relationship from is what cultivates the autonomy necessary to tend to the place of interconnection.

When we unconsciously move from our distortion (identified with our conditioned self and disowning parts of ourselves), we attract and are attracted to partners who embody what is in our own shadow. Similar to our own inner polarities, our partner embodies a polarity that we, ourselves, have diverged from within ourselves.

For intimacy to occur, we need both resonance and polarity in our relationship dynamic. Resonance is the quality of similarity that gives two people a shared meeting place or vibration. Polarity is the opposing quality that creates a charge in two contradictory ways of meeting the world. Resonance brings a level of comfort to the relationship, and polarity brings a stimulating sense of excitement to the relationship.

If there is too much resonance, the relationship will likely feel boring and practical. If there is too much polarity, the relationship will likely feel triggering and volatile.

Chapter 14

Relationships without Entanglements

The incredible transformation that awaits us all isn't going to happen in isolation, in therapy, or at a workshop. It will happen in the midst of a potential conflict or familiar relational dynamic when we choose to do the different, truer thing.

If we are not using our intimate relationships as a container for our personal growth, we are using them as a container to enact our old survival strategies that are no longer adaptive. The patterns set in motion during misattunement, abuse, and neglect were adaptive for our survival at the time we developed them. Our inner wisdom helped us to find a way to create homeostasis in a dysfunctional system that wasn't designed to empower us in our authenticity and wholeness.

When we continue to use those old survival strategies as our map for navigating relationships, we engage in an entangled relationship design where our distorted vital force gets jumbled up with other people's distorted vital force. Choosing to allow old imprints to inform our way of being may not seem like a choice at all. It may seem like following our conditioned patterns is the only way to be. When we can't see other options for how to be, we are asleep to our True Self. The light of consciousness is turned off, and our vital force cannot flow in its full alignment.

When we choose to follow our distortion, we are choosing to *not* look within to see what is being mirrored to us from the world around us. As we inhibit our own vitality from flowing, we inhibit our relationships from experiencing the full spectrum of clean, blissful connection.

Energetic Boundaries

The word "boundary" might evoke the idea of a barrier or

border to keep people out. While we can set limitations with our words and physical distance, our energetic boundaries are not intended to keep people out. The purpose of a boundary is to contact others while maintaining our own vibration. Our energetic boundaries represent our awareness of where we end and other people begin, making it possible for us to stay seated in ourselves as we contact with the environment. In this way, healthy, clear boundaries are in service of connection, they are the meeting place between ourselves and our environment.

When we are seated in ourselves and holding our own frequency, we can experience clean, healthy connection in our relationships without entanglement patterns.

Unlike physical boundaries or words, our energetic boundaries are seated in the more subtle aspects of who we are. With an attuned eye, we can see the energetic movement of the people around us. We can see the emotional weight they carry, the containment of their anger, the capping off of their grief, or the vibrancy of their essence. The *subtle energy* of our boundaries holds the vibration of our quality of presence and our availability to contact, which are our boundaries.

There are three types of energetic boundaries: Diffused, rigid, and flexible.

A *diffused* or open boundary system is the energetic quality of being permeable. Other people's thoughts, feelings, judgment, and projections easily make their way into our energy body. And as we hold other people's states as our own, we believe they are ours. With an open boundary system, we match the vibration of those around us and end up processing other people's emotions for them.

A *rigid* or closed boundary system is the energetic quality of steel. Our hard energy keeps other people's emotions and thoughts out of our system, and we maintain a sense of self that is completely separate from others. Not wanting to be influenced by others, we hold our own vibration firmly in reaction against others.

A *flexible* or healthy boundary system is the energetic quality of benevolence. In our healthy boundaries, we are in contact with our sovereign self, we can hold our own vibration, and we can see others with clarity and compassion. From here, we can engage in relationships with presence, curiosity, and choice. We can know what we want, what we think, and what it feels like to be us as an individual. We can also hear what someone else wants, thinks, or feels without needing to take it on as our own.

In the image below, we can see the three types of energetic boundaries that we can all cycle through.

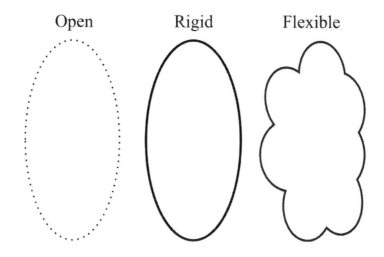

| Open | Rigid | Flexible |

When we have diffused energetic boundaries, we're not in contact with ourselves, and thus we cannot contact the environment in a healthy way. We try to get energy from other people or give our energy away, and we carry around energy that doesn't belong to us.

When we have rigid boundaries, we also deprive ourselves from the experience of making contact with others. Like an island, we defend our territory and close off from receiving deep connection. We also contain our emotions as a way to reject any evidence of being affected by others, unless our anger is needed to reestablish our impenetrable boundary.

When we have healthy energetic boundaries, we can stay in contact with ourselves as we contact another. Our healthy boundaries allow us to embody the transpersonal qualities of sovereignty and interconnection simultaneously. Without matching the vibration of those around us, we do not engage in entanglement patterns and we do not "otherize" people and keep them out. We stay aligned with our own Source of energy and occupy our full energetic sense of self. As we do this, we stay protected from other people's energetic hooks and entanglement patterns—while also having the capacity to stay in contact with them.

While many of us have a primary boundary that we hold energetically, it is possible to vacillate between all three boundary systems. When we feel resourced and securely connected with ourselves, we can have healthy boundaries. If a younger part gets activated and we leave contact with ourselves, our boundaries might become diffused in an attempt to get connection. Then when we're being reactive and resentful, we might close off our boundaries to keep other people out.

Energetic boundary systems are the subtle energy expressions of attachment styles (mentioned in Chapter 2). Since children are born with a diffused boundary, as they develop, they are constantly trying to find boundaries. How our caregivers are with their own boundary system affects a child's sense of self and sense of safety. A caregiver who is authoritarian (strict, demanding, and controlling) has a rigid boundary system. A caregiver who is permissive (lenient, tolerant, and accommodating) has a diffused boundary system. A parent who is collaborative (understanding, flexible, and in contact with themselves) has a healthy boundary system. These different parenting approaches affect the developing sense of self of the child and their attachment styles.

A person with a primarily open boundary system likely

has an anxious or insecure attachment style. Open boundary systems are usually indicative of an enmeshed relationship with a primary caregiver or sibling. Someone with a rigid boundary system likely has an avoidant attachment style. Rigid boundary systems are indicative of a relationship with a primary caregiver or sibling who was a boundary pusher. Similarly, someone with a healthy boundary system is likely securely attached. When a person moves quickly through all three in a state of dysregulation, they likely have a disorganized attachment style.

While our boundaries hold the energetic qualities of our attachment styles, our attachment styles come from our core wounding and live in our conditioned self. Alternatively, our energetic boundaries are an expression of the way we embody our essence and contact our environment. Once we create a secure attachment within ourselves, we can hold the energy of a flexible boundary system with more consistency.

Our boundary is the place in which we contact the world. When we interrupt our boundary with conditioned habits, we disturb our relationships with ourselves and others.

When we disrupt contact with our environment, we unknowingly shift the boundary in the direction we unconsciously think it needs to move to make sense of our state of being. For example, when I project my experience onto you, I shift my energetic boundary in favor of myself, making you responsible for the pain I feel. When I take in an introjection, I shift the boundary in favor of you, making your ideas more valuable than my own. When I turn in on myself in a retroflection, I shift the boundary in favor of you as I burden myself with the weight of all that is wrong in our relationship. When I move into a state of confluence, I make us one, dissolving the boundary all together in favor of everything else. And when I deflect, I shift the boundary in some other direction in favor of avoidance.

The more integrated and aligned we become, the more the positive expressions of contact boundary disturbances can emerge:

The positive quality of an introjection is being able to see another person's point of view; however, in our sovereignty we examine it and discern if we want to take that in.

The positive quality of a projection is being able to see someone clearly. Once the veil of our unfinished business is cleared and we develop the capacity to attune to our somatic experience, we can see others clearly and with intuition.

The positive quality of confluence is the transpersonal capacity for oneness. From a place of contact with ourselves, unity with others is a blissful spiritual experience.

The positive quality of retroflection is self-curiosity and introspection. Once we stop turning in on ourselves, we can see our own opportunities for growth more clearly.

And the positive quality of deflection is the ability to release tension. When we discharge tension consciously, we can come into even deeper contact.

Creating healthy energetic boundaries is similar to deepening our contact with our alignment: it takes practice and awareness. When we come off center, we find our way back to our home base with more grace and ease over time. There is an exercise at the end of the chapter to guide the setting of energetic boundaries. Practicing this often helps to anchor them into our awareness in a deeper way, making healthy connection with others more possible.

Boundary Exploration: Whether you have an open boundary system or a rigid one, self-trust is essential for healthy, flexible boundaries. Contact with yourself is the first step in learning to navigate the point of contact with others, and communication is the second step (which we will explore in later chapters). When you are in contact with yourself and have the skills to speak your truest truth, you can navigate boundaries in relationship in a healthy and honoring way. Remember, boundaries are the point of contact. Staying in contact with your inner being while relating with others is a practice that creates deeper connection.

Close your eyes and feel into your body. Take a couple of expansive breaths where you exhale and soften your jaw. Once you feel in contact with your body, take your hands and feel into your energetic boundary. With your hands, feel the edge of your energetic space. It may be farther than your hands or it may be close to your body or somewhere in between. Whatever is true about your boundary in this moment, simply feel it with your hands and breathe into your whole energy body with your breath.

Feel over your head, in front of you, and all around you with your hands.

Now imagine a person in your life with whom you have or have had a challenging relationship with is sitting across from you. Keep breathing into your energetic boundary, and place one hand in front of you like a stop sign and take your sternum (breast bone) with the fingertips of your other hand.

As you set this energetic boundary, it can be useful to imagine that the person is 2 inches tall. This is not to make them small, but to have them take up less space in your energetic field. If the relationship is very challenging, you may want to imagine that they are 2 inches tall and contained in a crystal pyramid.

Keep breathing, holding your hand in front of you, and tapping your sternum. As you do, say aloud, "I am here, and you are there."

Take another big breath and say it again, "I am here, and you are there." Repeat this until you feel your body settle and it seems like the person you are imagining believes you. If that doesn't happen, move them further away from you. Notice what happens in your body when you get space from them.

Then lower your hands and say, "I won't leave myself for you." Repeat this three times and let yourself surrender into your own energetic boundary.

Honoring Ourselves

The way we hold our energetic boundaries becomes more obvious when we are engaging in relationship with others. This occurs because our boundaries are undeniably connected with our relationship to our desire. If we have been conditioned to disown our desire, we have not yet cultivated the ability to hold healthy boundaries.

When we think that what we want doesn't matter, it's because we hold an unconscious misbelief that we don't matter. And when we think that we don't matter, we defer to what other people want. Doing our own shadow work where we claim our disowned desire, we can honor ourselves while in relationship. When two people have different desires, the way we relate to one another in this moment is the way we show up for relationship.

Among the many ways that our distortion contributes to relationship entanglements, self-betrayal seems to be the most insidious. As a conditioned habit of our attachment styles and energetic boundaries, we self-betray as a strategy to try to get energy and connection from others. Codependent patterns can cause us to deny our own needs and wants in an effort to keep connection with someone. From this conditioned pattern, we might think we are coregulating when in fact we are enabling a relational entanglement. In order to coregulate, we must be in contact with ourselves. Coregulation is the process by which we use our own nervous system response to find a resonant regulated state with another person. This cannot happen if we are not regulated, self-attuned, and have clarity about our sovereignty.

Self-betrayal begins with a subtle energetic collapse around our own sense of worth, and we rarely realize when this is happening. We might betray ourselves in small ways, like not speaking up when our feelings are hurt. Or we might betray ourselves in big ways, like having sex when we don't want to.

Any time we deny our truth, quiet our desire, or disown our power, we betray ourselves. In betraying ourselves, we give our will over to another person. We make ourselves less important than others, and we hide ourselves from the environment.

When our conditioned self still holds messages from childhood that we need to be selfless, accommodating, or pleasing in order to earn love and acceptance, we bring those misbeliefs with us into our relationships. These conditioned misbeliefs influence the way we reason with ourselves about why betraying ourselves is the right thing to do.

Although self-betrayal is an attempt at keeping connection and avoiding conflict, it is a certain path to disconnection and resentment. When our truth lives in the shadow of our relationships, we are choosing to show up for our connection in a way that is dishonest and self-harming. For example, if I were to engage in a sexual encounter with my partner and I wasn't honoring myself in doing so, I am harming myself and lying to them.

A misbelief that might underlie the dishonoring of myself in this way could be, "If I don't give them what they want, they won't love me." Beneath that misbelief, there might be another one that says, "My only value comes from what I offer physically." Underneath that idea, there is likely another misbelief that tells me, "My body doesn't belong to me." And in the shadow of that might be a very unconscious idea that "If I say 'No,' they will annihilate me."

Self-betrayal is part of our acquired, conditioned patterns that are intertwined with our gender development, cultural norms, and family patterns. Given the complex unconscious ideas that underlie the subtle movement of self-betrayal, it makes sense that not honoring ourselves would be the easy impulse to follow. We might think we're not harming ourselves and that we're getting what we want. However, that's not true.

On the energetic level, self-betrayal is an act of slowly killing the most beautiful aspects of ourselves: our truth. Keeping ourselves small and distorted, our vitality cannot flow under such conditions. And ultimately, when we don't fully show up for our relationships, they die, too. In the shadow of self-betrayal, we are unconsciously trying to control another person. We project what we think they will do in response to our truth and we hide our truth to prevent them from reacting in the way we project that they will.

Adding to the complexity of honoring ourselves is when we, ourselves, have conflicting desires. For example, if a part of me wants to have sex and another part of me wants to go get work done, knowing how to make a decision that honors the full spectrum of myself is more challenging. To honor ourselves every step of the way, even in the presence of ambivalence, takes an ongoing practice of checking in with ourselves and voicing what is true moment by moment.

When we try to get connection and safety through self-betrayal, resentment festers in the shadows. We give our will over to another, and then we resent them for it, even though they never asked us to betray ourselves.

Honoring ourselves is an act of dignity and self-love. It is also an act of true connection with our relationships. It is counterintuitive to take up our whole energetic space by honoring ourselves when we feel unsafe. The instinctive reaction is to get small when our safety seems compromised in a relational interaction, this is the effect of trauma. Paradoxically, closing in on ourselves creates less safety. Pushing out energetically to the edges of our energetic field allows us to stand our sacred ground and hold our own vibration. Here we hold ourselves in security and we enact the self-trust that we've cultivated by attaching to Self as Source.

When two people who are in their distortion have different desires, conflict and entanglement will likely ensue. Honoring our desires and navigating differences is where relationship happens. If we think we need to be the same to be in relationship, we allow someone else's desire to dictate reality through self-betrayal.

Without our desire voiced in our relationship, we are not present for the relationship. Desire is the meeting place of our boundaries. It takes courage to ask for what we want, and it takes maturity to hold our desires while negotiating how to be in relationship with a person who has different desires. The same is true for perspective: It takes maturity to hold our point of view while also listening to another person's different point of view.

Learning to honor ourselves in a way that keeps our relationships clean takes practice (which we'll dive deeper into later). At first, we might think that honoring ourselves and speaking our truth means that we express everything that's on our mind, telling other people about how they seem. But this isn't so. This is giving voice to our projections and resentments.

Honoring ourselves is about looking within, getting clear on what's true about our deeper experience—what we're feeling and wanting and needing—then giving that a voice. When we are fully honoring ourselves, we can coregulate with our partner. We can find resonance and stay in connection through emotional activation.

Slowing down and staying in contact with our physical sensations is our truest guide on the journey of honoring ourselves. Finding the courage to share our vulnerable truth with the people in our lives is the fire that ignites our vital force to come more fully into alignment. From here, we can cultivate deeply profound relationships.

Becoming Fully Aligned

When our unresolved pain causes us to search for unconditional love from another, we contort with conditioned patterns to try to earn their love and approval. We do this when we have forgotten that this is where we have come from, that unconditional love is who we really are. We forget that we are a messy, human expression of Source, as is our partner. We resist this and want perfect love that always feels blissful and easy.

Intimacy cannot happen in the presence of control and manipulation. To surrender our conditioned patterns and vulnerably release any attempt at control can feel uncomfortable and unattainable. Messy, human love that is infused with divinity is what we are here to experience. And the people we choose to explore the full range of our own messy sacred love with are the reflections we choose to see ourselves through as we make our way back to our own whole, unconditional self-love.

In our human form, on the level of ego, we are separate from one another. We have distinct bodies, diverse roles, various DNA, and varying levels of development, age, and awareness. We have diverse points of view, and different desires, values, and needs. We like different food, speak different languages, and have different hobbies. As far as the third dimension is concerned, we are separate. From this separateness, we often think that other people need to be different so that we don't have to feel what we're feeling. We forget our sovereignty and become focused on changing external stimuli.

In our Divinity, on the level of spirit, we are all connected. We have access to the same universal wisdom, consciousness, and energy Source. We are inherently whole, sacred, and infinite. We have access to power that is beyond what the mind can conceive, and we are so much more than our human form. As far as the fifth dimension of our higher-level spiritual Self is concerned, we are all on the same team, interconnected and unified as one. From this unification, we know that the way we meet ourselves is the way we meet the world. We remember to connect with Self as Source and become more fully aligned.

In the full spectrum of our spiritual humanity, we are *sovereign* human beings, responsible for our own actions, perceptions, and emotions. Nobody can "make us" feel anything. We simply are, by design, our living experience of ourselves in any given moment. At the same time, we are sensitive beings who are *inherently interconnected* with all of life. We affect one another, and we feel the impact of other people's actions and words and states of being.

Human relating is a complex exchange of energy and reflections. Having daily alignment and boundary practices (as outlined below) allow us to experience the baseline of our own vibration while seated in the core of our being. This makes it more possible to recognize when we come off center and to find our way back home. When we come out of alignment and find our way back to our Self, it's important to repair with the people in our lives. Hearing what it's like for others to be with us when we are off center, listening with empathy, and validating their experience is the way to repair. This is outlined in more detail in Chapters 15, 16, and 17.

In the image below, we see two people who are anchored into their alignment while holding the vibrational quality of healthy energetic boundaries. Their mind, emotions, and actions are all aligned with Source. They have both found their way through the matrix of their conditioned self and are able to embody their wholeness and sovereignty. They are connected to their Source of love, and they are staying seated in themselves as they contact one another.

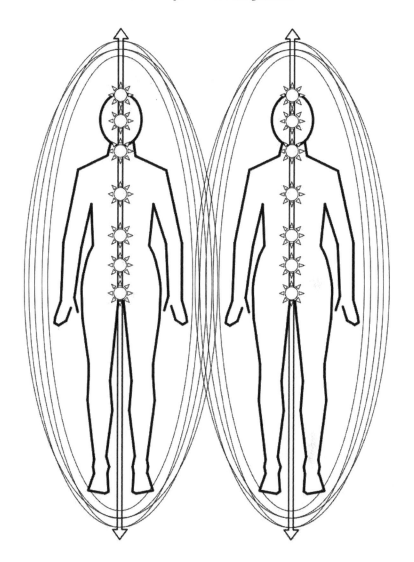

The way we hold our energetic boundaries becomes more obvious when we are engaging in relationship with others. This occurs because our boundaries are undeniably connected with our relationship to our desire.

The complexity of this is nuanced and delicate. In any moment we can slip back into the path of least resistance and see life through a lens of projection, and our distortions can hijack any interaction without warning. When our current environment mirrors an imprint of our wounding, our perspective in the present moment can easily be filtered through the past.

When we are not consciously in contact with ourselves, we are likely using old patterned ways of relating with others. Slowing down, we can bring more awareness into our whole being. We can stop following the impulses of the familiar patterns of our conditioned self. If we don't follow the impulse of our distortion and stay in contact with all that arises within us, we can feel the dysregulation that lives beneath our impulses. As we deepen into our somatic experience, we can bring awareness to the misbeliefs that guide the impulses to move away from ourselves.

Awareness makes it possible to discover new ways to be with ourselves and connect with others.

To really know, from the depths of our soul, that everything that is activated within us is ours to experience, we have agency for how we choose to be in the world. We no longer need other people to be something for us. Instead, we meet others in the way that makes contact possible. This is what it means to "be met," that we bring the quality of contact with self to our relationships and see if others do, too. If they aren't in a place to meet us in sovereignty, we stay aligned and in choice about how we want to be.

When we are still working out unfinished business from our childhood, it's common to look to others for our sense of safety. Wanting to be met, seen, and heard can seem very important. Needing other people to be a certain way so that we can feel safe and connected to them is an indication that we need to look within to see what our inner young one is wanting from us—not the person we are relating to. While it's true that the person we are relating to is also likely using their conditioned patterns, on our path of growth it is our job to cultivate our own internal awareness and navigate our own boundaries. We can share with the other person what we're seeing in them if they consent to our reflection, anything else is our attempt to control them to be different so we don't have to feel our own wounding.

"Being met" is less about other people's capacity to be sovereign and more about our own. When we are able to fully meet ourselves, we can fully meet the world as it is. When we have this degree of self-responsibility, being affected in the interconnectedness of the relationship allows us to deepen into our alignment as we see more nuanced aspects of our inner world with greater and greater awareness.

When we have diffused boundaries, it might seem like everything that arises within us does not belong to us. This is one reason why practicing holding our own vibration is so essential to clean relationships. Similarly, if we have rigid boundaries it might seem like other people need to be a certain way for us to open to connection. This is another reason why practicing holding our own vibration and creating a secure connection within ourselves is so essential to healthy relationships.

In the dance of human interactions, there is no greater dance partner than one who can stay seated in themselves while vulnerably opening to intimacy. We, ourselves, must be that dance partner, embodying the very thing we desire from others.

Fully aligned within ourselves, we integrate all aspects of ourselves in such a way that we move from the wholeness of our sovereign self. Two whole individuals, in contact with themselves who are able to make contact with one another, are experiencing the transpersonal living relationship called I-Thou. German philosopher Martin Buber (1923) first defined *I-Thou* as a way to give language to the transpersonal nature of relationship with all life. Contrasted by the I-It, where other beings and elements are reduced to objects that are separate from one's self, *I-Thou* is a framework for relating with other people and the world where we honor our interconnectedness in a sacred way.

When we are entangled in relationships, moving from our distortions, other people can unconsciously be viewed as an object to change or control. "If you were different, I wouldn't have to feel this pain." We disempower ourselves when we think someone needs to be different so that we can feel peace. Even if the other person is the object of our approval, pleasure, pain, or wounding, *I-It* is the way most people relate with one another. This occurs when we hold imprints of being treated like a "good object" or "bad object" by our caregivers. Children want to be seen for their goodness. Each time a child says "Watch me!" when they are doing something they are proud of, they want to know their goodness exists through our witness. When a child is mainly seen for the things they are criticized for, they orient towards the misbelief that they are not enough.

For example, if our caregiver punished us for making a mess by yelling at us and shaming us, we were being treated as a "bad object." Not seen for our humanity, their expectations taught us that we needed to be good for them in order to earn safety, love, and approval. If our caregiver rewarded us with praise for our good grades, appearance, or successes, they treated us like a "good object." By not asking us how we felt about our work, seeing our deeper emotional experience, or not acknowledging our motives for working so hard, they only saw us for the outer aspect of our actions.

When our caregivers were unable to see us in the full spectrum of who we were, we started treating ourselves as an object, thus learning to treat others that way, too. When we don't learn to attune to our inner subjective emotional experience, our conditioned self is shaped to objectify ourselves. With the misbelief that I am "bad" if I make a mistake, we put high standards on ourselves to try to be good. As an object, we do this at the cost of our own health, ignoring our need for rest and regulation, and often being mean to ourselves. When we believe that being a "good object" validates our existence, we seek approval from others at the cost of our own well-being.

Ignoring our somatic sensations, spiritual health, and emotional state, we treat ourselves as an object whose worth is dependent on something outside of ourselves. And when we meet ourselves in this way, we inevitably treat others as an object, too. When someone does something that we think is "bad" or "wrong" or we feel pain about, we project "bad object" onto them and miss the deeper aspects of their humanity. When we don't see an individual as a unique mystery, we are objectifying them.

Anytime we are not seeing someone as a mysterious, unique being we are trying to feel a sense of control. The use of labels is also part of the I-It and an attempt to feel a sense of control. Whether it's a diagnosis, a personality typing, or a flippant adjective, stating that someone is a label overlooks the humanity of that person. This is also one way we objectify ourselves, by describing ourselves with language that states that we are our diagnosis, personality type, or some other characteristic.

The deep curiosity of seeing another human being as mysterious and unknown from our seat in our alignment with the True Self is unfortunately quite rare. I-Thou is a place where we can see ourselves through the reflections of one another. The outer world is a holographic expression of our inner world, and the people in our lives are the most brilliant mirrors for us to see ourselves more clearly. This is not a state of confluence where our sense of self comes from others (that only leads to confusion and entanglement).

The interconnectedness of I-Thou is a place for us to see any aspects of ourselves that are being reflected back to us so that we can deepen into our own transformation and alignment. When we honor ourselves as whole individuals, how we feel in the presence of another person becomes both a mirror for us to see ourselves more clearly and a sacred encounter with the divine in the other. It's a sacred meeting of souls, where we can dance in relationship that is clean of entanglements, feeling more aligned for having had our time together.

Harmony's Story

After my divorce, I learned that I brought my attachment wounds and conditioned patterns with me when I left the marriage. Although I now know that I didn't *need* anyone, I didn't know how to be with someone if I wasn't trying to earn their love and approval.

A year after my divorce, I was more aware of my manipulation and self-betrayal in intimate relationships, yet I still wasn't sure how to honor myself. Ready to learn a new way, I enrolled on a 9-month training course in integral relational practices. I decided that I wouldn't date anyone in the training and I would use the experience as a playground to discover how to stay in the core of my being while in relationships.

The first 5 months of the training I was in a strong trauma response. My body would tremor in the fear of being seen by my cohort, and my old head trauma would cause me to dissociate and leave myself. Once I was able to stay regulated, I started claiming my shadow in relationship to my cohort. I would own my sexuality, I would ask for what I wanted, I would set clear boundaries, and I would acknowledge how powerful my presence was in the field of the training. This was revolutionary for me.

Being in a context with people who all agreed to be in relationship as a means for self-development provided me with the opportunity to heal my attachment wounds. We were in the workshop for an agreed amount of time, and as we explored the practices we were explicitly agreeing to be a certain way with one another in service of our growth and evolution. When I finally learned how to tend to the space where I could both honor myself and another simultaneously, I discovered sovereignty.

The old patterns of being accommodating, self-betraying, and keeping my focus on others were an attempt at regulating my system. When I finally chose to feel my dysregulation over following the patterns of my conditioning, I learned that being "in myself" felt so much better than leaving myself. Practicing this consistently and mindfully with a community of people who were are in this practice was a blessing.

I built the awareness and capacity to honor myself and others in a workshop container; however, I bring the skill with me everywhere I go. No matter who I am speaking with, I am committed to honoring myself, holding my experience as my own, and letting other people know how I feel in their presence. As I do this, I am *also* curious about what's happening within others.

My distortion thinks that there can be *either* my reality *or* yours. My True Self knows that there is *both* my lived experience *and* yours. This is the essence of a healthy, flexible boundary system.

A couple of years after I completed the training, I met my now husband, Christopher. My alignment within myself had me open to a new paradigm of relationship, one that is reparative, mutually respectful, and deeply loving. Knowing myself so fully, I know when I leave my alignment.

When I notice the old strategies arise, I slow down and feel what is beneath those impulses. I breathe and create more space around my conditioned patterns, which increases my consciousness in real-time. People often tell me that I am solid in myself, and this is what they are feeling. I prioritize my alignment and honor myself at every turn. Even in the midst of my distortion being triggered, I use my awareness to discover what is happening within me. Because I am committed to this practice in all of my relationships, my presence brings an aligned quality to the environment where other people remember how to honor themselves, too.

Exercise: Cultivating Healthy Boundaries

Part 1: Activate Your Alignment

Close your eyes and sense into your body. Simply notice what it feels like to be you in this moment. Starting at the top of your head, bring in presence and awareness through the crown chakra. Empty your mind as you bring in more presence and spaciousness into your head. As you breathe, make any vocalizations that feel authentic and supportive of moving energy.

Slowly move down the midline of your body, staying with each energy center for several minutes, noticing, breathing, and vocalizing, giving each energy center a tone. Bringing more presence and spaciousness to your throat, then slowly to your heart, your belly, and your root.

Every exhale, soften your jaw. As you soften your jaw, soften into your root. Surrender to your seat of security and safety. Breathing in all the way down to the earth and exhaling all the way down to the earth.

Once you feel anchored and grounded, bring your inhale up through the crown and exhale down through the root. Stay with this breath pattern as you breathe up and align with Source, and exhale as you touch your sacred connection to the earth.

Next, open your arms to the side as you inhale, and as you exhale bring your hand to the midline of your body, with the fingertips of your right hand facing up and the fingertips of your left hand facing down. Inhale and open, exhale bring your hands together and activate your alignment up the midline of your body, the core of your being. Feel the anchor down and the alignment up vertically to Source.

Remind yourself, "This is me. This is who I really am."

Part 2: Cleanse Your Energy Body

Start to notice any energy living in your system that does not belong to you and start to use your breath and awareness to give it back to whomever it belongs to (or put it in a vessel to return to Source, if you prefer). Imagine all of the emotions, judgments, projections, and energy living in your system that do not belong to you and are not yours to process leaving your energetic body.

Then, call on the cosmic realm for support: Say aloud, "I ask all of my angels and guides to identify, locate, and remove anything living in my system that does not belong to me. Any judgments, projections, thoughts or feelings that are living in my system and are not my assignment to process be removed immediately and returned to its proper source."

Then take a few more cleansing breaths and visualize or watch your energy body be cleansed of other people's energy that you are carrying around.

Next, call back any energy that you have given away and give back any energy that you've been carrying that doesn't belong to you. Any power, any clarity, and aspect of your energy that you have given away, call it all back and bring it to the midline of your body.

Breathe up and down the midline of your body, then breathe into the wholeness of your system, beyond your physical body. Take up all of the space that is yours.

You need to fully embody yourself and take up all of the space that is yours so that other people's energy can't come in. The moment you leave yourself, go over into their world and make them more important or disassociate to find safety is the moment other people's energy can come in and make a home inside of us.

Part 3: Setting the Boundary

Now that you are cleansed, use your hands to feel into the energetic space around you. This is your energy bubble. This is your space.

Put one hand in front of you like a stop sign. Take the fingertips of your other hand and tap your sternum, your breast bone. Breathe. Vocalize. And set your energetic boundary. If you have an open boundary system, you may feel clearer about the definition of your energetic space. If you have a rigid boundary system, you may feel a softening in your energy body.

Picture the people in your life who you have a challenging time individuating from and say, "I am here, you are there."

Say it with strength and certainty. Say it until they believe you.

From the midline of your body, push your energy out to the edge of your bubble. It can be counterintuitive to push your energy out. Most people hold their energy in to protect it, but that is an energetic collapse that actually allows other people's energy in. Take up all of your energetic space by pushing out so that if I were there sitting across from you, I would know where you end and I begin.

Then lower your hands and breathe. Attune to this feeling of individuation, where you are autonomous and sovereign and with healthy boundaries. The paradox of healthy boundaries is that the more we stay in ourselves, the more open we are to connection. Our heart can stay open when our system trusts us to stay in ourselves.

Remember, you are safer being embodied.

You are safer staying inside of yourself.

You are safer speaking your truth.

You are safer orienting toward your essential self.

You are safer saying, "No."

Exercise: Track Your Desires

Desire is the meeting place of our boundaries with others. When two people have conflicting desires, it can seem like one person will have to "win" while the other one has to "accommodate." Learning to honor the truth of our desires while also staying curious about the other person's desires makes collaborative problem solving possible. When we are in collaboration, everyone's desires matter and negotiation deepens the connection.

Practicing how to give voice to our desire is a gift to our relationships. Knowing what we want and asking for it makes it possible for us to show up for our relationships. Trusting another person to do the same and state their truth, is also honoring of our relationships.

There are two ways to do this exercise: either by yourself or with your partner. To be interdependent without entanglements we need to know what we want and cultivate the ability to ask for it. In addition, we need to trust other people's agency in knowing what they are and are not available for and know how to give ourselves what we want when others have a different desire.

How we relate with the people in our lives in the moments of differing desires is where relationship happens. There is a difference between *having a relationship* and *being in relationship*. *Having a relationship* consists of an explicit agreement that we are friends, lovers, monogamous, polyamorous, married, and so on. *Being in relationship* happens in the micro-moments of our interactions, such as when we and our partners have different desires about how to be in relationship. *Being in relationship* only happens in the present moment, whereas *having a relationship* is a mental construct or idea. We both get to choose how we want to be in relationship together; the growth happens when we are called to be both strong in our own desires and flexible about our partner's desires.

To do this exercise by yourself:

Choose one day to be your *Desire Day*. For the entirety of the day, look within to see *what you want* frequently throughout the day. Set a reminder on your phone so that at least once per hour you are pausing to look within to see what you want, separate from what your obligations are or from what other people want. This doesn't mean that you stop what you are doing to follow your desire unless this seems like it would be in service of your interactions being more aligned with your authentic expression.

To do this exercise with a partner:
Invite them into this experience by setting context and letting them know that this is a practice time for both of you to discover how to more fully own your desire and how to have more agency over what you are available for.

This exercise is very intimate and vulnerable. Even couples who have been together for decades find this to be edgy because being explicit about desires and boundaries is not something many people do on a daily basis. Because of this, create a really sacred container. Lay out a soft blanket, light some candles. Share any fears that might be coming up, and really slow down before you begin.

Each person will have a turn to be the one asking for what they want. The other person can either do what is asked, negotiate, or say they are not available for that. This exercise is a container for each person to stay in contact with themselves as they relate with one another around desire and boundaries. Both of you get to stay in touch with what is true for you and choose how you want to be together with awareness and agency.

Choose who will go first in asking for their desires, set the timer for 10 minutes, and begin! For the entire 10 minutes, the one speaking has the opportunity to ask for what they want and to get really nuanced about how they want it. For example, "I'd like you to rub my feet." If the other person is available for it and begins rubbing your feet, you get to change as much as you want about what is happening. "I want it lighter, harder, just the arch..." as long as it's truly what you want. Then if you want something else, you can change it. "Now I want you to touch my heart and gaze into my eyes..."

Then, when the 10 minutes is up, you can debrief how that was for both of you, and then switch roles. Once both of you have had a turn, negotiate how to be with one another moving forward.

Owning our desires together can become foreplay; however, if the desire for intimate pleasure is present, make that explicit and set context. Perhaps the context is that the person who typically doesn't ask for what they want continues to voice their desire every moment they become aware of it as physical connection continues.

If only one person wants physical connection and the other is not available for more intimate touch, talking about what is beneath these differences could create deeper connection.

If neither of you want to continue deepening into intimacy, have a conversation about how to navigate coming back into "real life" together. Perhaps even making a commitment to one another to ask for what you want with more clarity and being curious about what the other person wants with more interest.

Walkaway with Wisdom

If we are not using our intimate relationships as a container for our personal growth, we are using them as a container to enact our old survival strategies that are no longer adaptive.

There are three types of energetic boundaries: Diffused, rigid, and flexible. Our energetic boundaries represent our awareness of where we end and other people begin, making it possible for us to stay seated in ourselves as we contact the environment. In this way, healthy, clear boundaries are in service of connection, they are the meeting place between ourselves and our environment.

On the energetic level, self-betrayal is an act of slowly killing the most beautiful aspects of ourselves—our truth. Honoring ourselves is an act of dignity and self-love. It is also an act of true connection with our relationships.

It is counterintuitive to take up our whole energetic space by honoring ourselves when we feel unsafe. The instinctive reaction is to get small when our safety seems compromised in a relational interaction. This is the effect of trauma. Paradoxically, closing in on ourselves creates less safety. Pushing out energetically to the edges of our energetic field allows us to stand our sacred ground and hold our own vibration. Here we hold ourselves in security and we enact the self-trust that we've cultivated by attaching to Self as Source.

In the full spectrum of our spiritual humanity, we are *sovereign* human beings, responsible for our own actions, perceptions, and emotions. Nobody can "make us" feel anything. We simply are, by design, our living experience of ourselves in any given moment. At the same time, we are sensitive beings who are *inherently interconnected* with all of life. We affect one another, and we feel the impact of other people's actions and words and states of being.

The complexity of this is nuanced and delicate. In any moment we can slip back into the path of least resistance and see life through a lens of projection, and our distortions can hijack any interaction without warning. When our current environment mirrors an imprint of our wounding, our perspective in the present moment can easily be filtered through the past.

In the dance of human interactions, there is no greater dance partner than one who can stay seated in themselves while vulnerably opening to intimacy. We, ourselves, must be that dance partner, embodying the very thing we desire from others.

Chapter 15

Intentional Language

Word choice is meaningful. Depending on the place within us we're speaking from, our words are either giving voice to our distortion or our alignment.

When we've been engaging with our environment from our distortion throughout our life, the language patterns we've developed are likely allies of our distorted life force. If we continue the language patterns of our distortion, we reinforce our own distorted ways of thinking about ourselves and relating to others.

Our words hold a vibrational quality that mirrors the vibration that we, ourselves, embody. By repeating distorted language patterns, the vibration of our words expresses distorted energy. Our words influence the world around us in a similar vibration. By allowing our words to come from our distorted life force, we subsequently distort the environment around us. In doing so, we keep our internal matrix fixed and our life remains an expression of contorted conditioned patterns of our vital force.

When we find our way home to our center where life force energy can flow freely in alignment with Source, we can be in discovery about what language reflects and honors our alignment. Because our alignment flows with our emerging sense of self, there is no script for our essential self. The conditioned self has rules and ways that it must relate to the world in order to maintain its influence. The True Self is continually developing and evolving; therefore, the language we choose from our alignment resonates with the vibration of our essential life force energy.

The Language of Distortion

The place within ourselves that we speak from matters more than the words themselves. However, our word choice matters greatly. When we pay attention to the habitual language we use, we can cultivate more awareness about what is happening within us beneath our words.

For example, when a person says "It just feels like I can't do anything right for them," they are expressing many aspects of the filter through which they are seeing the world:

They have depersonalized their experience by using the word "It" instead of "I." In doing so, they are referring to themselves as an object, which likely comes from an introjection. They are disrupting contact with their direct experience, which creates distance from feeling vulnerable. They have minimized their experience by saying "just." This is a common way people remove themselves from the vulnerable experience of what is happening deeper within themselves. They've left themselves by paying more attention to the other person than their own feelings. The phrase "can't do anything right" is not a feeling, and it doesn't reveal what's truly happening for the person. They have subversively made themselves a victim to the person who they are trying to please. If the other person's satisfaction of their actions is the goal, the awareness of what would feel honoring to themselves is not present. It would appear as if this person has given their will over to another person and resents them for it.

This other person is being seen as "Source," as their reference point from which they are trying to earn approval. This one simple sentence is an expression of a distortion and an invitation to entangle.

Here are some other examples of how our language can contribute to an entanglement pattern:

"I'm experiencing you as (hostile or manipulative or controlling, etc.)."

This is an unconscious way people create entanglements

because they think they are giving voice to their experience but, really, they are giving voice to their projections.

Instead, if the person speaking focused on their own felt experience, they would be able to share impact when another person "seems" a certain way.

"It seems (hostile or manipulative or controlling, etc.)" is another version of this same entanglement hook. However, here the person speaking is talking about the other person as an object, not a subject.

"It feels to me like…" or "I feel like you…"

This is an unconscious way people create entanglements because they think they are giving voice to their feelings but really they are giving voice to their projections. However, they are not saying how they actually feel and are instead circumventing vulnerability by focusing on the other person.

Instead, if the person speaking focused on their own feelings and looked within to see the deeper aspect of what was happening for themselves, they could make contact with themselves and discover what was being reflected in the relationship.

"I'm feeling my walls come up and I'm realizing I feel (unsafe, dysregulated, scared, hurt, angry, etc.)" is a way to express how we feel instead of putting our feelings onto another.

"That makes me feel…" or "You make me so…" or "He/She/They make me so…."

These are examples of a person unconsciously believing that they have no agency of choice and their emotional well-being is at the whim of the way other people behave. Remembering that nobody *makes* us *feel* anything, our reaction is ours to own.

Instead of blaming the other person for our emotional state, we can look within to see if a younger part is activated and find out what that part needs from us.

"I'm noticing that as I listen to you, I feel (i.e., powerless, angry, scared, etc.). I'm imagining a younger part of me is activated right now, and I want to put my attention on my Self."

"You are being..." or "This person is being so..."

This is an overt attempt at claiming our subjective perception as objective truth, that how we see someone is how they actually are. When we have a strong emotional reaction to a person (like annoyance or anger), it's common to say "You are being so annoying" or "This person is so infuriating." However, because we feel annoyed or angry, doesn't actually mean the other person *is* this way. It simply means that something inside of ourselves is activated and we're putting the ownership of our feelings onto the other person.

When we acknowledge that what we experience belongs to us, we can give voice to how we perceive someone or the meaning that we are making of an interaction. This is necessary to stay in contact with ourselves and keep our relationships clean of entanglements.

Instead, we can give voice to how we're feeling ("I feel annoyed") and ask what's going on for the other person. Or we can say how the other person seems to us ("You seem like you really want my attention") then check it out ("Is that true for you?"). We can even combine them all ("I'm feeling annoyed each time you ask a question. You seem like you really want my attention right now. Is that true?").

Language is powerful, and we feel it in every interaction. Whether subtly aware of word choice or consciously tracking what is being said, the vibration of words can either create a murky entanglement or a vibrant expression of sovereignty where we honor ourselves and others.

Fully Owning Our Experience

Our ability to own that everything that arises within us is ours to experience is an element of sovereignty. This is also true for the words that we choose. Knowing that nobody "makes" us feel anything, our words can express the full ownership of our experience. Also knowing that our perspective and meaning making belongs to us and the way we see something is not objective truth, our words reflect the ownership of our point of view.

We might look at a person and perceive them as angry, but our perception does not determine anyone else's truth. That other person may feel exasperated, bewildered, or stunned. Their emphatic passion might seem like anger to us, based on our own past experiences or our nervous system response.

By saying to that person "You're so angry," we disown our experience and invite an entanglement, which might escalate to the person actually feeling angry. "You seem angry... is that true?" honors that we have a perception and the other person has their own truth. If our perception of another person's anger is a projection and not an attuned accuracy, there is likely an emotion activated within us that underlies the statement of "You're so angry." Perhaps what's true is that we feel scared. If we share this with another, we are being vulnerable as we honor what's happening within us.

Examples of ownership language:

"You seem..."

"You seem (this way) to me."

"I feel (sad, angry, happy, scared, hurt, lonely, guarded, etc.)."

"I have a story that (you want space from me)."

"I'm developing a story that you (want my attention)."

"I notice that I'm (feeling, creating a story, in a pattern, not in contact with myself, etc.)."

"I want..."

When we own our experience, our words are inarguable. No one can tell us that we don't feel scared. No one can tell us that we don't have a story about another person. No one can tell us that someone doesn't seem a certain way to us. And when we really hold the sovereign sense of ownership, we hold our perspective loosely. When we have a story about another person, we check it out with them so that we can discover what is true for them, assuming nothing. Assumption comes from projection, and when we check out our stories, we honor the other person as a mysterious, emerging being with their own experience of the situation.

However, if we say, "I feel like you're not attracted to me anymore," we are disowning our experience. This statement is arguable because the other person can say, "That's not true. I find you very attractive."

There are five basic human emotions: anger, fear, grief, joy, and love. There are many words to describe these emotions: for example, frustration is a degree of anger, and anxiety is a degree of fear. If we are owning our experience, when we say, "I feel..." the words that follow are about how we feel inside of our emotional body. If we say, "I feel..." and the words that follow are "like you are (distant)," we are not owning our experience. We are telling another person about themselves, which always creates the possibility for conflict.

One disowned statement can be the starting point of a long, entangled conflict.

Owning our experience can go a long way in keeping our relational interactions clean(er) of entanglement. As we're learning and emerging, we might slip into younger parts, distorted patterns, projections, and so on. However, if we attempt to own our experience with our words, we will be in the practice of keeping our contribution to the relationship clean. Supporting our own development of sovereignty through our language choice is an important shift in our developing sense of self.

Connection or Control

Words are powerful. The language we choose expresses how available we are to clean contact or how invested we are in controlling others and being right.

Most language is unconsciously devised to circumvent vulnerability and minimize one's truth. In our interpersonal relating, we are either communicating for connection or we are communicating for control (Campbell, 2001). When we have not yet cultivated the self-responsibility of our sovereign self, we have a tendency to choose words that either subtly or overtly try to exert our power over others.

The conditioned self unconsciously wants to control others. The True Self wants to create more love and connection. No connection has ever been strengthened by telling someone else what they've done wrong. By being really honest with ourselves about why we're communicating, we can see if our intention is to control or connect. If we truly want to connect, we vulnerably share what's happening within us.

Language intended to control another is often camouflaged as a joke, "Oh, you're always late" said in a jesting manner is an underhanded criticism that does not breed connection. It's an attempt at controlling the other person's behavior while circumventing vulnerability.

There is the objective thing that happened (the person was late), and then there is how we feel about it. "When you were late for our time together, I felt sad." This is a vulnerable reveal that can cultivate deeper connection. "I noticed myself making up a story that I didn't matter to you, and I can recognize that this comes from my old wound around my cargiver not showing up for my soccer games." This gets to the deeper cut of what was ignited in the interaction while also recognizing that this person is not our childhood caregiver.

Another way language is used to try to control another person is through criticism, which again circumvents vulnerability. Telling another person about all the things they do that impact us negatively diverts all of the awareness away from our own pain and hurt, focusing on the faults of the other person. When our words send a message of, "If you were different, I wouldn't feel this way," we are trying to get the other person to change so we don't experience our own discomfort.

Even if our words are expressing our vulnerability but we're sharing it so that the other person will change, we are communicating for control, not connection.

Any time we try to control another person, we aren't trusting their agency of choice in how they want to show up. Maybe the other person doesn't want to show up differently, and maybe we make up a story that they don't care about the pain or discomfort we feel in response to the way they show up for our connection. We then get to choose if this is a connection which we want to continue participating in.

Because our historical trauma is activated in relationship, it's easy to say that "If they weren't the way they were I wouldn't be feeling this way." Putting the ownership of our feelings onto another, we view ourselves as the victim and miss the opportunity for growth and integration. When we avoid looking at ourselves with the deep awareness and presence needed for transformation, we stay in our conditioning and our relationships continue to be messy and entangled.

When we are emotionally activated, it's common to start looping in stories about other people. In the emotional attunement exercise earlier in this book, we started the practice of honoring the emotions that are beneath the stories we make up. Beneath the loop of the mind, there is always an emotion driving that loop. And beneath the emotion, there is always a younger part that needs our attention. Instead of focusing on what the other person said or did or didn't do, looking within to honor our inner young one is the skill needed to stay in contact with ourselves and in our alignment.

The more we disown our emotions, the more they will come out sideways in language that does not serve the connection. The more we ignore our inner young one, the more we will try to get our emotional needs met by someone else rather than stay seated in our own Source of love. And the more we try to get our emotional needs met by someone else, more entangled our relationships become with our distorted patterns and misbeliefs. And when two people in a relationship are both ignoring their inner young one and trying to get their emotional needs met by the other person, the messier the dynamic becomes.

The more able we are to own that what is happening within us belongs to us, the more we can express ourselves with intentional worlds that clearly depict our truest truth. We can speak on behalf of our inner young one rather from this younger part. Speaking from the younger part, we blame and yell and spread our pain. Speaking on behalf of our inner young one, we vulnerably reveal what's happening within us and honor our pain as the doorway to a deep repair.

Two whole individuals who own their experience, hold their inner young one with love, and utilize language with intention and clarity can parse through any misunderstanding or differing desires, while ending up feeling closer and more connected for having had conflict. When the people in our lives seem to lack the capacity or interest to meet us here, it is still important that we do this work and embody our alignment no matter who we are in relationship with.

One aligned person relating with a person in their distortion can still keep their side of the street clean, so to speak. Not everyone is on the same timeline. If we truly have access to our alignment with Source, we don't say "Too bad" to those who don't. When we are truly full of divine energy, there is plenty to go around. Honoring other people's journey while speaking our truth is part of the dance of our own evolution in relationships. And as we learn, we can be discerning about who we let into our inner sphere.

Correction as Distortion

To find the voice of our truth, we must remember that our truth is always about us. It always gets to the deeper part of what's happening within us, and it gets to the core that is beneath that. To speak intentionally, we need to be mindful and aware of the inner layers of what's happening for us. It's very common for people to speak to their partner about what their partner did and call that their truth. But in our interactions, we have the opportunity to practice staying in contact with ourselves.

If our attention is on our partner and what they did, we have left ourselves and gone over to their world to point out their blind spots and distortion. From here, we end up speaking from our distortion. When we think "our truth" is our uncensored opinions and projections, we maintain conflict as the status quo.

Correcting our partner's disowned language, pointing out their shadow, or telling them what we wish they would have done differently is an expression of our own distortion. Even if our partner agrees with the things we are saying, finding our safety in our partner is a way that we slip back into our distortion.

In the image below, we see one person who has built the capacity to keep their vital energy flowing through their body while the other person acts from their distortion. One is not above the other. They are simply embodying different aspects of themselves. As long as one person can maintain their alignment, no entanglement will ensue.

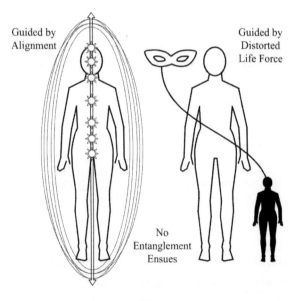

Guided by
Alignment

Guided by
Distorted
Life Force

No
Entanglement
Ensues

As we choose to do this deep inner work of being intentional with our language, correcting other people's language is a sneaky way the conditioned self criticizes and tries to control others so that we get what we think we need. Anytime our attention is on the other person correcting the words they chose, we have left ourselves and gone over into their world. Staying in contact with ourselves, continually coming back to what's happening for us is essential for staying in our alignment and seated in our hearts even if or when our partner is in their distortion.

We must slow down if we are to learn how to stay in contact with our Self as we relate to others. We must stay very present with what arises within us. The work is not about staying calm and contained — it's about fully contacting every emotion that is wanting to move through us.

We can frequently speed up to try to find a sense of control. Slowing down, looking within, and holding ourselves in loving awareness will allow us to stay embodied as we metabolize our emotions. We can hold space for ourselves, and perhaps we can hold space for our partner.

To look within ourselves to discover what is happening for us in the context of our relating with another human being is the way to stay in ourselves. This is a chance for a reparative experience, where we completely move through and metabolize the pain of the past in the context of the relationship. When we are able to stay seated in ourselves regardless of where others are meeting us from, we become the secure base for the deep repair to manifest, and it feels like liberation. When we stay in contact with our alignment no matter what, we set ourselves free from the trap doors of the past. This is the birthplace of conscious choice, where we can see clearly how we move, how others move, and how we want to be and whom we want to be with.

Exploration: Take a moment to close your eyes and contact a place in your body where you feel strong, grounded, and/or aligned. Once you find that place within, amplify it by keeping your breath and attention on it for several minutes.

Once you are connected to your sensation of grounding and strength, keep your inner eye anchored on this place as you slowly start to open your eyes. Any time you lose contact with the sensation, close your eyes and connect with it again. Keep breathing, and move slowly.

Eventually, keep your eyes open and look around as you stay anchored in the sensation and continue to breathe. This is a way to cultivate the capacity to stay in contact with yourself while also contacting your environment. Eventually, try doing this with other people. Stay in contact with yourself in this way as you look into another person's eyes. You can always close your eyes to reconnect with your power. Then slowly open them again and see how it feels to be both in contact with yourself and another person simultaneously.

The Language of the True Self

As we continually practice living from our alignment, discovering the language of the True Self is a journey in and of itself. It is in our choice of words where we get to really see how seated we are, how off balance we are, and how aware we are of our filter through which we are perceiving.

The True Self holds qualities of compassion, curiosity, connection, and collaboration. When we speak from the True Self, these qualities come through our words without betraying ourselves as we do. We can both honor ourselves and our experience while also speaking in a way that cultivates solution, safety, and connection.

Where our conditioned self wants safety and control, our True Self wants connection and freedom. If we think we need to find the right thing to say, our conditioned self is trying to control the outcome of our words. If we vulnerably express what is happening within us, our True Self is given space to express through us.

Our truth is always about ourselves. It's about a deeper aspect of our inner world that isn't obvious even to ourselves at first. We must look within to discover our truth and find the words to vulnerably express our present moment experience.

When we are in contact with ourselves, our words reflect our healthy aware state. Where conditioned habits and reactionary triggers disrupt contact, we can discover language that honors our connection with ourselves and others.

Without attachment to the outcome, without needing the person receiving our words to respond in a certain way, we simply use our awareness to give voice to what is happening within us. Meditation practice can provide us access to our witness mind, where we have a vantage point of our inner world without being caught up in the drama of our mind's stories. Bringing this into our relationships, we can witness ourselves and give voice to our conscious awareness.

Being connected to *Self as Source*—in flow with our vital energy—we get to discover how to express ourselves with both self-responsibility and compassion. No longer driven by younger parts or conditioned patterns, we can speak on behalf of those parts rather than speaking from those parts.

For example, if we were in an emotional trigger with our partner and our young one was activated, we might say, "You never listen to me. It's like I don't even matter to you and I'm all alone in this." Alternatively, if we are able to regulate through our trigger, contact ourselves and come into alignment, we can speak on behalf of our inner young one from our True Self. "I notice that I'm feeling hurt and I want to find a way back into connection with you. My story is that you don't listen to me, but I want to know what is true for you."

When we are really present and aware of what is emerging within ourselves, the vibrational quality of our essence influences our language patterns. Even if we are noticing an activation of emotions or mistunement in our system, we can notice what arises and discover in real time how our words can honor our alignment.

With our sense of self continually emerging, there are no rules for the language of the True Self. It's not as if we need to become unaffected by life to maintain the flow of our alignment. We simply need to be willing to contact everything that arises within us and take responsibility for metabolizing it and find the language of our truest experience.

Learning how to speak in a way that is resonant with our essence takes practice. As we speak our words, we can check in with our somatic experience to see if our own words resonate as truth. If they do not fully encompass our truth, we can try to find a fuller truth. As we do this, we can keep an eye on the inside to see if the vibration of our words resonates with our energetic body.

Harmony's Story

When I would give my will over to others, I would resent them for not treating me with kindness. Thinking that being nice would earn me love, I was angry when that wasn't so. Because I was not enacting with self-responsibility, my language was one of a victim whereby I blamed others for my state of being. *If they were kind*, I reasoned, *I would feel at peace*.

The day that I first realized my language was an expression of my conditioned patterns that set me up for victimhood, I started working to discover the language of self-responsibility. My anger was triggered by an encounter with my ex-husband where he complained about a diaper being left on the changing table. In my martyrdom, my mind looped in resentment with all that I do to take care of the kids, the house, and him while also working part-time without a nanny or housecleaner. I was building evidence for my self-righteous anger and I was ready to come at him with it as ammunition to "win" the inner argument happening within my own mind.

Once I noticed this distorted narrative and loop, I sat in meditation. I became curious about the theme of my looping thoughts, and I realized that something deeper was happening within me.

I got up from my meditation cushion and picked up my copy of *Nonviolent Communication* (Rosenberg, 2015). I started to work through the four steps of the communication tools outlined in the book. As I worked Step 1, I could not decipher the objective reality. My meaning making and narratives were so loud that looking at objective reality was effortful. Without judgment or interpretation, I slowed down to see what actually happened: My husband said, "You always leave the diaper on the changing table." To get to the simple words he spoke without clinging to his tone or labeling the statement as criticism was challenging.

Once I was able to identify that, I started working with Step 2, and I turned towards myself to discover how I felt when I heard that. To identify feelings that were about me—and not about him—also took effort. Without feeling like he didn't appreciate me (which is clearly not a feeling), I finally identified that I felt angry and hurt.

Working my way to Step 3, I realized that I had no idea what I needed or valued. I sat with this one for a long time trying to find the answer within myself. I thought about needing him to be nice, but that was about him. I thought about needing to be seen, but again that was about him. I thought about my values around tending to the children over keeping the house sparkling clean, and this one seemed the most clean and clear.

Finally, when I arrived at Step 4, I contemplated a request that I would ask of him. This was a little easier to identify. I wanted to make a request that he cleans the diapers up without pointing it out to me if he feels bothered by the way I prioritize the children over cleanliness.

By the time I worked through this process, I felt more

regulated. However, I was still unsure why this was so infuriating to me. Over years of working with clients, I discovered that there is a lot of value in giving voice to the stories we make up while we're in an emotional state. The narratives we create about another person are an insight into our own contact boundary disturbances. However, it is essential to own our narratives as ours, to use them as a key to discover what's happening within ourselves, and to share them vulnerably.

I also discovered over the years that there is value in looking at the part within ourselves that is activated. Identifying our inner young one or our subpersonality can be useful for our integration. Giving voice to this in relationship brings the full spectrum of our experience into the awareness field.

For example, in the situation above with my ex-husband, I would have said, "I have a story that cleanliness matters to you more than I do, and I think this comes from a part of myself that believes I'm unworthy of love." You can see here that while the story I was holding was about him, when I look to see what's beneath the story, I discover the place within myself that needs my attention.

Now in my life, when I share my stories and the underlying introjection, I share it vulnerably. I am showing myself to the other person in service of our connection. I share regardless if the other person can meet me in my vulnerability, and I do it so that I am in clean relationship with myself and others. Whereas before I would try to communicate in order to get someone to stop being in their patterns and meet me with love, now I communicate in order to dissolve my own barriers to love.

Exercise: Discover the Language of Self-Responsibility

When learning how to stay in contact with ourselves in the context of relationship, it is helpful to distinguish the interaction we had with another from the way we are affected by the interaction.

Keeping an eye on the inside, we can watch the movement of our inner world as we relate with others, knowing that this inner movement is our own experience of ourselves. I-Thou is our personal experience of the relationship while we are currently in the relationship. These two things, our impact and our experience of another person, can get conflated. This exercise is a simple method inspired by nonviolent communication (Rosenberg, 2015).

Think of a recent time you felt emotionally activated. The emotion could have been "positive" or "negative." All emotions belong to us. Even if someone does something to ignite our pleasure, the pleasure is still ours. Just like if someone does something and our anger is ignited, that anger belongs to us.

Once you have the memory of the emotional activation, write down the objective thing that happened. Without using interpretation, judgment, or stories, simply write down the objective occurrence. It can be as simple as, "My partner walked into the room." Maybe your partner seemed angry or distracted or heavy with depression. It doesn't matter how they seemed to you because all we want is to hone in on objective reality, not your perception (even if your perception was accurate).

Once you have written down your memory of objective reality, then write down how you felt. "My partner walked in the room, and I felt scared." If you made up a story about yourself or the other person, write down that story but own it as yours. "My partner walked in the room, and I felt scared. I started to make up a story that they were closing their heart off to me."

Now get curious about what was underneath that emotion. What part of you was activated? What was this part needing? Then write that down. "My partner walked into the room, and I felt scared. My inner young one was afraid that I was going to be abandoned, and she/he/they needed my reassurance that I will always love her/him/them."

Practice writing this out each time you feel emotionally activated in a relational interaction.

1) Objective thing that happened.
2) How you felt when that happened.
3) What story did you make up from that emotional place?
4) What part was activated?
5) What was that part needing from you?
6) What request does this part have of your partner?

Walkaway with Wisdom

Word choice is meaningful. Depending on the place within us we're speaking from, our words are either giving voice to our distortion or our alignment. The place within ourselves that we speak from matters more than the words themselves. However, our word choice matters greatly.

Our ability to own that everything that arises within us is ours to experience is an element of sovereignty. This is also true for the words that we choose. Knowing that nobody "makes" us feel anything, our words can express the full ownership of our experience. Also knowing that our perspective and meaning making belongs to us, and the way we see something is not objective truth, our words reflect the ownership of our point of view.

Examples of ownership language:

"You seem…"

"You seem (this way) to me."

"I feel (sad, angry, happy, scared, hurt, lonely, etc.).

"I have a story that (you want space from me)."

"I'm developing a story that you (want my attention)."

"I notice that I'm (feeling, creating a story, in a pattern, not in contact with myself, etc.)."

"I want…"

The language we choose and the way we express ourselves

indicate how available we are for clean contact or how invested we are in controlling others and being right. We can use any of these sentence stems from our conditioned self and contribute to a relationship entanglement. All the effort in the world cannot make up for our own lack of alignment. This is why alignment comes first, and language emerges from our internal connection with Source. Most language is unconsciously devised to circumvent vulnerability and minimize one's truth. Even if our words are expressing our vulnerability but we're sharing it so that the other person will change, we are communicating for control, not connection.

Any time we try to control another person, we aren't trusting their agency of choice in how they want to show up. Correcting our partner's disowned language, pointing out their shadow, or telling them what we wish they would have done differently is an expression of our own distortion.

To find the voice of our truth, we must remember that our truth is always about us. It always gets to the deeper part of what's happening within us, and it gets to the core that is beneath that. To speak intentionally, we need to be mindful and aware of the inner layers of what's happening for us. It's very common for people to speak to their partner about what their partner did and call that their truth. But in our interactions, we have the opportunity to practice staying in contact with ourselves.

The True Self holds qualities of compassion, curiosity, connection, and collaboration. When we speak from the True Self, these qualities come through our words without betraying ourselves as we do. We can both honor ourselves and our experience while also speaking in a way that cultivates solution, safety, and connection.

Chapter 16

Intentional Listening

While much of the work of coming into alignment is about cultivating awareness about our own patterns and connecting to *Self as Source*, we are not living in isolation. We are social beings who crave to feel seen and heard and in connection with others. As we discover and practice speaking from our sovereign self, learning how to listen is equally important as the words we choose.

When a person feels heard, they feel loved. Intentional listening is an act of co-regulation where our attuned presence invites the other person to soften into themselves. Feeling heard is regulating. Even if we don't agree with another person's perspective, putting forth effort to hear another person can cultivate the resonant qualities of love.

It's simple, really, and yet most people slip into patterns of wanting to be heard rather than listening. When neither person in a relationship feels heard, neither one is motivated to put their ego aside and listen.

When we want to be heard, it can be hard to listen to others. When we want to be right, it can be challenging to stay curious about what someone else is saying. Closed off to the interdependence of our living relationship, we might get louder and louder in an attempt to be heard while simultaneously not listening to our partner.

In a way, intentional listening is almost more important than the words we choose because this is where we create security. When the container of a relationship is a sanctuary where both people feel heard, both people feel loved and welcomed as they are. When the quality of presence we bring to our relationship embodies the desire to hear our partner, we create a secure connection in our relationship.

The Filter We Listen Through

With our language choice, the output of the words we choose can express the vibration of our distortion or our alignment. This is similar to the way we receive and hear the words of the people in our lives: We can either filter their words through our conditioned self or our True Self.

When we listen from our conditioned self, the filter we are listening through is tracking for evidence against ourselves or the other. Instead of an open mind of curiosity and empathy, the conditioned self personalizes, twists, resists, or tries to fix or change what the other person is saying. For example, if I have a wound that tells me I am not lovable, I will be listening to my partner's words through that filter. Anything said that touches this wound will become my focus and I will miss the rest of their message. Personalizing their words as evidence of my not enoughness, I might defend against my partner rather than really hear what's happening for them.

When a person is speaking, they are telling us about themselves. Even if their words are about us, when we really listen, we can learn about them. The way they saw what happened, how they're feeling, what they're wanting, etc., is embedded within the words they choose.

In the image below, we see two people who have rigid boundaries and are looking at the same situation through different filters. Even though there is one objective reality, the perception of that reality is skewed by the way it is being perceived. It is the same with how we listen: there are the objective words that were said, and then there is our perception which we filter them through.

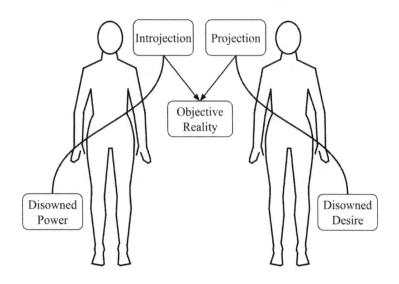

Knowing that everything the other person says is about them, even when their words are about us, we can listen without personalizing their sentiment. We can try to see the interaction through their lens, and we can relate from our most sovereign self, without reacting, blaming, or being driven by shame.

As we set down the filter of our conditioned self and listen with an open mind of curiosity, we can hold the vibrational quality of loving awareness. Without reacting or cutting a person off midsentence, we can simply hold space for their perspective to be expressed. Setting our ego aside, we can listen with love even if we have a different point of view.

In the image below, we see one person with flexible, healthy boundaries who has the capacity to stay in alignment with Source while listening to a person who is identified with patterns of their pain and conditioning. The person speaking has an open boundary system and is speaking from their distorted life force. The listener is listening in such a way that the distorted narrative of the other person is filtered through a lens of clarity. This type of listening prevents entangled and distorted patterns from intensifying.

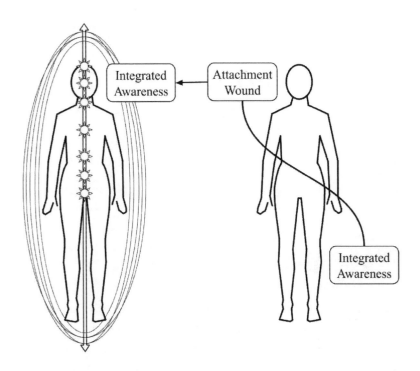

As we listen to another person from our sovereign sense of alignment, we can fully immerse ourselves into their world with deep curiosity while also staying in contact with ourselves and giving them complete space to be themselves. When we stay seated in our alignment and set our own perspective aside, we can listen with an open mind and open heart. To open our minds and really hear what it's like for the other person in the moment while also staying in contact with ourselves is a practice in relational presence—where we treat the other person as we would like to be treated *without* dropping ourselves.

In this type of listening, we can hear the other person's distorted narratives without getting hooked into entanglement patterns. We can give them space to speak, and when they are complete and feel heard we can express our perspective. Since our ability to see with clarity can get clouded by projections, this type of listening is our own practice in building our capacity to differentiate our perspective from our projections.

Listening beyond Words

As we listen to our partner, they will be telling us what they think and feel. Listening to the words they are saying is important. We learn a lot about what's happening with someone from what they say.

When we are seen beyond our words, we know that we are in the presence of someone who sees us for all of who we are. By paying more intention to the person who is speaking than their words, we attune to our partner in a way that honors their whole being.

The subtle energy body can offer us more information about a person than their language. For example, if our partner says, "I really don't like what happened yesterday, but I'm over it and I just want to move on," we can pay attention to those words and move on. However, if we notice that as they say this their energy body seems heavy and sad, we might reply, "I hear that you want to move on, but when I look at you, I think I'm sensing that the sadness is still here. I want to be sure moving on is really what you need right now."

Listening to the vibration of our partner's energy expression is the deep level of attunement that we all long for in relationships. It is a skill that takes practice to develop. However, simply trying it out and seeing if the way we track the subtle energy body resonates with our partner will give us more information. Even if what we think we're hearing in the subtle body is inaccurate, taking the risk and speaking to it lets our partner know that we are at least trying to attune to their essence. Holding what we think we're seeing loosely and listening to the correction of the true experience of our partner lets us know if we were projecting or attuned.

The Power of Curiosity

There are two times when people tend to forget to be curious about another person: when they themselves are emotionally activated or the other person is.

To be curious about ourselves when our attachment wound is activated is part of our own inner work. To be curious about another person when our own wounds are activated is also part of our work and can be quite regulating.

When we notice that something seems off in our connection with another person, learning to give voice to how we experience the point of contact is clarifying. By honoring ourselves and the other person, we can bring conscious awareness to the space between us with curiosity.

Creating space for another person to be vulnerable and share what's happening in them is a gift to our relationships and our intimacy. For example, if the other person seems distant, we can name "I feel distant from you" and then we can ask how the other person is or if there is something happening for them. To do this with a genuine heart of wanting to bridge the gap with love, we create an opening for deep and meaningful conversations.

Conversely, if the other person seems emotionally activated, we can still name how we're sensing our relational contact. For example, if the other person seems anxious and insecure, we can say that lovingly, "I'm wondering what's happening for you right now?" This can be a way to bring consciousness to our relational field. Or, "You seem anxious. I'm wondering if there is anything you need from me." Or "I notice something in the field between us. Are you noticing anything?"

Giving voice to the subtle, implicit field between us is essential for our connection to be clean. This is especially true when it seems like ourselves or the other has forgotten that we each have our own energy Source within ourselves and have left our alignment.

Seeing and sensing one another while holding an open mind of curiosity is a skill to develop. Please note that we are not stating that what we see is objective reality. The words are not "You're super needy right now. What's going on with you?" Our words are powerful, as is our expression of our words. When we are seated in our own alignment, we create an opening in which to foster genuine curiosity about the other person. This genuine curiosity allows us to fully notice them.

Even if we've been married for 40 years, our partner is still a mysterious being who we will never fully know. We will never know what it feels like to be them, what they think, where they move from, or what their deepest expression is. We might glimpse it, we might think we get it, and we might even extend a lot of curiosity in service of really knowing our partner—and yet we will never know them with the depth that we know ourselves.

Clean, sovereign relationships cannot exist without curiosity. A curious mind is a healthy mind. Assuming nothing, we can stay open to another person's subjective world and stay curious about what their words mean. Maybe when they use the word "sad" they mean loss, hurt, longing, or something else. Maybe when they use the word "grumpy" they mean distant, frustrated, tired, or something else. In our curiosity, we can really hear the essence of another person's message, and this in itself, is good medicine.

When we stay curious about another, it's important that we don't leave ourselves. Keeping an inner eye on the inside, we keep at least 40% of our attention inward and 60% outward on another.

Curiosity and compassion without contact with ourselves and healthy boundaries is enabling. We need to be in ourselves to have a place to connect from. If we go totally over into another person's world with all of our attention on them, we've left ourselves. Without dissolving the boundary between us and another, as we listen, we might try on what it's like to be them.

For example, if our partner says, "I really wanted you to support me by making dinner tonight. You know that I've been busy with work and school, and when I come home to see you watching television, I feel so frustrated. It's as if you don't even care about me."

Instead of defending and explaining why we are watching television, we can stay curious about our partner and try on what it's like to be them: "I hear that you would have felt supported by me if I had made dinner. I want to sense into what you're saying to make sure I'm really getting it: I'm imagining what I would feel like if I had worked a full day and took an exam at school... I can already feel the stress in my body. Then I'm imagining walking in here and seeing me sitting on the couch, looking as if I've been waiting for you to get home and make dinner... when I try that on, I can really feel the frustration and deep desire to feel supported by me."

Trying on what it might be like for our partner to be in relationship with us when they feel upset by our actions is a transpersonal level of empathy. We fully put ourselves aside and listen with our whole body. We stay curious about their experience, and we honor the way they are affected by our actions. Even if we have reasons and excuses and defenses for our behavior, putting ourselves aside and holding the presence of empathy is the deep listening that creates a healthy, secure relationship.

Reflective Listening

Reflective listening is the most potent way to show a person who is talking that you are listening. It helps them to see themselves more clearly. It helps you to avoid seeing what they said through your own filter. It helps to keep the whole of the communication clean and clear.

Some people have mastered reflective listening at work, but

at home have a harder time utilizing the skill with their partner, kids, parents, and friends. Other people have cultivated the skill at home and have a harder time bringing it to work. Other people have no practice in this skill at all and have never received this type of meaningful relating where they feel heard. When we feel heard, we feel loved. Our reptilian brains begin to settle and our vagus nerve begins to orient to the feeling of safety.

Practice reflective listening frequently in all of your close relationships. In moments of conflict with an intimate partner, reflective listening is *the* most important tool in keeping the conversation clean of entanglements. As you reflect, if you can also validate at least one part of what your partner is saying that will calm the nervous system even more.

There are four types of reflective listening to practice in your intimate relating:

Key Word Quoting: As you listen to your partner speak, repeat the most *charged* or *important* words back to them as both a reflection and an invitation to continue.

Example: They say "I'm feeling really frustrated with you!"

You can repeat, "Frustrated... with me..." and if you like you can follow this with, "Tell me more."

Word for Word Summary: As you're listening to your partner, reflect back the whole of what they said using their words. This is really useful in making sure you're getting what's happening for them so that they feel heard.

Example: They say, "When you left the dishes in the sink yesterday, I was so frustrated because you know how much it means to me to be able to come into the kitchen and cook without first doing all of the dishes. It's like you don't care about me or the agreements you've made to me."

Then you reflect, "You're frustrated because I left the dishes in the sink yesterday, and it's really important to you that you can come into the kitchen and cook without first doing the dishes. Because I agreed in the past to do my dishes before leaving the kitchen, you're feeling like I don't care about you and the agreements I've made." Then you can follow that with, "Did I get that?" and "Is there anything else?"

This shows curiosity for your partner and the impact you've had on them. Without defending or explaining (and without word policing their disowned language) you simply open your mind with curiosity about what it's like for them right now. And if you're also able to validate some part of what they said, that would be honoring of the I-Thou and the impact you had in the relationship.

Paraphrase: As you listen to your partner, you paraphrase in your own words what you think you're hearing. This takes a high level of listening skills that needs to be cultivated over time. However, when done with attuned skillfulness, a really good paraphrase can have a person feel even more heard than if you used their own words to summarize what they said. However, some people *really* like hearing their own words repeated, so it just takes trial and error to learn the map of your partner.

Example: They say, "I can't believe that you just made such a big purchase without even considering having a conversation with me about it first. It's like you don't even think of our money as ours... it's just yours to do with as you want."

Then you paraphrase, "It sounds like you're really upset that I just bought the car without first talking it through with you. It makes sense to me that it would seem like this action would have you think that I see our money as mine, and not ours."

You can see here that the language is changed and a validation was woven into the paraphrase.

Clarifying the implicit: As you listen to your partner, they might be implying something without saying it explicitly. Clarifying the unspoken feelings is a great way to get clarity on what is underneath their words instead of allowing it to permeate the unconscious or the relationship field. This is a way to make what is implicit, explicit.

Example: They say, "I need more affection, more physical connection."

You say, "It sounds like you might be feeling unimportant or lonely. Is that true?"

They say, "No. I've been feeling rejected and unattractive."

You say, "To you it seems like I find you unattractive? Like I've been rejecting you?"

They say, "Yes. This is so vulnerable to share. I've been holding it for so long."

You say, "I hear that this is really vulnerable. I didn't know you've been holding this."

In this example, by clarifying the implicit we can see that the partner was circumventing vulnerability and hiding something really tender. If the clarifying question intended to get at the unspoken feelings that haven't been expressed, there could have been meaning making and made-up stories about what was happening that were inaccurate. Clarifying the implicit is an essential way of keeping intimacy clean of assumptions.

Harmony's Story

As a psychotherapist, I am constantly paying attention to the field between myself and a client. To me, the quality of our contact gives me more information than the words a person is saying. As a client speaks, I am listening for the deeper cut of what they are saying. If a client comes in talking about their partner, I am looking at the deeper place inside of them that needs to be heard and seen. In transpersonal counseling, this is known as "paying more attention to the storyteller than the story" (Kurtz, 2001).

Throughout a session, a part of my awareness is tracking if the thing the client is talking about is happening right now. Just as relationship only happens in the present moment, healing happens only in the present moment. By asking myself, "Is this happening right now?" I am looking for openings to being in relationship with a client in the present moment as I create openings for their healing.

For example, a client might say, "Because I was seeing the thing that no one else was talking about, I was never safe to ask questions as a child. If I asked a question, I would have hurt them. Harmony, why can I see these things with you but I can't talk to other people about it?" The thing in the past that the client was looking at emerged in the therapeutic room. Because I am tracking the present moment expression of the wound, I say, "Thank you for asking me this question. This is a very valid question and I am so glad you asked. I see that your young one didn't feel safe to ask questions, and I want him to know that I welcome his inquisitiveness." When I do this, a lot of emotion arises in the client. Had I simply answered the question, I wouldn't have been present with my client.

When we listen to a person's whole system rather than their words alone, we make contact with them. This is what people long for in their intimate relationships. It can be quite frustrating to a client that their therapist can hear the essence of what they are saying but their partner, parent, and friends cannot. Understanding that most people walk around identified with their distortion, we can stop looking to others to be heard deeply and start listening to ourselves in the way we long to be heard. When we are practiced at listening to ourselves deeply, we embody our alignment more solidly. We then bring this quality to our relationships and listen with an open heart even when others are unable to provide this for us.

When I am holding space as a clinician, I am intentionally staying seating in my alignment with my True Self. To hold a transpersonal therapeutic container, I must set my persona aside and embody the vibration of my essence. Outside of the therapeutic container, my persona and conditioning reemerge. Although this happens less now that I am more aligned, it is my ongoing personal work to be aware of my habitual patterns and thoughts as I engage with my husband, children, and friends. Noticing when I am looking to other people for my validation, I become aware of when I leave myself. This is my indication to look within to see what my inner young one wants.

Once I become aware of what's happening deep within myself, I can speak to my implicit sense of my relationship with another and create an opening for a meaningful conversation. For example, my husband has a long list of projects for his business and his home that keeps him very busy. When this goes on too long without his intentional slowing down and bringing his full presence to our relationship, I start to become subtly activated. Because he is not harming me, it can be challenging at times to identify why my mind is looping in thoughts of dissatisfaction.

My parents divorced when I was young; I didn't see my father very often, and when I did see him, he was always busy. My father never did anything to harm me, but his lack of presence was very damaging. The imprint of the masculine that I have from childhood is one of neglect. As a child, I learned to be okay with this and I assumed that this was the way that dads were.

Because my husband and my father are very similar, it is very easy to slip into a projection where my young one feels hurt and neglected. As an adult, I have the capacity to give this a voice and create an opening in my relationship. My husband is very receptive to my desires and wants to know what's happening for me even if his conditioned self doesn't slow down to check in.

"I notice that I am feeling lonely. I'm wondering what's happening for you?" is a way I might begin to bring awareness to the implicit field between us. Without blame, resentment, or walls, I share my experience and invite him to share his own experience.

"I'm feeling overwhelmed by my list of projects and I keep thinking that I need to stop to connect with you but it's so hard for me. My fear of rejection keeps me doing things to try to please you."

My heart softens, and I feel closer for having had this conversation. He slows down and touches me and looks into my eyes, and we regulate and breathe in being seen and heard. Encounters like this are reparative for both of our systems. This is how we create a secure connection with one another in our relationship.

Exercise: Be a Mirror
Choose one day this week where you will be a mirror for the people closest to you. Using reflective listening, simply reflect what you're hearing them say. If you're talking to your parent, your child, your best friend, or your partner, simply repeat their words back to them and summarize what you hear them saying.

As you listen, pay attention to the subtle energy of the person, as well as the essence of what they are saying. This may seem like a challenging concept to bring into relationship, yet attuning to the deeper aspect of what a person says deepens our connection with them.

For example, if you are talking on the phone with your parent, and they say, "You never call me. Your sibling calls me every day. You're just too busy to pick up the phone and check in on me."

You might reply, "It sounds like you want me to reach our more, and I'm imagining that you think I don't care as much about you because I call less."

After you spend the day being a mirror, journal about how these interactions differ from your typical interactions with these people.

Walkaway with Wisdom
The way we listen can either filter their words through our conditioned self or our True Self. When we listen with our conditioned self, the other person's words are distorted through

our filter. When we listen with our True Self our clarity and presence cultivate connection and regulation.

Knowing that everything the other person says is about them, even when their words are about us, we can listen without personalizing their sentiment. We can try to see the interaction through their lens, and we can relate from our most sovereign self, without reacting, blaming, or being driven by shame.

Listening to the vibration of our partner's energy expression is the deep level of attunement that we all long for in relationships. It is a skill that takes practice to develop. However, simply trying it out and seeing if the way we track the subtle energy body resonates with our partner will give us more information.

Giving voice to the subtle, implicit field between us is essential for our connection to be clean. This is especially true when it seems like ourselves or the other has forgotten that we each have our own energy Source within ourselves and have left our alignment. Creating openings for connection with a genuine heart of wanting to bridge the gap with love, we invite more emotional intimacy into our relationship. Here are some examples of opening communication when something feels implicitly off in our connection:

"I feel distant from you. I'm wondering how you're feeling right now?"

"I think I'm noticing distance between us and I'm curious to know if there is something happening for you?"

"I'm wondering what's happening for you right now?"

"You seem anxious (sad, quiet, frustrated, etc.). I'm wondering if there is anything you need from me."

"I notice something in the field between us. Are you noticing anything?"

There are two times when people tend to forget to be curious about another person: When they themselves are emotionally activated or the other person is. Creating space for another person to be vulnerable and share what's happening in them is a gift to our relationships and our intimacy.

Reflective listening is the most potent way to show a person who is talking that you are listening. It helps them to see themselves more clearly. It helps you to avoid seeing what they said through your own filter. It helps to keep the whole of the communication clean and clear.

There are four types of reflective listening to practice in your intimate relating:

Key word quoting, where you repeat the most *charged* or *important* words back to the other person as both a reflection and an invitation to continue.

Word for word summary where you reflect back the whole of what they said using their words.

Paraphrase in your own words what you think you are hearing.

Clarifying the implicit feelings beneath what the person said.

Chapter 17

Revealing Our Truth

The discovery of our truth takes more awareness and more self-curiosity than simply speaking our opinions. Our truth is not our uncensored thoughts and feelings, these are our projections and wounds. When we reveal our truth, our words are about us, we share a deeper aspect of what's happening for us, and we vulnerably speak to the less obvious part of our inner world.

There is a tendency in relationship to hide our inner experience. Even when we are aware of what's happening within us, revealing our deeper experience feels vulnerable, which is something we tend to sidestep. Instead of sharing it, we live with our truth concealed within us, left unspoken. As a result, we feel more distant from the people in our lives and they feel distant from us, too.

On the opposite end of the spectrum, some of us disclose everything we are feeling, thinking, and wanting without discernment. We lay all of our dirty laundry out to be seen, and we end up pushing people away with our oversharing. Even though it might seem like we're being vulnerable, the excessive expression of our deeper truth takes up a lot of space in relationship and can actually be a barrier to real connection. People in our lives feel overwhelmed by our sharing, and they might even tell us that we're "too much."

Most people polarize between these two extremes: hiding or oversharing. There's a sweet spot in the middle between these two expressions, and it involves staying in contact with our alignment.

Vulnerability Creates Deeper Connection

Getting clear on our intention for communication, we ask

ourselves "Am I communicating for connection right now? Or am I wanting this person to be something for me?"

There are many reasons we can come up with to hide our truth. We might think that other people won't be responsive. We might think that our truth will disrupt connection. We might think that the unskillful ways we tried to share our truth in the past is evidence that we should never do it again.

When we hide our truth, we are unconsciously trying to control the way other people perceive us. When we overshare our truth, we are unconsciously trying to get other people to be something for us. In both cases, we are working out our unfinished business in our relationship, perpetuating patterns of our distortion.

When we don't reveal our inner world to others, it is often the beginning of a path of self-betrayal. Hiding what is true for us because we are uncertain of how others will receive our words gives our power over to the other person. Waiting for other people to be empathetic enough or conscious enough to hear our truth is a way that we disrupt contact with ourselves and others. The truth of our deeper experience deserves to be voiced, regardless of our perception of another person's capacity. Although, our own discernment is part of our sovereignty and it's not our job to be vulnerable all the time.

Communicating our truth in service of connection means that we surrender any attempt at controlling the way other people perceive us. In this great act of letting go of control, our intention is connection; however, we are not speaking "for" the other person. We are speaking for ourselves, so that we have a voice and honor the full range of our deeper experience *without* projecting our pain onto the other.

Revealing our truth is simple. With an eye on the inside, we share the present moment sensations and feelings we're experiencing in a succinct sentence. We talk about the map of our inner world as we stay curious about what's happening within us.

Our truth is always inarguable.

For example, "I feel like you don't care about me," is an arguable statement that is about the other person. "You seem inconsiderate," is also an arguable statement about another person. Although "You seem..." has more of a quality of owning that this is how you seem to me, it is still a jab at the other person and circumvents our felt experience of ourselves.

Without discharging our experience or projecting our "truth" onto another, the practice of revealing is a practice in honoring the full range of our experience while staying fully seated in ourselves. With a sovereign sense of wholeness and dignity, we show ourselves to others by letting them know what we feel like in relationship to the interconnectedness of the meeting point of "I" and "Thou."

It's counterintuitive to turn towards ourselves, speak about our present moment sensations and only reveal about ourselves. We are conditioned to leave ourselves, talk about our stories or ideas, and talk about what the other person has done. However, if we consider that instead of living in a house of windows we actually are looking into mirrors (Perls, 1973), this practice makes good sense.

When we reveal, we look within to see how we feel.

Then we look even deeper to find the feeling beneath the first layer of our experience.

Then we look even deeper yet to discover the birthplace of why we are feeling this way in relationship with the other person at this moment.

Although looking within ourselves may seem like a simple formula, it is not always easy, especially in the midst of intense emotional reactions. To completely honor the truth of our inner experience, we need to wholly and completely let go of any illusion of control we have over the way others might perceive us.

Similarly, we must remember that our truth is *always* about us and *never* about anyone else. The complexity of this is that our truth usually emerges in relationship with another person, so it seems like talking about what the other person said or did to ignite this feeling within us would be reasonable. However, what is ignited within us is ours, and no one made us feel anything.

One way to think of revealing our inner world is to share impact, letting other people know how we feel in relationship to them. For example, if your partner walks into the room and kisses you, sharing your experience of yourself as you are affected by the kiss is the way to bring your experience of the relating in that moment to the awareness field.

Start by stating the objective thing that happened, "When you kissed me..." Then simply share how you felt/feel, "I felt tingly inside," or "I felt my body tense up," or "I noticed my mind start making up stories about you and I'm excited by the meaning that I'm making about that kiss." There are infinite ways one can be affected by a kiss. These few examples are to highlight the way we are impacted. Contrast this with a statement like, "You make me so uncomfortable when you're all over me all the time." This does not communicate the impact in a clean, authentic way, but instead puts the emphasis on the other person and deflects vulnerability.

The murky place where sensitive beings can feel muddled in relationship is when we sense something is happening with the other person in the moment we are impacted. For example, if I feel tense when my partner kisses me, I might be sensing that they are feeling irritable and the kiss is obligatory. If I blame my tightening in my body on them, I've given them my power. Noticing my own tension, I have the opportunity to stay in contact with myself, give voice to what is arising inside of me, and check in with my partner about what's happening for them. Even if they are feeling irritable, they did not cause my tension—this was simply the way my system in my design was responding.

Keeping an Eye on the Inside

In order to reveal our inner world to another, we must have an eye on the inside. We observe our inner world from our witness mind, and then we speak from our witness, not from the emotion. Even when we are emotionally activated, we can learn to speak on behalf of our pain rather than from our pain.

When a younger part is activated, we most likely don't realize that this is the case in the moment. However, our emotional reaction is an indicator that something deep is coming to the surface. If we speak from the emotion, we speak from our younger part. We say things we typically wouldn't say, and we react in ways that aren't typical for us in a regulated and aware state.

Clues that a younger part is activated:

We are blaming the other person for our feelings.

We want the other person to be different so we can feel okay.

We are unable or unwilling to be curious about the other person's perspective.

We want to disappear.

We look to the other as proof that we are lovable.

We betray ourselves to try to please the other person.

We quiet our truth and feel small.

We think we are responsible for the other person.

We feel trapped.

We feel powerless.

To be in an experience where a younger part is activated and stay in a healthy, aware state takes tremendous practice, and it is possible to do this. When we become aware that big emotions or an antiquated narrative is rising to the surface, we can learn to stay in contact with our Self and offer love to our inner young one. Giving ourselves what our young one needed at the time, we attune to our emotions, we see ourselves, and we love ourselves unconditionally. From this place, we can speak on behalf of our emotion and younger part, without speaking from them. When we speak from them, we are projecting. When we speak on behalf of them, we are in our sovereignty.

This is where the practice of revealing inner experience can really create deep intimacy in relationships even when there is conflict. The sentence stem, "I notice..." is a way to illustrate that we are aware of what's arising within.

For example: "I notice that my emotions are starting to grow in strength, and my mind is creating stories against you. As I slow down and look within, I can touch the place in me that felt voiceless as a child, like my opinion never mattered. Now I'm in touch with my sadness, and I have a lot of compassion for my inner young one. They really want to be heard by you. And I'm going to slow down to make sure they feel heard by me, and remind them that you are not the parent who ignored me."

Noticing our inner world happens in the present moment. We discover what is happening within us as it's actually happening. Giving voice to our lived experience from a place of self-responsibility is an ongoing practice of staying in contact with ourselves as our experience unfolds.

When we first practice revealing, we might not recognize how we were affected by an interaction until much later. It is good practice to go back in hindsight and share, "Earlier, when we were talking, I didn't realize how big my emotions had become. In hindsight, I can see that a younger part of me was activated, and this part was projecting (Mom/Dad/caregiver) onto you. I know you're not the person who ignored me when I was a child, and yet when it seems like you're not hearing me this part of me seems to take over. I've spent some time connecting with this part of me and I want you to know that I take full responsibility for my reaction."

With an eye on the inside, we can have a baseline of what it feels like to be us alone, separate from our relationships. Then we can keep an eye on the inside and know our experience of ourselves in the moment of relating with others. Again, this *does not* mean that we feel this way because of the other person. It simply means that in our design, with our attachment wounds, conditioning, sensitivities, etc., this is what is arising within us as we interact with this person. From here, we get to decide what we want to do with this information about ourselves. When we consider that a different person could have a completely different response or reaction to this same experience, we can see more clearly how our own imprint contributes to the way we are affected by a situation.

Revealing is the path to honoring ourselves and cultivating deep intimacy, while also creating more agency. When we reveal, we are honoring ourselves as human beings with a vast inner subjective experience rather than ignoring what happens within us and treating ourselves as objects.

Harmony's Story

I have been a very skilled hider throughout my life. Hiding my pain and my truth was an expression of my trying to appear perfect. I thought that if I told other people how I really felt, especially if I was telling them how I felt hurt by their actions or words, they wouldn't want to be in connection with me. I hid my inner world and tried to be what I thought others wanted me to be for them, thinking this was the only way to get connection.

This strategy was my trauma response. I didn't trust that my experience mattered because I had been hiding it since I was an infant. This preverbal strategy was all I knew of being with my pain, and it was reinforced when I was 4 and my dad left. By not having my voice present in the field around me, no one ever knew I was suffering. This set me up to endure emotional abuse from people who had narcissistic traits, including gaslighting me into believing their reality was the only reality that was true.

As I shared in Chapter 14, when I went through the 9-month integral relationship training I worked through much of the dysregulation that occurs in my system when I am seen. During that time, I learned how to reveal myself to others. As I practiced the art of sharing myself to those around me, I realized that I had never actually shown up for a relationship. By hiding, there was no place for others to contact me. Showing myself to the people in my life felt so life-affirming that I also wrote a self-help memoir called *Reveal: Embody the True Self Beyond Trauma and Conditioning* (2018).

Writing *Reveal* was a cathartic experience that felt like a complete whole, where my story was greater than the sum of its parts. Although I felt more current and whole for standing within my story and showing myself to the world, my conditioned self was frightened to the core. I wrote *Reveal* to use my story of how I overcame the distorted life force within myself, and to share that story I needed to highlight other people's distorted life force, too. My conditioned self was scared because I let go of any attempt at control by publishing my story. Any pretense of perfection and any strategies I developed to keep me safe were set down.

Two weeks after I published *Reveal,* I met my husband. On our first date, I asked him to do a relational meditation with me (detailed in the exercise below). Just 30 minutes after we met, we were revealing our present moment experience of our inner world with one another. I didn't know at the time that he, too, was also a masterful hider. However, seeing his capacity to be in contact with himself while sharing with me what was arising within him had me trust that we could cultivate deep intimacy together.

This vulnerable experience of showing ourselves to one another set the foundation for our relationship where we are in the continual practice of staying seated in ourselves in service of our connection. When either or both of us are emotionally activated in our wounding, we can remember to stay in contact with ourselves when we're dysregulated. By keeping our inner eye anchored into our deeper experience, we have the capacity and language to stay vulnerable even when we're hurting. Where the shadow tendencies of projective identification unconsciously try to hurt another person when we're hurting, we instead create openings for connection by contacting our own hurt.

My conditioned self previously thought I would be annihilated for speaking my truth. Now I know that I annihilate myself when I don't. There is no place to contact me in relationship if I don't share what is happening within me as I sit with you. By sharing my inner world in the context of relationship, I show up in a way that is congruent, where my expression and words match how I'm feeling.

Every group I lead, class I teach, and relationship I engage in, I bring my inner eye into myself and let other people know how I feel in their presence. My congruence calms the social field in which we contact one another. Since our amygdala is always scanning the environment for unknowns, judgment, physical threats, and incongruence, my reveal eliminates all four of these threats because people know what is happening within me.

Practicing noticing what is happening within myself while in connection with others also influences my work as a psychotherapist. Awareness of the I-Thou is the transpersonal point of contact where therapeutic transformation is possible. Noticing my experience of myself as I sit with a client gives me vital information about where my client is disrupting contact. By using present moment felt sense therapeutically, my awareness amplifies the healing potential of my clients. Because they are seen beyond their words and beyond their persona, they feel safe enough to contact their barriers to connection. The processing of these blockages in relationship with me brings them closer to embodying their essence in relationship with all people.

Exercise: Practice Revealing

To Practice Alone: Notice Your Experience of Yourself

To practice revealing when you're not with others, you can cultivate the skill of keeping your inner eye gazing within as you move through your day. While you're working, doing the dishes, talking on the phone with a friend, intentionally keep attention within and notice your experience of yourself.

Even if you're alone in your home, say aloud how you're feeling. Example: "As I am doing the dishes, I notice my mind is wondering and I'm wanting to move my attention into my body." Or "As I'm working, I notice I feel depleted and resistant to this task."

The idea is that we are in a constant practice of getting more in touch with what's happening within us as we move through the world. Staying in contact with ourselves in the present moment, noticing whatever arises within us, without trying to fix it, analyze it, or make it go away, offers us an access point to our emerging sense of self.

Practicing this alone allows us to build the skill for when we are engaging with others. Eventually, we're able to stay in the moment as we notice how we are affected in an interaction and what we are noticing about ourselves.

Practicing with a Partner: Relational Meditation

This is an exercise to do with another person. Your intimate partner, roommate, or even someone you just met can be a good practice partner.

The first step is to set context, which gives us the parameters from which to explore this communication technique. The only rules of this practice are that you speak on behalf of what is happening within you in the present moment.

You may notice that your attention is on the person across from you. In that instance, you simply name that you are unsure of what's happening within you because you have more attention out than in. I want to invite you to be curious about why that might be. Why would you have more attention out than in? What would be underneath that impulse for you?

Set the timer for 10 minutes.

To begin, you'll sit across from your practice partner and close your eyes. Take a scan of what it feels like to be you in this moment. Use your breath and awareness to welcome everything you find within you. This is a time to connect with yourself. It's not possible to connect with another if you don't first connect with yourself, knowing what it's like to be you as a separate individual. After a few breaths, slowly open your eyes and look at one another while also keeping your inner eye connected to yourself. This, in and of itself, takes practice.

As you eye gaze, practice meeting halfway between you two, meaning don't allow your attention to go all the way over to your partner. Meet in the middle.

After a few moments of silence looking at one another while keeping some attention within, the first person to speak will say, "Being here with you right now, I notice..." Then they'll say one thing about them. Speaking on behalf of their witness mind, they'll simply say one thing they notice about themselves.

Then the other person will say, "Hearing that, I notice..." and they'll say one thing they notice about themselves.

Example:

Person 1: "Being here right now, I notice I have a wall up and I feel distant."

Person 2: "Hearing that, I notice that I feel open and welcoming of that wall."

Person 1: "Hearing that, I notice that I soften a little bit."

Person 2: "Hearing that, I notice that I feel my seat in my chair and my feet on the floor."

Person 1: "Hearing that, I notice I have some tension around my heart and my mind is wandering to stuff I have to get done."

Person 2: "Hearing that, I notice that a part of me feels lonely, like I'm here by myself."

And so on...

Note: The sentence stem is NOT "Hearing that makes me feel..."

Nobody ever "makes" you feel anything. As a sovereign being, everything that arises within you belongs to you, and the words in this game are powerful in reinforcing this concept.

To practice this exercise, you need to be curious about what's happening in you in relationship with another. In Gestalt psychotherapy this is called the "I-Thou" of the relational field, where I have an experience of you experiencing me.

At first when practicing these skills, you may need to close your eyes to know what's happening within you. That's okay, but be sure you're exploring why this is the case. Be curious about what is challenging about having your eyes open and give voice to this part of you. Then, explore what it's like to do this exercise with your eyes open.

Walkaway with Wisdom

Our truth is always inarguable. It is *always* about us and *never* about anyone else.

To completely honor the truth of our inner experience, we need to wholly and completely let go of any illusion of control we have over the way others might perceive us. The discovery of our truth takes more awareness and more self-curiosity than simply speaking our opinions. Our truth is not our uncensored thoughts and feelings. These are our projections and wounds. When we reveal our truth, our words are about us, we share a deeper aspect of what's happening for us, and we vulnerably speak to the less obvious part of our inner world.

When we don't reveal our inner world to others, it is often the beginning of a path of self-betrayal. However, discernment is part of our sovereignty and it's not our job to be vulnerable all the time.

Revealing our truth is simple. With an eye on the inside, we share the present moment sensations and feelings we're experiencing in a succinct sentence. We talk about the map of our inner world as we stay curious about what's happening within us. Noticing our inner world happens in the present moment. We discover what is happening within us as it's actually happening.

Chapter 18

Conscious Relating

Internally, we set the foundation for our transformation in meditation by bringing more awareness to our sense of self. As we learn to differentiate between what the world has taught us about who we are versus who we actually are, we become highly aware of our conditioned patterns. This awareness is the springboard for discovering a new way of showing up to life, where we are aligned with our hearts, our truth, and our essence.

As we create a secure relationship with our inner young one, we become attuned to our own needs and we attach to *Self as Source*. In doing so, we honor our unique inner matrix while also honoring our interconnection with all of life. As we metabolize unfinished business, we become more updated and current, our outdated strategies are reexamined. All of this give us the space and awareness needed to be intentional about how we are with ourselves and others.

Bringing deeper levels of presence into our whole being, we create more and more space around our conditioned patterns that we no longer are compelled to follow the impulse of outdated habits. In this spaciousness, we are left with a fertile void, where there is silence in our minds and bodies.

Without old trauma beneath the impulses of our thoughts and actions, our bodily sensations soften into quiet stillness. Without contact boundary disturbances impeding our ability to be present with life, our minds open in expanded wonder. Without our life force being distorted by inner polarities, we embody our essential self.

Where before we related to others from the "I-It" of objectification, we learned to relate to others from the "I-Thou" of interconnection. From the fertile void, we are able to relate to the world from the "I-Divine" of our collective true natures.

Our quality of presence is expanded, and expansiveness is the quality of our relationships. Remembering that the universe is not separate from ourselves, every encounter becomes a deep meeting of the Self.

Being in Relationship

There is a difference between *having a relationship* and *being in relationship*. When we *have a relationship*, there is a sense of obligation and ownership. In some cases, there is a propensity of the mind to think of a person as our possession, indicated through the language of wanting to "find our person." When we want to have a relationship, we unconsciously want that relationship to bring us wholeness and fulfillment. This is a drive from the ego and leads to entangled relationships where we can easily fall into patterns of conflict.

Having a relationship does not in any way indicate that we know how to *be in relationship*. Being in relationship requires our attention and presence to be anchored in three places: **We must be aware of ourselves, present with the other, and tend to the point of contact with quality attention.**

Relationship and contact only happen in the present moment. Through words, touch, actions, and silence, our relationship can either thrive in life-affirming connection or suffer under oppressive attempts at control and manipulation. When we are identified with our conditioned self, we are preventing ourselves from being with another person with true presence. When we are in alignment, we create space for our relationships to thrive in an environment that honors the wholeness of all people.

When our conditioned self is the driving force of how we relate to others, we argue, blame, and betray ourselves. We see our partner as "other" and we can easily forget that we want the same thing and that we are on the same team. Couples frequently argue about something (like money, chores, sex, etc.), instead of looking within to see what is activated or being curious about what is happening for the other person. With an updated and current way of being in the world, we no longer work out our unfinished business and unprocessed emotions on our partner.

When we tend to our relationship with mindful presence, we hold the intention that everyone present is a sacred being. On the level of Spirit, we are all on the same team and we all want the same thing. When we are able to notice our own lived experience, we are fully present with ourselves. When we are able to be curious about the other person's lived experience, we are fully present with them. When we are tending to the place we contact each other, we are fully present in the relationship. It is this capacity for presence that makes it possible to *be in relationship*.

Staying in contact with ourselves, we can have agency over how we want to show up for life. We build trust in ourselves over time as we continue to meet the world from a place of being seated in our bodies. Solid, aligned, and securely connected to our young one, we hold ourselves in whatever arises within our inner world. Emotional self-attunement is a powerful practice where we can develop the skills to be the "I" that does not objectify one's self. This, of course, allows us to meet others as a "Thou" and not an "It."

The more capacity we develop to honor others in the full range of their humanity, as a "Thou" who is not an object of our projections or a figure to fill our own void, the more able we are to touch higher frequencies of our own divinity. Rather than looking to others to be our "Source" of love and wholeness, we align with our *Self as Source.* In doing so, we bring qualities of our higher vibrations into this dimension, and we honor the people in our lives as sacred.

To be in relationship, we must slow down. Slowing down and

creating potent moments of silence can be more intimate and connecting then anything we say or do. Relationship happens in the present moment. It is not a past construct being projected onto this moment and it's not a fantasy of what could happen in the future. Each moment we are able to be fully present in our connection with another is a moment we are in relationship.

Sacred Connection

The spiritual dimension of *being in relationship* has practical elements to navigating this dimension. When we tend to our relationship as sacred, we begin to experience the alchemy of our "we-ness," where our essential energy is touched by that of another. Connecting with another from this higher-level vibration creates a quantum connection, where 1+1=infinity.

In our ego relationships, our energy is being depleted by finding all of the different ways to make this relationship "work" so that we can maintain possession over our partner. Conversely, when we are cultivating a sacred connection, our energy is enhanced and up-leveled because we come together. Whereas our ego relationships are depleting, our sacred connections are enlivening. We are able to bring more sacred energy into the world when we are able to touch higher levels of divinity through our connection with other human beings. This is the positive side of our interconnection.

When we are able to maintain our own vibration and engage in sacred connections, we touch higher frequencies in our system. Our high vibrational energy amplifies. From here, all connections become sacred, and our presence on this planet creates a cumulative effect that amplifies the higher frequencies of humanity.

In the next section of the book, we will dive into the embodied energetic practices that contribute to sacred connections. For the purposes of this section, we will focus on the practical communication tools to navigate our interconnection.

The 4 Rs of Conscious Relating is a template to help us tend to our relationships with sacred presence. Maintaining contact with ourselves and curiosity about another in day-to-day life requires tremendous mindfulness. We may slip into paying more attention to the tasks of our lives than tending to the space between us with care.

Looking within takes conscious effort. Accessing the deeper cut of our inner world requires tremendous self-curiosity and self-awareness. Being mindful of how we relate to others is a lifelong journey.

Conscious relating is an unscripted endeavor where we bring quality attention to our lived experience of the relationship. To do this in the midst of an interaction with another person— slowing down, looking within, and being curious—allows us to maintain a healthy, aware state of being. These practices ultimately help us to tend to our sacred connections with mindful awareness.

Relational Practice

Here are four key communication concepts for being in relationship:

Reflect: When your partner says something about the relationship or themselves, pause. Rather than responding with your thoughts, reflect what you hear the other person saying. Reflection is a summary of what you're hearing and how the *other person seems.*

When you reflect, rather than respond, you slow down and bring more awareness into the interaction. You have the opportunity to make sure you've heard the other person accurately, and the other person has the felt experience of being heard.

After you reflect the person's words, you can also reflect what you think you're seeing in their subtle energy body. Once you share how they seem, ask if that fits for the person. If they correct your attunement, reflect what you hear them saying about how they feel.

Receive: Once you've heard what the other person has said, notice how you feel as you receive their words. As you bring more awareness into your inner mind-body process, welcome everything within you. Notice the layers and texture of your experience. Notice if walls or defensiveness emerges. Without reacting, simply be mindful of your inner world.

Without identifying your own experience as "truth," be curious about how you are receiving the words of the other person. Keeping an eye on the inside, seat your attention at the deepest place in you that is impacted by their words.

Reveal: Share what you notice within yourself using ownership language. "I notice that I am..." "I feel..." "I seem...." or "I'm starting to develop a story that..."

When we reveal, we are letting someone know what it's like to be with them. By remembering that everything that arises in you belongs to you, you fully own your experience. From this place of contact with yourself, your words are inarguable.

Relate: After you share impact with your reveal, ask the other person how that was for them to hear. Being curious about how your words land with them keeps the interaction relational and clean, honoring both people who are in the connection.

As you relate, *pay attention* to the quality of your connection with the other person. Notice the alchemy of your interaction and how "we seem" together. On the level of Spirit, we are all on the same team and we all want the same thing. When we tend to our relationship with mindful presence, we hold the intention that everyone present is a sacred being.

Harmony's Story

Throughout my entire life, I longed to feel loved. I longed to feel like I was worthy to be loved. I had a romanticized delusion that my worth and enoughness was only possible if a healthy, conscious man wanted me. From my wound of not-enoughness, I searched outside of myself for evidence of my worth and lovability.

Because I was identified with my wounds, I attracted and was attracted to partners who reflected my wounds. Longing for love from another, I held the unconscious delusion that I would only be whole if I got what I wanted, that my wholeness was dependent on getting the love of a conscious, healthy man. This misbelief perpetuated my looking for love outside of myself, which kept me identified with my wounding. When my relationships were painful and conflictual, this misbelief had me wanting my partners to be different so I could be whole. With these patterns, I set myself up to always feel broken.

Recognizing that real love is neither painful nor earnable, I started orienting towards a different way of being. I began to bring love and attention to the part of me that searched for love from others, "I see that you want to feel loved," I would say to myself, "I will always love you." I would wrap this subpersonality in light and love, and I would breathe in a way that was self-loving and self-compassionate.

With a high level of awareness and real-time practices of being self-loving, I was in conscious relationship with myself. And although it might seem obvious, at the time it was revolutionary to me that a conscious relationship with myself was necessary if I were to have a conscious relationship with another.

When my inner younger one is activated, she believes that she will die if she doesn't get the attention and love that she longs for. This is because my wound is tied up with a near-death experience. Being able to give myself what I want, I tend to myself with love and care. Meeting myself in this deep, loving way is what makes it possible to meet others in a deep and loving way.

I can hold space for my husband, children, friends, and clients even if I have something going on inside of myself.

Knowing that there is no urgency, that I will have my turn, that I will not drop my experience for ever, I can set my own self aside for some time and stay curious about what's happening for the other person.

As I listen, I keep an eye on the inside so I don't drop myself completely. I listen and then I reflect in an effort to slow down the conversation and stay in contact with myself and the other person. I allow myself to feel impacted by their words, and then I let them know what it's like for me to be with them, always revealing my truth in the most vulnerable way possible. Then I check back in with them to see how that was to hear.

This is more challenging when I feel under resourced, in which case I ask for time and space to regulate. Knowing that what is happening within myself is important and deserves attention, creating space for myself is an act of self-love. Since the world is not separate from myself, when I love and care for myself, I love and care for the whole universe. Remembering that consciousness is elevated awareness, I use my conscious relationship with myself to relate consciously with others.

Staying curious about what is happening for another person *while staying in contact with what is happening for myself* brings more awareness to the often murky place in relationship, where we are *both* sovereign *and* interconnected.

Because my capacity holding space for other people is so large, part of my growing edge is asking for this level of attention in return. When I share what's happening for me, my husband will often start responding and reacting. When this happens, I pause him and I ask him to tell me what he heard me say. If he didn't fully hear me, I repeat myself and ask him to reflect again. Once he's gotten that, I let him know what I feel, "I feel my whole body soften as I hear you reflect what's happening for me. Now I'd like to know what's happening for you."

We each have our own subjective reality, and there is room for both without conflict when we are conscious of ourselves and the other. My reality doesn't dictate his reality, nor does his reality dictate mine. I don't betray myself for him, nor does our relationship have room for his self-betrayal. He is my beloved, a sacred being with whom I get to walk this journey of life with. I want him to feel heard and loved, just as he wants me to feel heard and loved. When we are aligned with Self as Source, there is ample love and space for both of us. Our sacred union amplifies the field around us in quantum ways, where we can positively impact the world even more because we are in conscious relationship with ourselves and one another.

Exercise: Practicing Relational Conflict Resolution

When we feel hurt or angry after an interaction with a loved one, sharing our deeper truth can be messy. If you are holding on to resentment, judgment, or fear, this will get in the way of your connection with your partner. Similarly, if we share what's happening for us in a way that has our partner feeling blamed, we will surely be met with defensiveness.

Learning to communicate effectively about how you are feeling is an offering of clean connection. In the aftermath of a conflict, coming back to clean communication offers us the space to express our truth. The most important aspect of this is that we hold the intention of strengthening our connection, instead of avoiding or projecting that we want to feel closer because we chose to have a difficult conversation.

As we learn this relational way of cleaning up conflict, we may want to process our feelings alone with this framework before coming to our partner. This can help garner clarity before bringing it to the person we are wanting to communicate with.

Note: The person bringing the communication will be called the "Giver" and the person receiving the communication will be called the "Receiver."

Step 1: Giver, state your intention and see if the other person is open to having a conversation:

"I have something I'd like to talk with you about, and I'm bringing it to you because I want to feel closer to you. Are you available for that right now?"

*This step is important for a few reasons.

If you are communicating to get your partner to be different, to express blame, or to vent, you are not ready to communicate your deeper truth. When you are clear that the reason you want to talk is to feel closer, this is the point at which you are ready for a mature dialogue that will serve your relationship. Letting the receiver of the communication know that this is why you want to talk will support both of you in being more open for connection.

Asking the receiver if they are available for the communication is important because if it is not a good time for both of you, it is not a good time. Having the person consent is essential for a mutually respectful conversation.

Step 2: Get a shared understanding of the moment you are discussing:

Get clear on the objective moment that you want to talk about, and then ask the person you are communicating with if they remember that moment. Objective means just the facts that cannot be argued with. Without interpretation, what objectively happened between you that has you wanting to talk right now?

It is important that both of you clearly remember the moment and agree that it happened before you move on.

Example: "Do you remember when you said that I am 'just like all of your exes'?"

Notice that there is no judgment, interpretation, blame, or story about what happened.

Get confirmation: The other person might want to clarify, "That's not what I remember saying. I said, 'That one time when you got upset that I didn't cook for you, you reminded me of my exes' — but that you do so much for me — it's very different."

Spend time getting shared reality making sure that you have

a clear starting point of the moment you are about to talk about. Sometimes this step alone can untangle some conflicts and miscommunication.

Once you both have agreement on what happened and what was said, then (and only then) are you ready to move on to the next step.

In this scenario, the couple agreed that the person said, *When you expect me to cook for you, you remind me of my exes, but you do so much for me that it's very different.*

Step 3: Giver, state your feelings and explain while owning your emotions and stories:

"When you said that, **I felt hurt and frustrated**... it seemed to me like you were lumping me into the same category as your exes and **I started creating a story** that you think I'm using you the way they did. I'm realizing now that I was so triggered by the first part of what you said that I missed what you said about our relationship being different."

It is important that the feeling you choose is actually a feeling and not your story about the other person. There are **five basic human emotions: fear, anger, sadness/grief, love, and joy**. Hurt (used in this example) is a degree of sadness, and frustration is a degree of anger.

It is also important to notice that in this communication the person shares their story and they are fully owning that this is their story. Projecting one's story would sound like "You lumped me in with your exes and you think I use you" or "You think I'm lazy and you never appreciate me." In the ownership of your story, you respect the dignity of the receiver of the information and you also own what's happening for you.

Step 4: Receiver, reflect what you heard and let the giver know how you feel as you listen:

Now it's time for the receiver of the communication to reflect what they heard and share what that was like to hear.

Receiver: "I hear that you felt hurt and frustrated when I said you remind me of my exes when you expect me to cook for you, and that it seemed like I was lumping you in the same category as them, and then you started creating a story that I think you use me... and that you were so upset with the first part of my statement you had missed how I said that you do so much for me that it's different. Did I get that?"

Giver of the communication confirms and has the opportunity to clarify or expand. Example: "When I hear you reflect that all back to me, I can see that a younger part of me that felt unappreciated by my dad was activated." The receiver would then reflect again.

Receiver: "Hearing that, I feel a lot of regret and empathy. I wish I would have worded that differently because I want you to feel appreciated by me and I feel a lot of compassion for your young one."

Step 5: Receiver, find at least one part of the person's story that you can **validate**.

"It makes sense to me that you would feel hurt thinking that I didn't appreciate all you do for me... and it also makes sense to me that you feel frustrated thinking that I lumped you into the same category as my exes."

Step 6: Both of you state one thing that you wish you would have done differently, and one thing you wish the other person would have done differently.

Receiver goes first. "I wish that I would not have compared you to my exes at all... and I wish that you would have told me at the time you felt hurt because I would have wanted to amend this right away."

Giver goes second: "I wish I would have slowed down and asked you to clarify... and I really wish that you would have brought up our agreements around chores in a way that was about us and not your exes, because I want to hear the impact I have on you."

Step 7: Giver: State the solution (if needed).

The person who brought this topic up can ask for what they want moving forward, which is always done as an invitation.

"Would you offer some words of appreciation with me now?" or "Can we have a conversation about our division of domestic duties?" or something else.

The receiver gets to decide if this is something they are available for.

Walkaway with Wisdom

As we unlearn what the world has taught us about ourselves, we are able to bring deeper levels of presence into our whole being. We empty ourselves of our conditioned patterns, and we are left with a fertile void where there is silence in our minds and bodies.

Relationship and contact only happen in the present moment. When we are able to notice our own lived experience, we are fully present with ourselves. When we are able to be curious about the other person's lived experience, we are fully present with them. When we are tending to the place we contact each other, we are fully present in the relationship. It is this capacity for presence that makes it possible to *be in relationship*.

To be in relationship, we must slow down. Relationship happens in the present moment. It's not a past construct being projected onto this moment and it's not a fantasy of what could happen in the future. Each moment we are able to be fully present in our connection with another is a moment we are in relationship.

When we are able to maintain our own vibration and engage in sacred connections, we touch higher frequencies in our system. Our high vibrational energy amplifies. From here, all connections become sacred, and our presence on this planet creates a cumulative effect that amplifies the higher frequencies of humanity.

There are four key communication concepts for *being in relationship*:

Reflect: Rather than responding with your thoughts, reflect what you hear the other person saying.

Receive: Once you've heard what the other person has said, notice how you feel as you receive their words.

Reveal: Share what you notice within yourself using ownership language. "I notice that I am..." "I feel..." "I seem...." or "I'm starting to develop a story that..."

Relate: After you reveal, ask the other person how that was for them to hear. As you relate, pay attention to the quality of your connection with the other person. Notice the alchemy of your interaction and how "we seem" together. On the level of Spirit, we are all on the same team and we all want the same thing. When we tend to our relationship with mindful presence, we hold the intention that everyone present is a sacred being.

Part 5:

The Undefended Heart

Chapter 19

Doorway to the Heart

Our hearts hold the most tender and expansive qualities of divine love. When the heart is occupied by unprocessed pain, the purity of our heart is covered with protective mechanisms that are intended to keep us safe. This can all be happening below the level of awareness and become more obvious when we're feeling under-resourced or emotionally activated by hurt, loss, fear, or anger. The more closed off we are from our hearts, the more our mind is active with narratives and meaning making that are an attempt at control and self-protection. Our self-protection can be expressed through blame, resentment, and looping in stories of our version of reality. As we close off from our hearts, the mind collects evidence to justify our self-protection.

The habitual ways we stay closed-hearted eventually harden the subtle energy body of our heart center. The wall that was built to protect us becomes a barrier that keeps us hardened to connection. And with plenty of justification as to why another should not be allowed back in, we cling to our patterns and keep ourselves cut off from the most vital access point of Source moving through our alignment.

The qualities of an undefended heart are the qualities of a child. Without self-protection, a newborn baby is open to giving and receiving pure love. Their subtle energy body is soft and open, and there are no defenses, blame, or stories to pull them away from their Source of love. Having just come from Source, the purity of the heart is untainted and undistorted. In order to survive the environment around them, the child eventually learns through observation and experience to contain the most essential part of their inner world. At the time, the child didn't have the capacity to survive on their own, so closing off their heart and protecting their innermost sanctuary within the deepest part of the heart was wise. However, they simultaneously began to close off from their Source of love, healing, and trust.

The Protected Heart

When we were born, our vital force flowed through us with ease. Without learned patterns or an ego, all of our energy centers were open and our subtle energy body was fluid. We were born as the pure expression of vitality, fully self-regulated. Because we didn't yet see ourselves as separate from our environment, our minds were infinitely creative and curious.

Children feel a sense of belonging and safety when they are seen and welcomed for the full range of who they are. When children are only seen for a miniscule part of who they are, they adapt by rejecting parts of themselves in an effort to find safety and belonging. In childhood when we felt rejected, violated, ignored, disempowered, or scared, we created strategies to survive our experience. Part of this adaptation included covering up and closing the most tender, vulnerable part of our inner world: our hearts. In an effort to feel safe, we rejected our own innate wisdom, self-love, and self-acceptance, which are the inherent qualities of Source expressed through our hearts.

A closed heart might evoke the idea of a wall or barrier to connection or vulnerability. While this might be one expression of a closed heart, trying to get other people to love us is also a sign of a closed heart. Blame, anger, desperation, obsession, and self-hate are also indicators that our hearts are closed.

The generous abundance of Source cannot fully flow through us when our hearts remain closed. When we are closed-hearted, the ego has more power. The mind thinks that we need to control to find safety and defend our reality as "the" reality. With a closed heart, love becomes a commodity. Instead of having a beautiful, intimate exchange of pure love, we engage in a "tit-for-tat" love that is more like a game. Although we originally closed our hearts to find safety, when we engage with life from this place, we feel less safe.

From this closed off place, we close off from our True Self. We close off from the qualities that live within our pure, undefended heart. Vitality, compassion, generosity, collaboration, exploration, and creativity are divine qualities that come from the Source that beats our heart. To fully embody our True Self, we must trust ourselves enough to open our vulnerable tender heart even when it seems unsafe to do so.

With defenses in place, intimate relationships can be full of pain and conflict. With our defenses down, our relationships can be a life-affirming place of pleasure, support, affection, and honoring the sacred connection.

With clear boundaries, we can be both soft and strong simultaneously. Our systems feel safe to open when we trust ourselves to honor our truth, our power, and our boundaries. Without needing other people to be a certain way in order for ourselves to be openhearted, we can stand our sacred ground. We can honor the full range of our experience while we stay in contact with our tender hearts.

Exploration: Before we can soften into our undefended heart, we need first acknowledge and feel the walls around our heart. By closing our eyes and placing a hand over our heart, we can begin to bring awareness to our own self-protection. Touching our barriers around our heart, we bring the quality of compassion and love to the wall.

Without trying to make the wall go away, notice it's there. Acknowledge that it was formed at a time when we needed a way to protect ourselves. We thank the wall and breathe around it with complete and total gratitude.

Then, we notice what the wall is protecting. Bringing our awareness to the center of our hearts, we bring the quality of our presence directly to the most tender and vulnerable place within ourselves. Noticing the felt sense of our hearts, we bring more presence and curiosity into our Source of love. With our attention seated in our heart's energy center, we can direct our breath to wrap our heart with compassion and love. At first, we might feel nothing. If this is the case, we can notice how "nothing" feels. As we keep our attention in our hearts, we tap into the stored pain, resentment, and grief that is blocking our access to our experience of pure love, joy, and connection.

Staying in contact with our heart as we move stored emotions, we are walking through the doorway to our pure, wise heart. Touching the soft spot beneath the hardness, we touch the power of spontaneous enlightenment, where we are motivated by great compassion for all beings. As we do this, our attachment to the illusions of the conditioned self and separateness falls away. We can touch the most sacred and loving qualities of our True Self when we contact our softness. We can nurture gratitude, forgiveness, generosity, compassion, and appreciation, bringing the qualities of open-heartedness with us as we interact with the world.

The Cloaked Heart

When we realized that our caregivers were not capable of holding the vibration of their essential self, we decided that we weren't safe being openhearted. As we unconsciously closed off from our hearts, we established somatic and subtle energy patterns around and within our heart chakra to keep ourselves protected. When something was happening in the field around us that had us feel unsafe, we cloaked our heart's essence.

Physically, our shoulders moved forward. The muscles around our chest tightened, and our breath stopped moving in its full capacity. We placed an energetic veil over our hearts to protect the pure love that resides within. As we do this, the heart's pure love becomes cloaked and our ability to be in connection with others becomes inhibited. Whereas closed heartedness is a wall to keep people out, a cloaked heart is an energetic movement of hiding, hiding the truth of our full expression.

As children, when the world around us was a stressful and unsafe place to be, retreating behind a cloak was a masterful way to stay in the environment while mitigating potential harm. Because the adults around us were closed off from their hearts, it was healthy for us to create a place within our own inner world to retreat. Retreating into the sanctuary of our hearts, we constructed a little closet or hiding place internally. Over time, keeping our Self cloaked and hidden became a habit.

When these patterns became fixed parts of our personality, they stopped being healthy and instead impeded our ability to stay in contact during intimacy. The cloak is an unconscious tool of self-regulation. When we feel unsafe in relationships, the dysregulation of feeling unsafe is mitigated by retreating to our hearts and showing people what we think they want to see. We cover up our truth, our wisdom, and our True Self when we are uncertain if we'll be accepted for who we really are.

All people want to feel safe to be in relationship. But when we think that our safety comes from others, we cloak our vulnerable hearts and track other people's behavior as our cue for when we can come out of hiding.

Because these patterns were developed in childhood, it makes sense that we would think other people need to be a certain way for us to show our vulnerability to them. This is often where the delusion of "too muchness" is seated, where we collect evidence that other people can't handle our big love, expressive emotions, or desire to connect. "I need to contain my emotions to keep people close" is a younger strategy that was an adaptive way to survive a childhood where our caregivers were emotionally immature, violent, or absent. As an adult, however, when we have an experience of being too much for other people, we are in all likelihood working out our attachment wounds on others. We have left contact with ourselves and want the other person to make space for all of us when we, ourselves, haven't yet learned how to do that.

As we process unresolved experiences, it becomes more obvious when we are projecting onto other people and how our projections reinforce our cloaked heart. Working with our inner young one, we can tell ourselves, "I can make room for all of our emotions, needs, and desires." Holding ourselves in our full experience, we contact our *Self as Source*, which makes it possible for other people to experience contact with us.

With our cloaked hearts covering our essence, our conditioned patterns have more influence over how we interact with the world. In adulthood, our habitual barriers around our heart keeps us from experiencing deep intimacy. To stay openhearted when something is happening in our relationships that we don't like is counterintuitive. The intuitive response is to follow our cellular memory of closing off to stay protected. However, when we close off from our hearts we close off from our *Self as Source* and we become reactive. And when we are reactive, we end up entangled in conflict and ultimately less safe and less protected.

Even when the environment around us seems safe, our Self may still be hidden in our heart if we are following the impulses of our conditioned self. For example, if my heart is cloaked and I am aware of loving my partner, my love is not pure. If I say "I love you" with protective barriers over my heart, my words hold a vibration of wounding, pain, and neediness. Blocked off from my own Source of love, the words "I love you" are not aligned with the pure love that I Am.

Similarly, with a cloaked heart we can perform acts of love for our partner, but the behavior is not coming from a place of pure love. The low vibration imbued in the action will likely engender a tit-for-tat ego tracking.

The pure quality of unconditional generosity is what lives

within the undefended heart.

To remove the cloak, to set down the shield, and to open the doorway to our own hearts repairs and retunes our energy body at the deepest level. We invite Source to move through us in our interactions with others, without needing anyone else to be anything for us. Our sovereign Self has the capacity to uncloak our hearts and honor ourselves as we expose our True Self.

This is how we are designed to be, with an undefended heart.

Before we learned to contort and hide in order to fit into the world around us, we were designed to be entirely openhearted. Seated in our undefended hearts, we embody the pure love of our essence.

It may seem as though the cloak is what keeps us safe, but it is in our full alignment where safety is created. To stay aligned when the world around us seems unsafe is to hold the vibration of our Self. Without matching the vibration of the world around us, we stay seated in ourselves in such a way that we cannot be pulled off center by someone else's distortion.

As we continue to practice deepening into our somatic experience, it becomes easier to notice when our hearts are cloaked. For example, maybe we are feeling relaxed and soft in our bodies and then our partner walks in the room and our body tightens around our shoulders and chest. This is an indication of a somatic memory of self-protection. Even though the threat is not currently present, the pattern continues to disrupt our ability to stay in contact with ourselves and others simultaneously.

When we become aware of this pattern, we can consciously choose to soften into our bodies and regulate through our tension patterns. We can stay seated in our hearts and use our breath to bring more awareness and compassion to the barriers that we have built against love. The heart needs five things to feel safe to open: 1) To have the sense that we are in contact with ourselves, 2) To have a deep trust in ourselves to speak our truth, 3) To have trust in ourselves to ask for what we want, 4) To fully trust ourselves to honor our boundaries, and 5) To trust our ability to see the other person clearly and fully. When we trust in ourselves in this way, our heart opens as we no longer think we need to control the other person.

Where there is openheartedness, there is healing. Where there is pure love, there is wholeness.

True intimacy happens when we let go of any attempt at control. We trust ourselves enough to open to another, and we release the cloak that has been covering our heart. We show our sacred self to the other, and we see the other as sacred. From here, we joyfully explore our sacred connection.

Openheartedness Sows Openheartedness

When we rest in our hearts, the flow of our vital force through the channel of the core of our being is uninhibited. Divine love from within creates more growth and change than any thought or effort we exert. Coming back to the self-regulated, openhearted state of wholeness that is our birthright, we find our way home to ourselves. Healing happens spontaneously in the presence of divine love.

As we open the doorway to our hearts, we move closer to the essence of our own divinity. As we keep this door open and fully occupy our hearts when we contact the environment, we nurture sacred connections and a sacred life. To experience our own Self in the context of intimate relating without any disruptions to contact inhibiting our presence, we resonate at a vibration that invites those same qualities in other beings into our field.

The world around us is a holographic expression of our inner world. As we use the context of any and every relationship to see ourselves more clearly, we find our way back to our Self. Once we are seated in our alignment, our relationships reflect that congruence.

The more self-regulated and openhearted we remain, the more the people around us feel regulated and openhearted. The sacred experience we have of being embodied is reflected by the people around us also experiencing their sacred Self in our presence. Finding resonance with our alignment, rather than reacting against our polarity distortion, our relationships become the sacred container where we fully show ourselves to another. With our heart wide open, we can reveal our authentic Self to the world, knowing that whoever resonates with our essence we will be attracted to, as they will be to us. And for those people who don't resonate with our authentic expression, we can love them on their way out.

All of our conditioned patterns are defenses to protect our heart. Once our heart becomes undefended, we might notice that our conditioned patterns bubble to the surface to try to protect us. Welcoming our protectors with love, we can be with our barriers to an open heart with tenderness and compassion.

Harmony's Story

Feeling unsafe in relationship caused me to hide my pain and truth throughout my life—this also caused me to cloak my heart. Unsure if I was safe to be openhearted, my True Self would hide behind the cloak covering my heart, while my personality presented the illusion of love and care. Listening with curiosity, offering help, being accommodating, and nourishing others with healthy food had the appearance of being loving and caring. However, because my heart was cloaked, I was moving from my conditioned patterns and trauma response to try to earn love.

My conditioned self is a set of patterns and misbelief that are my own barriers to the love that I am. I am pure love.

When I engage with my husband from my conditioned patterns, my mind thinks he needs to be a certain way so that I feel safe enough to open to him. *If he were really present and open hearted*, my young one thinks, *then I can open my heart to him*. If I follow this well-worn path of staying closed and cloaked, I am inviting conflict and separation into our relationship.

Knowing that my safety comes from within myself, I can look within to see what I need from myself to feel safe. Bringing presence into my heart, I look at my walls surrounding my heart. With my inner eye, I bring more awareness and appreciation to my walls. I thank them for protecting me. I breathe love around them as I stay curious about what I need to feel safe. Once I find my words, it is typically something very simple that I need.

"I want to open to you," I say to my husband, "and I think I need to hear something from you first. If it's true for you, tell me that you want to see me. Tell me that you want to be here with me and that you love me."

This is my vulnerable request in service of our connection. I'm essentially asking him to remind me that he is not my dad—which is where I learned to hide my pain from the masculine. My young one would have felt safe to stay in my heart with the masculine had my father been present with me and saw me for my whole self. Instead, I cloaked my heart—and decided that I wasn't enough to be loved—to prevent myself from feeling the pain of having a disengaged father.

While it's true that we need to attach to *Self as Source* instead of looking to others as our source of love and enoughness, it is also true that healing happens in relationship. My wounds were created in relationship, and my deepest transformation occurs in relationship when I choose to do the different, truer thing. When I can connect with myself in a conscious and loving way, asking my husband to be a loving presence for me is one way I bring my healing into relationship.

"I'm right here and I love you. I want to see you, Harmony. I want to see all of you."

Hearing his words, my heart melts as I cry, "Will you say it again, please?"

When this happens, he repeats these words as he looks me in the eyes until the cloak has vanished and my heart is open. My openness happens not because of what he said, but because I trust myself enough to honor my walls and ask for what I need. My whole system softens when I speak my truth and honor my full Self in relationships with others.

The co-regulation he offers me when I make a vulnerable request is a deep repair in my system. Whether or not he has something happening in him that ignites my walls is irrelevant to my own work—this is his to look at and be with lovingly. My work is to look within myself and act in ways that are a reflection of my self-responsibility. My making the request nurtures our intimacy, just as his availability to be present with me in this way does, too. My openheartedness sows openheartedness.

Exercise: Your Resonant Heart

If, as the Sufi poet Rumi states, our "task is not to seek for love, but merely to seek and find all the barriers within [ourselves] that [we] have built against it," the journey inward to find the authentic resonance of our heart is the path to love. Because when we resonate at the frequency of the undefended heart, the matrix of the world around us reflects that back in enigmatic and resounding ways.

To find the resonance of your own heart, close your eyes and turn your attention inward. Take a few loving breaths, sighing with the exhale as you soften your jaw. Breathing in with self-care, exhaling with sweet surrender.

As you continue to breathe in this way, begin emptying the mind and bringing more presence into your head. Inhaling with self-love, exhaling with sweet surrender.

After a few moments, bring that presence down into your throat. Emptying your throat and bringing more awareness into your neck. Stay with the breath pattern, softening your jaw with every exhale.

Now bring your attention to your heart, the seat of your soul. Direct all of your presence and breath into the center of your heart and notice any sensations or emotions in your heart. Without trying to change the sensation or figure it out, simply notice what it feels like in the center of your heart. Notice if there is a barrier of protection over your heart. If so, take your hands and place them where the barrier is. Hold your hands here, bringing your attention to the protection over your heart. Take a few loving breaths to the barrier, validating and honoring it.

Then become aware of what is being protected. Bringing your attention deeper into your heart, notice the most vulnerable part of you. Keeping all of your presence on your tender vulnerability, keep breathing in self-love and exhaling sweet surrender, softening your jaw.

Hold your vulnerability with care and love, and now begin to breathe in the breath of forgiveness into each chamber of your heart. Allow any and all stored pain, frozen trauma, resentment, grief, shame, and anger to be touched by the breath of forgiveness. This isn't about being okay with what others have done, this is about clearing out the pain that is being held in the heart so that you may resonate at your true vibration.

Continue to breathe and notice the sensation in your heart. Find the resonant words or tone that express the truth of your heart. Maybe the word is honor or love or truth. Maybe the tone is a sign or a song or a noise. Repeat the words or tone 3 to 4 times, amplifying the resonance of your heart.

Finally, make a commitment to your heart. Find the words of this commitment that are true to you. "I will always honor you" or "I will continue to come back to you and listen to your truth" or "I will stay seated here, in you" or "I will practice bringing in the vibration of Source through you in all that I say and do." Then write down your commitment and keep it somewhere you will see it.

Exercise: Finding Resonance with a Partner

Because polarities create so much intensity in a relationship, learning how to find resonance with our partner is a very gentle skill of coregulation. You can do this practice with anyone—your partner, your children, your clients, your friends, etc. Its purpose is to create a vibrational quality in the relational field that both people resonate with. When the tendency is to ignore our inner world and have conversations, we unconsciously match other people's limbic vibration.

Choose one person to begin. Both of you close your eyes, and the first person will share three sensations you feel in your body in the most detailed way possible. Speaking slowly and deliberately, describe the quality of the sensations, the size, the depth, the color. If it changes as you focus on it, describe that, too. And if this sensation needs something from you, describe how you are going to care for this sensation and then do that before moving on to the next sensation.

The idea is that you are contacting, resourcing, and grounding in the presence of another. As you do this, the other person is tracking their inner world, noticing how they are affected by hearing about yours.

For example, "I'm aware of a sensation in my chest. It's fluttering, like a butterfly. Its pace is quick and it seems a bit scattered and untethered, but tickly at the same time. I'm going to take a few breaths, making more room for it, and I notice I want to shake my arms and wave them around, so I'm going to do that, too... there... it's starting to settle more... now I'm aware of my legs. They feel solid and strong. They're warm. I'm going to take a few breaths into my legs as I move my feet around to feel the earth... now I'm aware of my feet. They're cold. I notice an impulse to reach down and touch them, so I'm going to do that now. (Rubs feet. Takes a few more breaths.) There, I feel complete."

And then the next person goes. Each person will get three

turns, and as you find resonance, keep noticing how you're influenced by what the other person says.

This is a good exercise to do on walks, during snuggles, or after a conflict.

Walkaway with Wisdom

Children feel a sense of belonging and safety when they are seen and welcomed for the full range of who they are. When children are only seen for a miniscule part of who they are, they adapt by rejecting parts of themselves in an effort to find safety and belonging.

With defenses in place, intimate relationships can be full of pain and conflict. With our defenses down, our relationships can be a life-affirming place of pleasure, support, affection, and honoring the sacred connection.

Our hearts hold the energetic qualities of our unhealed old grief. When the heart is occupied by unprocessed pain, the purity of our heart is covered with protective mechanisms that are intended to keep us safe. The habitual ways we stay closed-hearted eventually harden the subtle energy body of our heart center.

All people want to feel safe to be in relationship. But when we think that our safety comes from others, we cloak our vulnerable hearts and track other people's behavior as our cue for when we can come out of hiding.

Touching the soft spot beneath the hardness, we touch the power of spontaneous enlightenment, where we are motivated by great compassion for all beings. As we do this, our attachment to the illusions of the conditioned self and separateness falls away.

The more self-regulated and openhearted we remain, the more the people around us feel regulated and openhearted. The sacred experience we have of being embodied is reflected by the people around us also experiencing their sacred Self in our presence.

With our heart wide open, we can reveal our authentic Self to the world, knowing that whoever resonates with our essence we will be attracted to, as they will be to us. And for those people who don't resonate with our authentic expression, we can love them on their way out.

Chapter 20

Sacred Embodiment

If anything is sacred, the human body is sacred. Instead of being treated as a revered organism that beholds wisdom beyond the limitations of the mind, our bodies bear much of the burden of lived experiences.

Our bodies hold trauma inflicted by others.

Our bodies hold trauma inflicted by ourselves.

Our bodies hold our distorted life force energy.

Our bodies are the object that our conditioned self projects upon.

Our bodies are the object that other people project upon.

Our bodies are blamed for the way our choices impact them — including overeating, lack of exercise, and acquired diseases and infections resulting from our own behavior.

Our bodies are blamed for not having more energy.

Our bodies speak to us in pain.

We tend to ignore the body's pain and become upset with our body for hurting.

We detach from our bodies.

Our bodies hold other people's energy.

Our bodies hold the somatic memory of all of our experiences.

Even with all of the burdens our bodies carry, the unwavering presence of our somatic intelligence, our ability to heal, and our ability to become more embodied is astounding.

Relating to Our Body

As with all aspects of our conditioned self, the way we relate to our bodies is learned. Regardless of our level of athleticism, weight, or perceived attractiveness, when we are taught to ignore our somatic sensations and emotions, we are taught to disconnect from our bodies.

When we learn to disconnect from our bodies, we walk around in a disembodied state. This may seem impossible because we do, in fact, have a body. However, our relationship to our body is one of disconnect, dissociation, and objectification. When we are disconnected from our body, we feel detached, like our soul is not seated in our body, and we avoid looking within our bodies to check in with how we feel. When we dissociate from our bodies, we are in a trauma response where we feel separate from our body, our thoughts, and our emotions, like we're not present and aware of ourselves or our surroundings. When we objectify our bodies, we degrade ourselves down to being an object and we actively ignore our body's sensations, like our body is something to control and depersonalize.

As we were developing our conditioned self, we likely experienced or witnessed body judgment, body shaming, or dissociative behaviors (like alcoholism, overeating, and physical violence).

Body shame is an introjection, an acquired belief about the human body left unexamined. Body judgment is a retroflection, turning in on ourselves. Objectifying others is a projection, putting our judgment onto the people around us. Dissociation is an adaptive response to trauma, where our inability to regulate causes our soul to leave contact with our body.

Some of the thoughts we might have that express these learned ways to relate to the body are as follows:

"I don't belong here in this life."

"I'm not safe in this body."

"This body doesn't belong to me."

"There is something wrong with me because of this body."

"I don't deserve pleasure or love because of this body."

"I need a distraction because there is too much discomfort in my body."

The way other people treated our bodies does not need to

be the status quo for how we relate to our bodies. The people around us may have reduced our bodies down to an object, seeing our bodies' appearance as proof of our worth and our bodies' wisdom as inconsequential. Other people's ideas about us do not need to be our ideas about us.

Looking in the mirror and judging the body as *good* or *bad* is to treat ourselves as an "It" rather than a "Thou." Even when the judgment is "positive" it is still an objectification and conditional praise. Viewing other people's bodies as an object to judge is a reflection of the way we think about our own bodies.

Although we have a long history of media and industries built upon the notion that our worth comes from our physical appearance, this is not the purpose of the body. Power structures in society fuel the dehumanization of Black and Brown bodies, non-binary bodies, and female bodies. White male bodies have also been objectified by the very systems that keep them in power. The harm that has been inflicted on Black, Indigenous, people of color, non-binary folks, and women live within ancestral patterns, introjections, somatic memory, and are perpetuated by systems in place. To continue to objectify our own bodies is to continue to give these harmful systems influence over our internal world. Radical self-love and acceptance is a revolutionary act of taking our power back and deconstructing systems built on our self-hate.

When we relate to our bodies from our conditioning, our distorted thoughts and behavior impacts our physical bodies. Instead of listening to our bodies, we shame our bodies. We apologize for our bodies. We give our bodies to other people to do with as they please. We push our bodies to perform better, to look different, or to stop feeling a certain way. We suppress our bodies' messages rather than listen with compassion.

When we try to change our bodies, we ignore the very message that our body is trying to communicate. Relating to our bodies as a living entity, rather than an object, we can begin to treat our bodies with the attention and care that we crave. Similar to the practice of creating a secure connection with our inner young one, we can create a secure relationship with our bodies, where we listen to our body and trust its inherent wisdom.

No matter how misused, violated, or ignored, our bodies hold the capacity to come into the full expression of our health. We each have varying degrees of disembodied ways of relating to being in a body. The journey to sacred embodiment is the journey back home. Once our soul is fully seated in our body, we feel the three dimensionality of our physical presence. We land in ourselves, and this allows us to move through this dimension fully aligned.

Disembodiment makes it possible for our distortion to persist. Embodiment makes it possible for our essence to be fully here in this world, aligned with Source.

Our alignment exists within our physical body, and our physical body is not separate from our alignment. Relating to our bodies as a sacred vessel, as the body for divine presence, we can be in discovery about what thoughts and behaviors align with our truest truth about our bodies. We can reclaim our bodies when we reclaim our alignment. We can allow other people to hold their values and beliefs about bodies, and we can be in discovery about what is true for us.

Beyond Objectification

We cannot both objectify ourselves and raise our consciousness simultaneously, that would be a distortion. However, this tendency to objectify is not something to reject or disown. If we shame ourselves for objectifying our bodies, we reinforce our distortion. In claiming our own tendency to treat ourselves as an object, we paradoxically have more choice in how we want to be with our bodies.

Bringing more awareness to the tendency to shame, judge, or disconnect in our relationship with our body, we can be in choice about how we want to live beyond objectification.

When we learn to treat our bodies like an object, our conditioned self violates the temple that we are here to occupy. Body judgment and shame disregards the divine being who is housed in that body. Disconnecting from our bodies causes a spilt between our soul and our presence in the third dimension.

Our body is the place for our soul to be present in this world. It's our home, our vessel. It's the expression of boundless life itself through us. We must be in our bodies if we are to create our life consciously. If we are to be fully in our purpose, we must be fully in our body.

This flesh, this shape, this body is sacred.

Every bit of the physical body is a reflection of our presence here on this planet. And when we treat our bodies as sacred, we become part of the collective body for more high vibrational energy here on the planet. To experience our divine essence embodied, we can be both an aligned and flawed human, simultaneously.

Being embodied is *not* about being in shape, looking amazing, and being physically active, although this might be a result of becoming more embodied. Living beyond objectification is to attune to our own subtle energy body. Slowing down and bringing more awareness and presence into our physical vessel, we can tend to the nuances of the way our somatic intelligence communicates to us. In the field of counseling, we call this a bottom-up approach to processing. By taking sensory information from our bodies and honoring that, even if our minds haven't collected all of the information, we are contacting our bodies beyond objectification.

Learning to relate to our bodies as sacred, we nourish our bodies with attention and intention.

We breathe in a way that feels like self-care.

We touch our bodies in a way that feels like self-love.

We think about our bodies in a way that feels like unconditional acceptance.

We feed our bodies in a way that feels like every meal is a sacred offering to our temple.

We move in a way that feels like a joyous expression of our vitality.

Loving awareness, compassion, and kindness is the very thing our body deserves. Honoring our body with the sacred presence of attention, we can learn in each moment how to live beyond objectification.

Too Much

One of the reasons we tend to disconnect from our bodies through cognitive bypassing, over-exercising, over-eating, over-drinking, and so on is because our conditioned self holds a belief that our experience is "too much." Because our caregivers were unable to stay present and attuned during our emotional expressions, we acquired an introjection that holds the misbelief that we are too much. Being overwhelmed by an experience that felt like "too much" turned into "I am too much."

If we're afraid that we're "too much," we try to contain our emotions and detach from what we're feeling. In rejecting our lived experience, we disconnect from our embodiment. Because we didn't have a loving presence to help us co-regulate as children, when we're in relationship with others we believe that they will not be able to co-regulate with us. In fact, we might even hear this from the people in our lives, telling us that they experience overwhelm in our presence.

While it's true that our emotions are our own to experience and metabolize, there is no such thing as being too much. When we look to others to be our corrective parent, their experience in relationship with us might be too overwhelming for them. They might be trying to set a boundary when we try to get energy from them, which is reasonable. It is important that we remember that we have our own energy source within us and to learn how to self-regulate when other people aren't able to be a source of co-regulation.

Some of the obvious ways energy exchange occurs in relationship is through attention, listening, action, touch, sex, and money. Conversely, through the subtle self, energy is exchanged below the level of awareness. Someone with an open boundary system can unconsciously give their vital energy to someone else, depleting themselves to energetically find connection with the other person (i.e., making the other person "God"). Someone with a closed boundary system can unconsciously acquire other people's energy, drawing all of the vitality to themselves in an attempt to feel powerful (i.e., wanting to feel like "God"). Someone with a healthy boundary system is in touch with their own energy source and trusts that other people will find their way to theirs, as well, which is generative and honoring (i.e., we all have our own access to Source).

When we feel emotional overwhelm and either contain our experience or try to get other people to give us their energy, we are using outdated survival strategies. These survival strategies persist in the presence of our disconnection from our sacred embodiment.

For some of us, having an attachment wound of being too much can have us try to get really small physically so we don't take up too much space. For others, having an attachment wound of being too much can have us turn to food and take up a lot of space physically as a way to hide. The polarity between "too muchness" and "containing and hiding" is common. As children, we managed our dysregulation to try to keep stability in our environment. We vacillated between wanting our needs to be met and trying to meet the needs of the people around us. As with any polarity, these two extremes are indicators that we have left contact with our Self.

Within this attachment wound, we hold the delusion of too muchness. If we look within and see where our internal experience feels too much for ourselves, we can begin to touch our wound. Being with our attachment wound consciously and lovingly, we can learn how to make space for our full experience and process our unresolved emotions. The wound of "too muchness" is often seated in rejection and turns into self-rejection. This means that when this wound is activated, we likely look to others to accept us and make a lot of room for us.

Remembering that we have our own energy Source within ourselves, we can practice accepting ourselves and honoring the full range of our experience. When we fully accept the full range of our expression, we no longer grasp at other people to be the source of our okayness. By honoring the way our body holds our experience, we are treating ourselves as a divine being when we tend to our inner world in this way. When we contact our Self in our body, we can be in true contact with others.

Harmony's Story

My body has always been an uncomfortable place to be. Having a traumatic brain injury caused me to dissociate as an infant and have chronic pain. Throughout childhood, I was frequently obese and I frequently dieted. My mom was overweight and she was perpetually trying to find the magic cure to get to her to stay at a reasonable weight, and this is how I learned how to be with my body.

I was also chronically ill as a child. With unusual symptoms, I saw many specialists who tried to figure out why I couldn't walk or hold a pencil. My body ached all the time, and I actively resisted being in my body until early adulthood.

Conditioned with an image-conscious ego, my body has been a "thing" to control rather than inhabit. Although I vacillated between periods of overriding my body's physical cues by over exercising and undereating, and honoring my body's physical needs by listening when I'm hungry and resting when I'm tired, my mind has had a persistent message about my body.

311

My conditioned ideas about my body claim that my worth is dependent on my physical appearance. Therefore, my ego is constantly judging my physical appearance, with a strong focus on my weight.

One day, about 10 years ago, I was sitting in meditation and I heard from deep within, "Be the body for God." I sat with the vibration of these words and contemplated this message. Realizing that I was unsure how to be the body for God, I went on a quest to discover what this truly meant for me. I thought about how I would treat a divine deity if they came for dinner. I would offer her the most nourishing food and see her as sacred. I would not judge her body and reduce her down to physical form. I would see her whole being and be grateful that she had a body so she had the ability to visit me and grace this earth with her presence.

I realized that treating my body as I would any life-giving deity was necessary to nurture my vital energy. Nurturing my vitality occurs with more than the food I eat—it also happens with the thoughts that I think and the words that I speak. It happens with the way I move, the way I sit, and the way I touch myself and allow myself to be touched. As a sacred being, this body that I inhabit is also sacred.

Recognizing that my body responds to the food I choose to eat, the movement I choose to enact, and the thoughts I choose to hold, it is not my body's fault if it hurts, holds extra weight, or feels badly. My body is simply communicating with me about the way I relate to her. When I eat too much for too many days in a row, my body lets me know by gaining weight. When I think body-shaming thoughts, my body communicates with me by closing off or hunching over. When I override my body's needs, my body communicates with me by becoming unwell or exhausted.

Sacred embodiment is about so much more than listening to my body—although that is essential for our well-being. Sacred embodiment is the deep knowing that my physical symptoms and state of being are an expression of my spiritual alignment. For my healing to fully manifest, coming back into alignment and bringing more high vibrational qualities of Source directly to my pain is necessary.

Suppressive medication suppresses my symptoms, but it also suppresses my connection with Source. I can't pick and choose what I suppress. Medicine for my spiritual self, such as homeopathy, Chinese medicine, nutritional medicine, energy medicine, functional medicine, Ayurvedic medicine, and plant medicine, ignite my vital force and bring me back into alignment. This does not mean that I disregard or discount the medical model. It simply means that I honor my spiritual self by nurturing my vital force, and if something manifests in my system that requires allopathic medication, I consider it as an option. I do not look to systems that try to control my body through force or suppression. I look to systems that honor the full spectrum of my humanity and see my body as a sacred vessel.

When I really think about this, it is miraculous. My body is responding to the way I treat her. Blaming my body for that would be counterproductive. Listening to my body and appreciating the way my body communicates with me, I am enacting self-responsibility. From this stance, being in a body feels empowering and exciting. In this life, I get to be in this body doing the work of bringing a high vibrational frequency to the world around me. The deep gratitude I have for my body as my sacred vessel is profound.

Exercise: Body love

To do this exercise alone: After you take a shower, put some lotion on your hands and intentionally rub it on your body in service of deep self-love and body appreciation. As you rub your feet, thank your feet for walking you through life. As you rub your legs, thank them for holding you in power and strength.

As you rub your belly, thank your belly for being a source of such wisdom and beauty.

Do this with every part of your physical body.

When you are done, take a few breaths and begin to move your body in a way that feels joyful. Naked and embodied, feel the bliss and joy of being in this temple.

Look at your naked body in the mirror and tell yourself, "You are the body that brings more consciousness onto the planet. You are the body for the divine Source of all Life."

To do the exercise with a partner: This exercise is about sacred sensuality, where one person touches the other in devotion to the sacred. This is not about sex or climax. It is truly a practice of being with yourself and your partner in the intentional experience of sacred embodiment. Because of the conditioned ideas we have about touch and sex, this might be a stretch. However, if you are ready to fully embody your True Self, this exercise is a tool to support you in doing so in the presence of another in a vulnerable way.

To begin, create a sacred nest with pillows and a soft blanket or sheepskin. Light some candles and keep the light on. Both you and your partner will get naked for this practice, so make sure that the temperature in the room is comfortable. Get some nice oil or lotion, and perhaps play some sacred instrumental music.

Choose who will be the receiver first and who will be the giver.

Sit down and face one another. Look into one another's eyes and bow to the divine within each of you. Then, take turns stating your desires, fears, and boundaries. For example: "I have a desire to surrender to your touch, I have a fear that I will stay stuck in my thoughts, and my boundary is that there is no penetration or kissing." Each person takes a turn.

Once that is complete, the receiver will lay down on the blanket naked, and the giver will begin by looking at the receiver as a sacred being. Visually taking in their body, slowly look at the shape of this divine embodiment of love and light. See this being as if you are seeing them for the first time. Receiver, keep breathing up and down the midline of your body, sighing with the exhale and softening your jaw. Giver, you will also breathe in this way, at your own rhythm to stay in your body as you put attention on your partner. Giver, as you do this, hold your hands over your partner's body without touching them. You are simply attuning to and touching into their energy body as you honor them as divine essence.

Starting at the receiver's feet, the giver will put some lotion in their hands and with intention place your hands on the receiver's body. Do this with great presence. Hold your hands here on their feet without rubbing their feet. You are simply making contact with presence as you continue to breathe.

Giver, attune to your partner and when you feel like you are in contact with yourself as a sacred being and the receiver as a sacred being, sensually move your hands and rub their feet. Receiver, keep breathing and taking in this sacred gift. If emotions arise, let them flow. If you want to vocalize, let yourself be heard. Keep moving the energy in your body as you honor yourself in the most sacred way in the presence of your partner.

Giver, use your essence to express your appreciation for your partner's divinity embodied. Then slowly move your hands up as your rub your partner's legs. Receiver, keep breathing. Remember, this is not sexual. It is sacred sensuality.

Continue to rub up the body in a rhythmic, attuned motion. Move your hands over their genitals without turning this into a sexual encounter. Continue moving up their hips, stomach, chest, arms, face, and head... slowly... with attention and presence. All the while, receiver, continue to breathe, take in the presence, love, attention, and touch.

Once the entire body of the receiver has been touched in devotion to the sacred, look into one another's eyes, hold one another, and luxuriate in the energy of the connection. Perhaps say a few words of how this was for you, and end with a bow where you honor and appreciate one another for this experience.

When you are complete, you will likely want to wait for a different day and time until you change roles. Make this commitment to allow each of you to have this sweet and loving devotional touch.

Walkaway with Wisdom

Even with all of the burdens our bodies carry, the unwavering presence of our somatic intelligence, our ability to heal, and our ability to become more embodied is astounding. As with all aspects of our conditioned self, the way we relate to our bodies is learned.

When we learn to disconnect from our bodies, we walk around in a disembodied state. When we relate to our bodies from our conditioning, our distorted thoughts and behavior impacts our physical bodies. Instead of listening to our bodies, we shame our bodies.

When we feel emotional overwhelm and either contain our experience or try to get other people to give us their energy, we are using outdated survival strategies. These survival strategies persist in the presence of our disconnection from our sacred embodiment. Disembodiment makes it possible for our distortion to persist. Embodiment makes it possible for our essence to be fully here in this world, aligned with Source.

Our body is the place for our soul to be present in this world. It's our home, our vessel. It's the expression of boundless life itself through us. We must be in our bodies if we are to create our life consciously. If we are to be fully in our purpose, we must be fully in our body. This flesh, this shape, this body is sacred.

Chapter 21

Conscious Sexuality

The way sexuality has been distorted through the lens of our collective shadow and conditioning is truly one of the most twisted ways our life force gets manipulated. Distorted sexuality is rampant. From the subtle ways we betray ourselves to the overt ways we fail to honor the other person, the expression of our distortion in our sexuality can reinforce our warped vital force.

Body shame, disowned sexual desire, objectification, misused power, and so on have tainted the pure and transcendent qualities of sexuality. In doing the practices in the chapters leading up to this one, we have already begun to clear the conditioned imprint of sexuality. To arrive at this place, where we consciously tend to our relationship with bliss, sexuality, and embodied pleasure, we come full circle.

We all come from orgasm. This means that bliss is our original state. As we experience life and our energy becomes distorted, we get further and further away from the inherent bliss that arises from being fully aligned with Source.

The open flow of energy that was ours when we were first born can move through us again with conscious sexuality. When we disarm ourselves of our disruptions to contact, claim our shadow, and open the channel of vitality that aligns with Source, our sexual expression can be a complete cycle of experience where we no longer have unfinished business preventing us from full, embodied presence.

Sexual Transformation

Our sexuality is an essential part of our sacred expression. As we get closer to intimacy, our vital force becomes amplified. The alchemy of intimately sharing our bodies with another person increases the volume of our somatic sensations and energetic vibrations. If our vitality is distorted, our distortion becomes amplified.

In an attempt to self-regulate, it is common to leave contact with our bodies and use strategies that close off our natural flow of vitality. When our bodies seem like an unsafe place to be, deepening into our somatic experience during a sexual encounter might not seem possible. If we close off from our experience, we might withdraw from contact by dissociating, tightening our muscles, trying to perform or please our partner, or stopping the intimate encounter all together.

Bliss comes from our embodied alignment with Source. When we effort for pleasure, we inhibit bliss from flowing through our channel of vital energy. We might climax, but the transcend qualities of true pleasure are repressed and the full range of our energetic flow is inhibited. Acquired ideas and habits around sexuality cause us to try to *make* pleasure happen. Our effort is antithetical to pleasure itself and it is an attempt at playing "God." The real work of conscious sexuality is not about creating pleasure and bliss, it is about opening to our inherent ecstatic energy and experiencing our natural state as we are.

Learning to stay in contact with ourselves as we ride the waves of emotion and sensation, we develop the capacity to be present for our sexuality. Staying with our breath, maintaining contact with our bodies, and allowing our emotions to flow through us, we can discover new ways to move through the full range of our experience as our sexual intimacy amplifies our vitality. When we stay with ourselves and all that arises in our sexual experience, any blockages to our alignment that inhibit our energy centers from being open can move with conscious sexuality.

If we have experienced traumatic violations to our sexuality, maintaining contact with our bodies during physical intimacy can be challenging. The dissociative patterns that were adaptive when the trauma occurred require a lot of presence and awareness in order to shift. Similar to developmental trauma, the range of sexual trauma is vast. However, any violation to our sacred embodiment that does not honor our sexuality as sacred can be traumatic.

To honor ourselves as sacred, and to be with a partner who also sees our true essence, we can take back our bodies and our sexuality. We can create a new way to be with our pleasure. We can fully sense into our genitals and occupy our full presence here in our body. This deep level of presence can be emotionally overwhelming, which is why it takes practice and self-trust. Learning to stay within our window of tolerance, where we are regulated and aware, will help us to metabolize past traumas and experience true, surrendered bliss.

Moving slowly, feeling each moment of our experience, we can regulate. As we regulate, we can stay embodied.

Reminding ourselves that we are safe, that we are consenting to this sexual encounter, we can fully occupy our bodies and be in choice about how we want to be with our sex. When we stay connected to our bodies and deepen into our experience, we are honoring ourselves as sacred beings. When we encounter sexuality from this Self-honoring, we can become more aligned for having shared ourselves with another.

When our vitality flows in an open channel of alignment, sexuality can amplify any vibration that we are holding that is not the vibration of bliss. We might become more aware of energy blocks and old grief. Tears might begin to flow or a guttural scream might need to be released. Staying with everything that arises within us, we develop the capacity for our energy to flow more freely. This practice makes it more possible for our sexuality to be a transcendent experience that brings us closer to the Source of life.

To stay with our body, our breath, and our bliss can feel vulnerable. With all of the barriers to contact met with awareness, our sexual expression supports the de-armoring of our barriers to love. We experience the pleasure and bliss that is seated in our vital alignment with Source, and we fully show ourselves to another uninhibitedly. When we experience orgasm from this deeply embodied place, the bliss is beyond anything the conditioned self could have fabricated. However, orgasm is not the goal—staying in contact with ourselves moment by moment and getting more in touch with what's arising within us in the only place to get.

It takes tremendous self-trust to hold ourselves in this experience. We've cultivated the secure connection with Self in order to go to these deep and wild places. As we experience the upper reaches of our pleasure with another, it's important to remember that this bliss is ours.

The mind can assign positive emotions and experiences onto others in the same way it does with the negative ones. Just like nobody *makes* us *feel* angry, nobody *makes* us *feel* blissful. It is through our contact with our Self and our capacity to move through the full range of our experience that creates a space for transcendent sexuality to occur. If it doesn't happen with our partner, it is not our partner's fault—just like if it does happen with our partner, it is not our partner's power that made it so. Everything that occurs within us is ours.

Self-Pleasure

The practice of staying in alignment during intimacy is just as important to practice when we are alone in self-pleasure as it is to practice with a lover or lovers. Even in self-pleasure the images and messages of our conditioning can maintain their power at the forefront of our awareness. De-armoring when alone can still require intention and focus.

Self-pleasure as a conscious sexuality practice is the beginning of a return to wholeness, where we are fully responsible for ourselves as we move closer to our union with universal bliss.

To clear the imprint of what sexuality and bodies "should" be like requires us to have a felt experience of what our sexuality truly is beyond those ideas. To be with the purity of our own pleasure is the deepest surrender. Turning off the pornography and quieting the fantasies in our minds, we can simply be with our breath, our body, and our pleasure.

Even when no one is watching, this is still a vulnerable and transcendent experience.

When our antiquated conditioned patterns are active in our minds and bodies, achieving climax is a release of energy. When our minds are empty and we are fully present with ourselves and aware of our sensations, orgasm is an integrating experience where we touch the edges of our whole being all at once.

Although transcendent orgasm is blissful, it is not the goal. There might be a propensity to limit our exploration of pleasure when alone, focusing on our genitals. Discovering ways in which we can experience our own bodies in new ways cultivates even more capacity for pleasure. Touching more parts of our body than only focusing on our genitals and keeping the breath moving freely as we relax our muscles can provide us space to surrender into bliss.

Intentional Pleasure Practices

To be fully present with a lover is one of the most transpersonal, expansive experiences a person can have. To slow down and fully experience a kiss, a touch, and the feeling of our bodies together is a powerful place to start.

To consciously move beyond our conditioned patterns of sexuality is an internal practice. However, being explicit with our partner and creating a container for sexual exploration with consent is foundational in conscious sexuality practices. Many people feel shy talking about sexuality with the very person they have sex with. Giving voice to our desires, intentions, fears, and boundaries can be a huge stretch when we are clinging to our conditioning.

That's okay.

We must allow the shyness to be present. We must let the fear have space. Allowing ourselves to feel awkward and uncertain is part of the vulnerability that brings us back to our undefended heart. Over time, the more we practice and move through the uncertainty, the more self-trust we build.

If conscious sexuality was talked about in the media and in our collective society, it would be easier to have these conversations and set these intentions. Unfortunately, the makers of the movies and television series are identified with their distortion, thus their programs are a representation of their shadow and conditioned beliefs. Mainstream imagery of sexuality is a product of the collective shadow around sexuality. Self-betrayal, misuse of power, and the myth of purity are at the core of these visual representations.

Two (or more) sovereign individuals who are clear about what they want, what they're afraid of, and what their boundaries are can explore sacred sexuality in a deeply honoring and relationally clean manner.

The foundation for sexual exploration is context. Making our desires, fears, and boundaries explicit to our lovers is paramount in creating an experience based in shared reality of the intention of the interaction. In the Tantra tradition, this practice initiates any physical intimacy.

For example, if my partner and I were to decide to be physically intimate, we would sit across from one another and each have the opportunity to share our desires, fears, and boundaries. I might say, "My desire is to stay embodied in my own energy system. My fear is that I will try to perform for you. And my boundary is that I am not available for any penetration."

Then my partner would reflect what they heard to let me know they understood and agreed. Then they would share their desires, fears, and boundaries, "My desire is to explore deep pleasure with you. My fear is that I might do something you don't like. And my boundary is that we don't analyze what is happening between us." Then I would reflect what my partner said to let them know I understood and agreed.

In order to be intentional about our sexuality, we need to meet another from our "adult"—not our inner young one. In order to be explicit about the context we're available for, we need to have access to our deeper truth. If we don't have the capacity yet, we can make a guess at our desires, fears, and boundaries—then as the encounter happens, we learn more about if our spoken words resonate with our deeper truth.

Once both partners have expressed their desires, fears, and boundaries, we begin to breathe. Looking into one another's eyes, we breathe into our hearts, into our bellies, and into our sex centers. Tantric breathing (explained in more detail at the end of this chapter) activates our kundalini energy and ignites our alignment with Source.

After 5–10 minutes of activating breath, we move closer together. One person sits on the other person's lap, with their legs wrapped around their partner, and we continue to breathe the tantric breath. This is the practice of staying in our own energy center aligned with Source as we make contact with our physical bodies.

From here, we continue to breathe and experience our pleasure as we rub our bodies together, touch one another, and experience the sacred essence of one another. If the context included a boundary of no penetration (as stated in the example above), this sacred sexuality encounter has no penetrative sex. But that does not mean that this is not a sexual encounter. Through breath and touch, we might reach climax. But again, that is not the point. The intention is to practice honoring ourselves and one another as sacred, sexual beings.

Over time, we build off of these practices and learn more skills and build more capacity. We might decide to play with polarities in sexuality, where the person who is typically the pleaser becomes the dominant one, and the person who is typically in charge becomes submissive. When we bring the polarities into greater consciousness through sexual relating, it is never to hurt or harm. It is always to invite more integration and alignment into the dynamic of the relationship.

If we have a history of sexual abuse, the context we might have of wanting to feel safe could be having our partner ask our permission before initiating any new movement or touch. Or perhaps we want to direct everything that happens and name our desire with nuance as it arises.

As long as there is intention, consent, and clear context of how we agree to be with one another, conscious sexuality can be a fun exploration of transformation.

Harmony's Story

My sexual healing has been the deepest transformation I have experienced. Learning how to differentiate from my conditioned self and honor my body as sacred, I learned how to experience sacred sexuality. For me, it's impossible to live a sacred life and not practice sacred sexuality.

In my youth, sexuality was a dehumanizing experience where my first sexual encounter was a traumatic violation. Thinking that saying "No" would cause me more harm, I went along with the violation as if my own self didn't matter. I learned to be okay objectifying myself, believing that my pleasure didn't matter.

Once I realized the way I was dehumanizing myself, I polarized to the other extreme and became the dominant one who dehumanized others. My heart was closed to intimacy, and so I used other people for my own pleasure. Since this also felt like a violation to my own soul, I stopped having sex for many years. I wanted to discover a new way to be with a lover, and I had no idea where to begin.

I attended my first Tantra workshop when I was in my mid-twenties. The idea of sacred sexuality wasn't new to me, as both of my parents were open about their exploration into sacred sexuality. It was actually my dad who suggested I attend this workshop. Although I come from a family that honors sexual expression, I didn't think I was worthy to be met by another person in this way. I didn't view myself as sacred, and I thought no one else would, either.

Over the years, as I've deepened into embodying my own Self as sacred, I have been in a continual practice with my own sexuality. While workshops and books have been useful, the real-time practice of staying in touch with my spiritual self as I breathe and honor my own Source of pleasure and bliss has been the most transformative. Although I wanted to practice with a partner, it was important for me to practice on my own with a yoni egg first (detailed below).

Quieting my mind, dropping into my body, and inviting aligned bliss to flow through my kundalini as I self-pleasure is transformational. This practice gave me space to build the capacity to embody my sacred Self with a sexual partner.

When I met my husband, he wanted a spiritual connection with a woman and was unsure how to bring this to our sexual relationship. We attended many sacred sexuality workshops together, and I taught him many techniques. As it was with myself, he needed to learn how to be in his own body and align with his sacred Self in order to meet me in this deep way. With his conditioned Catholic values, he's needed to open more fully to the beauty of his sexuality. Also, as a masculine being raised in a time when men were misusing their power over women, he carried a lot of sexual uncertainty. He wanted to be a safe man, and that meant containing his sexuality.

To move through the confines of sexual shame together, we are in continual discovery of how we want to be with ourselves and one another. There are moments when we move closer that his conditioned self wants to please me to earn my love, and my body freezes. He becomes afraid of being rejected, and I become afraid of being dropped. Slowing down, we practice staying in our own energy Source with our breath as we eye gaze. This is sex. Without even touching, pleasure moves through our kundalini as we clear blockages in our own systems—sometimes jolting with the bliss of the movement of energy.

The alchemy of our sacred connection becomes even more potent when we move closer and touch one another from this place. Staying in contact with ourselves, we begin to contact one another. We continue to breathe and to look into one another's eyes. Our union heals the deepest trauma and violation within my body when we meet one another in this way. With my whole body relaxed and open, experiencing climax from this place is 100 times more pleasurable than an effortful orgasm.

I feel more aligned and more connected to my Self when we are intentional about our sacred sexuality practices. Not every encounter is like this, but when we practice our devotional exercises our intimacy and connection feels like the most sacred gift of being in a body. Life feels more vibrant, and my creativity flows with more ease.

Exercise: Tantric Breathing

Our innate pleasure arises from being—not from trying. In our alignment with the Source of bliss, our embodied presence in our intimate relating can facilitate levels of transcendence that we couldn't otherwise access on our own. Whether you do this breathing practice alone or with a partner, keep your awareness and presence on the surrender of the exhale. Softening into our body, we can be more open to pleasure and to Source.

To do this exercise alone: Close your eyes and start to breathe in and out of your mouth in a circular rhythmic pattern where you don't pause at the top or the bottom of the breath. Inhale, then exhale and allow your jaw to soften.

Direct your breath into your heart. Inhale into your heart,

then vocalize with your exhale and soften your jaw. Repeat this for about 2–4 minutes where you breathe into your heart and give it a tone, give your heart a voice with the exhale. What does your heart sound like in a vocalization?

Keep your attention in and breathe in a way that feels good to you.

Next, direct your breath into your belly, your power center, and vocalize with your exhale. For about 2–4 minutes, breathe into your belly and give it a tone with the exhale. What does your power center sound like?

Then, breathe into your root chakra, your sex center, and vocalize with your exhale. For about 2–4 minutes, direct your breath right into your root chakra, and give it a tone. What does your sex center sound like?

Lastly, breathe into all three, heart, belly, root, and give all of them a tone with the exhale. Repeat this for about 5 minutes.

If you feel inclined, you can continue to breathe and touch your body. Feel the pleasure of rubbing your arms, your face, your legs, or your genitals. Continue to breathe as you drop into the pleasure of being in your body. (For bodies with vaginas, a yoni egg can be a great accompaniment to self-pleasure meditation. It can awaken our contact with our genitals in new and significant ways.)

To do this exercise with a partner: Sit across from your partner, either cross legged on the floor or in chairs with backs. Alternatively, you may choose to sit closer, with one person sitting on the other person's lap facing them with their legs wrapped around the other. Either way, face one another as you breathe. Gaze into one another's eyes.

Take a few cleansing breaths as you look at one another, then start to breathe in and out of your mouth in a circular rhythmic pattern where you don't pause at the top or the bottom of the breath. Inhale, then exhale and allow your jaw to soften with every breath.

Direct your breath into your heart and vocalize with your exhale. Repeat this for about 2–4 minutes. Breathe into your heart and give it a tone, give your heart a voice with the exhale. What does your heart sound like in a vocalization?

Your breath does not need to be in sync with your partner's, but it can be. Don't make an effort to inhale and exhale at the same time. Keep your attention inward and breathe in a way that feels good to you.

Next, direct your breath into your belly, your power center, and vocalize with your exhale. For about 2–4 minutes, breathe into your belly and give it a tone with the exhale. What does your power center sound like?

Then, breathe into your root chakra, your sex center, and vocalize with your exhale. For about 2–4 minutes, direct your breath right into your root chakra, and give it a tone. What does your sex center sound like?

Lastly, breathe into all three, heart, belly, root, and give all of them a tone with the exhale. Repeat this for about 5 minutes.

Keeping the eye gaze, just breathe in a way that feels good. Let any stored emotional energy move as you do this entire practice. Cry even if you don't know what the tears are about. Laugh even if there isn't a story that is funny. Feel awkward even if you've been with your practice partner for 20 or more years. And feel the orgasmic bliss that is in the root even when there is no stimulation.

Let your energy flow up the center of your body.

If you both desire, you can grind your bodies into each other, touch one another, and eventually make love. If you choose to move into this deeper level of physical intimacy, be sure to have explicit consent and stay with the breath as you enjoy your own bliss and alignment in the presence of your lover.

Walkaway with Wisdom
The way sexuality has been distorted through the lens of our

collective shadow and conditioning is truly one of the most twisted ways our life force gets manipulated. Body shame, disowned sexual desire, objectification, misused power, and so on have tainted the pure and transcendent qualities of sexuality.

As we get closer to intimacy, our vital force becomes amplified. The alchemy of intimately sharing our bodies with another person increases the volume of our somatic sensations and energetic vibrations. If our vitality is distorted, our distortion becomes amplified.

When our antiquated conditioned patterns are active in our minds and bodies, achieving climax is a discharge of energy. When our minds are empty and we are fully present with ourselves and aware of our sensations, orgasm is an integrating experience where we touch the edges of our whole being all at once.

To honor ourselves as sacred, and to be with a partner who also sees our true essence, we can take back our bodies and our sexuality. We can create a new way to be with our pleasure. To stay with our body, our breath, and our bliss can feel vulnerable. With all of the barriers to contact set aside, our sexual expression supports the de-armoring of our barriers to love. We experience the pleasure and bliss that is seated in our vital alignment with Source, and we fully show ourselves to another uninhibitedly.

Chapter 22

Living in Alignment

Alignment is the deep honoring of the boundless energy of life itself being expressed through us with clarity. It is not a belief system. It's a felt sense of our most authentic expression. It's who we are when we feel most like ourselves. It's not a peak experience we have at a retreat or a place of enlightenment that we reach. It's the way we engage with the world, day by day, without contorting or distorting, without hiding our betraying, and without managing or controlling.

When we are aligned, all of our actions are an expression of Source moving through us. As we practice living and loving from the True Self, we will slip into conditioned patterns along the way. Life is messy, and we have no control over how or when our stress response is activated. When we do notice the somatic expression of our pain and conditioning, we can continue to choose to be in the practice of staying in contact with all of the layers of our felt experience as they emerge.

Staying calm and peaceful is not the goal. Staying embodied and regulating through our emotions is the goal. The conditioned patterns are an attempt at self-regulation, and we must feel the dysregulation in order to contact ourselves. Honoring our bodies as sacred, we can attune to the sensory information being communicated from our somatic intelligence. This provides us the spaciousness and awareness necessary to choose a different, truer way to be in the world.

As we stay in contact with ourselves, we also tend to the way we contact our environment. From our alignment, we can honor the people in our lives as sacred, sovereign beings. Together, we can deepen into our alignment and continue to emerge into our truest expression.

Lifelong Learning

As we transform and learn new skills, our development is not linear. There is no right way to transform. There is no direct path to unlearning old patterns.

It can be quite painful to see the ways our distorted life force and survival strategies have caused or continue to cause pain in our relationships. Becoming aware of our patterns is the most important undertaking in our transformation because our own awareness is what allows us to be in conscious relationship to ourselves and the environment. Once we are awake to our conditioned patterns, we will likely fall asleep again and again, forgetting how to live from our essential self. Although this might feel like failure, there is no possible way that we can take a step backwards on our path. We are either stepping forward consciously, awake to our essential self, or we are stepping forward unconsciously, using conditioned patterns.

Before we are aware of our distorted patterns, we are unconscious to our own ineffectiveness. We walk around, oblivious to our destructive ways of being and seeing the world, wondering why life is so challenging and painful. As we cultivate awareness of our own distorted patterns, there is a tendency to be hard on ourselves for not being more evolved or more effective. Although we might see the patterns, we may not yet be sure how to respond differently.

Eventually, we develop the awareness and courage to be more authentic and intentional with how we show up for life. Although we are choosing to do something different, it takes all of our attention and intention to do so.

Over time, we go back to being unaware, then we see our patterns again, then we get frustrated with our own incompetence, then we make choices consciously and find our way again. With practice, we develop enough capacity that we no longer need to put any attention on staying in contact with ourselves and honoring our alignment with Source—we simply do it unconsciously.

The stages described here are adapted from *The Four Stages of Competence* (Broadwell, 1969):

Stage 1: Unconsciously incompetent: This is when we are unaware of the patterns of thinking and behaving that inhibit our ability to experience the life we long for.

Stage 2: Consciously incompetent: This is when we develop the awareness of our patterns, but we are not sure how to do something differently.

Stage 3: Consciously competent: This is when we use our conscious choice to do something different and truer to our essential self.

Stage 4: Unconsciously competent: This is when we have the capacity to do the different, truer thing without needing to think about doing it. It's integrated into our way of being.

When we are learning any new way of being, there is a flux in the way we move through these stages. It is not a linear path of unconsciously incompetent, to conscious incompetence, to conscious competence, and then to unconscious competence. We move between them all (as pictured below) sometimes with great frustration and sometimes with great elation.

In the image below, we can see that there are various ways to come into and out of our own ability to be integrated, aligned, and sovereign. Devoting ourselves to our alignment requires that we dedicate ourselves to seeing our own unconscious behavior.

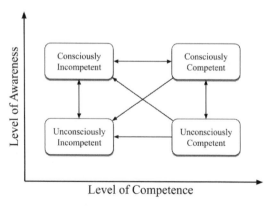

As we continue on the path of self-development, sometimes old patterns reemerge, seemingly out of nowhere. We may have thought that we had moved beyond a certain wound or fully healed an aspect of our old trauma. Then something happens in our world and the pattern is ignited all over again. This is an opportunity to metabolize and heal unfinished business more deeply.

Anytime we become more aware of our distortions, we own our blind spots and conditioning. This, in and of itself, brings us closer back to our home base where our life force energy is aligned with Source. As lifelong learners, there are no failures in relationship; there are no wrong turns on this sacred journey. There are simply lessons that when met with conscious awareness can bring us closer to our alignment with Source.

Apologizing to those we harm when we act from old patterns of conditioning and trauma is an act of atoning the way we showed up. "I'm sorry you were negatively impacted by me," is not a true apology. A true apology acknowledges the way that we contributed a maladaptive or unconscious energy to the interaction. "When we were talking yesterday, I felt scared that you might be angry with me. Because I was moving from fear, I wasn't in my heart. I apologize for reacting with such intensity. I want to learn how to listen from love." When we clean up our side of the street, so to speak, we amend our energetic output. This supports our living in alignment, even as we clumsily learn how.

Working with Affirmations

Once we bring more awareness into the patterns that sabotage ourselves and our relationships, it can be useful to work with an affirmation. Our words are powerful, and speaking what we are ready to claim for ourselves can help to anchor the new way into our bodies.

Using the sentence stem, "I am ready for…" state with clarity what aspect of your transformation you are wanting to shift. Think back to the patterns of your conditioned self and your younger parts, and write down what inner misbelief or pattern you want to transcend.

Examples:

"I am ready to honor my truth."

"I am ready to honor my boundaries."

"I am ready to stand in my power."

"I am ready to open to real love."

"I am ready to learn how to love myself."

Choose an affirmation that feels 100% reflective of what you are ready for. Then take a piece of paper and fold it in half or draw a line down the middle. On the left-hand side of the paper, write down your affirmation. On the right-hand side of the piece of paper, write down all the reasons why your mind says this is not possible, why you don't deserve this or aren't capable of it. Get it all out.

Then again, on the left-hand side of the paper write the affirmation, and on the right-hand side write down all the reasons your deep unconscious says this isn't possible, even if you repeat the same things.

Do this five times, and end with "And I am ready *(your affirmation here)*."

Cycle of Alignment

Because of the human propensity to fall asleep to the True Self and to turn off the light of awareness, it is so, so important to see our relationships as a container for our own spiritual development. To receive the gift of reflection in relationship while also knowing where we end and another begins (i.e., not personalizing our partner's projections or state of being) is the offering of sovereignty.

Fritz Perls (1973), the creator of Gestalt counseling, said "We live in a house of mirrors and think we are looking out the windows." This way of seeing the world keeps us looking to others to change, believing that if other people treated us a certain way, we would feel okay. The propensity to look outside ourselves keeps us out of alignment with our own Source of energy and power. By turning inward with gentle introspection, we can be in discovery of what is being reflected to us from those around us. We can look to find where our shadow holds what the other person is reflecting. We can discover what younger part is being activated. We can look at our own distorted narratives and pain with love in order to come back home to the core of our being.

When our partner also does their own inner work, we can be a reflection of our highest vibration to one another. This experience touches the highest vibrational alchemy where our sacred embodiment is even more sacred because we have learned to dance in such a way that we strengthen our sovereign alignment with every step.

We all have deep wounds and we are all infinite essence. Where we move from, where we see from, and where we choose from is the key to our sovereignty. Fully responsible for ourselves, we are the creators of our life. In conscious choice, we are a victim to no one. This is not about manifestation—this is about doing the deep inner work of integration so that we move from our wholeness and have that integration reflected back to us. When we honor ourselves in this way, all beings are honored. When we speak our truth with clarity and ownership, all beings have more of a chance to be heard and seen. When we return to wholeness and heal the deepest wounds within, all beings benefit from that healing.

In the image below, we can see the cycle of alignment.

We begin with our alignment with the True Self, then the environment feels unsafe and we become dysregulated.

In an attempt to regulate, we develop/use conditioned patterns, and subsequently we engage with the world from our distorted vital force.

Eventually, we look within to discover how we leave our alignment, and we become aware of the holographic expression of our inner world being reflected back to us through the outer world.

From here, we create a secure connection with our inner young one and find our way to sovereignty.

Then we meet the world from our most integrated, emerging sense of self.

Cycle of Alignment

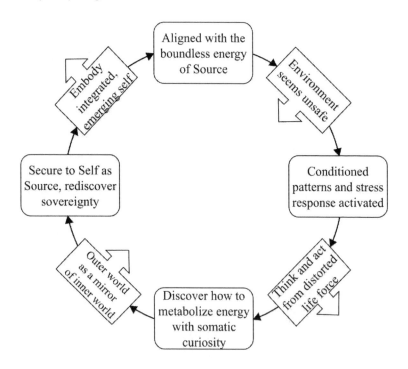

Our alignment is a gift to this world. Our truth and dignity and boundaries are part of planetary restoration. The more able we are to hold the vibration of sacred embodiment in the presence of others, the more God consciousness there will be on this planet. We are—with all of our flaws, all of our patterns, and all of our misbeliefs — the living expression of Source. The distortion of our life force energy is the distortion of Source, which serves no one. The clarity and strength of our life force energy is the vibrancy of Source shining through you, which serves all beings.

To be kind to ourselves when we slip into the patterns of our distorted life energy, and to maintain daily practices that bring us back into alignment with the core of our being is how we, with all of our blind spots and flaws and attempts at control, can live a sacred life.

Harmony's Story

The more experience I have living primarily in alignment with Source, the clearer it becomes that any movement I make from my distortion creates a wonky effect in the world around me. When my alignment was less developed, the distorted actions I took were immensely self-harming. Giving my body over to others as if I had no worth, pretending everything was fine when I was suffering inside, and hiding my wisdom out of fear that I would be annihilated if I spoke my deepest truth caused my life to be a distorted reflection of my survival strategies. Living from my conditioned patterns, my life was askew and nothing felt quite right.

When I engaged with the world from my adaptive survival strategies, I was completely asleep to my True Self. I knew conceptually that there was more to myself, but I was unsure how to embody my truest expression. As I devoted myself to practices that bring me back into alignment, my life force energy became retuned, back to its original state. As life happens, my life force can become mistuned again when I feel under-resourced, especially when the outside world closely resembles a past experience that was traumatic for my inner young one.

Keeping my energy flowing up the core of my being is an ongoing devotional practice to bring more of the vibration of

Source to the planet. Every morning, I sit in meditation and attune to my infinite, unbreakable bond with Source. I open up my system to deepen into my embodiment of the True Self. With intention, I look in my mind's eye for the places where my spirituality can be most useful and practical to the world around me. With my children, my husband, my clients, and students, I ask that the vibration of Source be at the center of all that I do, all that I say, and all that I am.

Once I get up from my meditation cushion, I bring the qualities of my own aligned energy of Source with me into all of my relationships. If social norms induce self-betrayal or hiding, I still honor my truest truth. When the grocer asks, "How are you," I answer with the most authentic truth available to me in that moment, "I feel grateful for the ability to buy so much healthy food, and I'm also carrying a lot of stress in my body from working so much. How are you?" As the grocer responds, I listen with great care and compassion. I see the person speaking, not just the role they are playing in my life at this moment.

When something happens in my relationships that is stressful enough to pull me off center, I look within and I notice the places in which I left my authentic expression. Even though I am aware of the way the other person is projecting onto me, my work is to look within and stay curious about what the world around me is reflecting back to me. I amend the distortion within myself and with those who I was off center with.

For example, sometimes students interrupt me while I'm leading a practice or lecture, and sometimes I am totally welcoming of this. In a learning environment, full engagement is healthy and generative. However, there are times when at the moment of interruption, I have a ping inside that this particular disruption is off in some way. The ping I experience is my intuition, and it might be that I am sensing the students' dysregulation, projection onto me, or some other expression of their distortion. When I disregard my intuition and prioritize the student, my life force energy is distorted.

In these moments, it is increasingly imperative that I slow down and stay in contact with myself. Pausing the student, revealing that something is happening within me, and making space for me to find my seat, I prioritize my alignment over answering the question. This is important because when I don't do this, everything in the classroom is unsteady. My steadiness in my alignment is vital for my leadership. Where there is lack of contact, there is lack of leadership. And for contact to happen, I must be in contact with my Self.

As I have come more fully into alignment, the movements I make from my distortion are more obvious. More often than not, I can catch myself in real-time and realign as the interaction occurs. However, when I don't catch myself, I always go back and amend my own contribution to the dynamic. Whether it is a student, a friend, my husband, my children, or anyone else I contact, I reach out to the person let them know what I can see in myself and what I wish I would have done differently. Repairing when I am off center is essential for bringing my full Self into the world.

For example, if I am under resourced with my children, I might rant from a place of martyrdom. "I do so much for you, and you can't even clean up when I've asked you five times do so?!" Since I rarely rant to my children, when I do so I feel incredible regret and shame. I take some space, I sit in meditation and come back into my heart. When I am seated in my Source of love, I repair with them. "I want to apologize for raising my voice. I've been feeling a lot of stress lately, and I'm sorry I took it out on you. I want you to feel loved by me, and I also want you to help out more by cleaning up after yourselves."

Since they were little, I have apologized to them with genuine love every time I have acted from an under resourced, unconscious place. I make room for them to tell me how they felt when I raised my voice, and I validate their experience with empathetic listening. "It sounds like you were surprised that I was so upset. That makes sense to me. You two were playing quietly when I realized you still hadn't cleaned up. I wish I would have reminded you in a way that felt loving."

They spontaneously will frequently validate my stress, too. "Mom, it makes sense to me that you were so frustrated. We kept forgetting that you asked because we were already doing something else."

As the relational leader of my family, staying aligned with Source is my highest priority. When I am out of alignment, I prioritize cleaning up my contribution to the interaction. Even though I am a flawed human who makes mistakes, I still have access to the wisdom of Source to amend those mistakes.

Living and loving from my True Self requires conscious intention. When I am in alignment, I honor myself, stay embodied, voice my truth, and move from my essential self. From alignment, my life flows, where I feel the rightness of being alive. From this place, my relationships flourish, where there is playfulness and joy in my connections. Beyond the pain and conflict of my conditioned self, meeting life from my alignment allows my inner and outer world to be a reflection of the purest and truest expression of my Self.

Exercise: Each Day Is a Sacred Opportunity to Move from Our Alignment

In the Morning: Begin each day in prayer and meditation to remind yourself where you want to live from.

First thing in the morning, sit on your meditation cushion, close your eyes, and notice what it feels like to be you. Notice what pulls the attention of your mind. Notice the sensations in your body. Notice your breath. Without trying to change anything about yourself, simply bring more presence and loving awareness into your being.

After 10–20 minutes of sitting in silence, say a prayer of intention.

Example: "May Your presence, Your vibration, Your love, and Your consciousness be at the center of all I do, all I say, and all that I am. Please guide my actions and make clear the way."

In the Evening: End each day with meditation and forgiveness to clean up any and all ways you've met the world or your relationships from your distortion.

Sit on your meditation cushion and close your eyes. Notice what it feels like to be you, without trying to change anything. Bringing more presence and awareness into your being, begin to cleanse your energetic body of other people's emotions, judgment, projections, and so on that do not belong to you. And then take back any way in which you gave away your power, projected onto others, or met the world from your distortion. Ask the cosmic realm for support as you clean up the energetic field with breath and awareness.

After several minutes, say, "I ask for forgiveness from anyone I offended today, either knowingly or unknowingly. And I forgive those who have offended me today, either knowingly or unknowingly."

Take a few breaths here, allowing yourself to rest in the amending of the way you showed up today. With every exhale, open your jaw, sigh, and surrender.

When you lay down to sleep, imagine a sweet energetic tent around you protecting you from other people's thoughts or energy making their way into your deep unconscious so that you can feel safe enough to fully surrender into a nice, sweet sleep.

Walkaway with Wisdom

As children, when the environment felt unsafe, we became dysregulated. In an attempt to regulate, we developed patterns and thoughts that helped us to feel more in control. Because these thoughts and patterns are not aligned with our true nature, our vital force became distorted. Over time, we became identified with our learned thoughts and patterns, and our distorted life force influenced much of how we showed up for life.

As we start to look at our pain and our patterns, we're no longer identified with it. Our curiosity has us make space for our wounds, and this space increases our awareness and choice.

When we are dysregulated and under resourced, our conditioned impulses and thoughts are more likely to hijack our state of being. The more we look within to discover how we leave our alignment, the more we can see that the world around us is a reflection of our inner world—deciphering the holographic expression represented in the outer world is much of the work of coming back into alignment.

Once we can see the wound that is being shown to us, we get to create a secure connection with our inner young one. The more we hold ourselves in unconditional love, the more we find our way to sovereignty—where we are fully self-responsible and no longer react against the environment. Meeting the world from our most integrated, emerging sense of self, our inherent joy can be expressed. No longer dependent on other people for our safety, our self-trust makes it possible for us to be in our full expression.

Remembering our essential self is an exercise in awareness. The seductive nature of our habitual patterns can lull us into forgetting our true nature. With promises of safety and control, the conditioned self is persistent in its stance. The unwavering presence of our True Self is such that we simply need to remember how to come back to ourselves.

Alignment is the deep honoring of the boundless energy of life itself being expressed through us with clarity. When we come back into alignment, we access the pure love and joy of our untainted essence. Life becomes a playground for our authentic expression when we embody the True Self. We get to explore how we want to be with ourselves and the world in each moment of life. No longer driven by outdated beliefs and behaviors, being current with ourselves makes it possible for us to be fully present with our environment. Our presence influences the field around us, and the whole world comes more into alignment when we do.

Living and loving from the True Self is a way of being, it's not an achievement. In our continual evolution, we get to discover how we want to be with our thoughts, our emotions, our bodies, and our spiritual Self. Knowing that we are here to be in our full expression, we embody our alignment with dignity in all of life's experiences. Because we have a secure attachment to Self as Source, we no longer give our power away, play small, or try to earn the right to exist. With the openheartedness of a child, we bring the qualities of pure love, creativity, and curiosity into our lives as we continually emerge into who we are becoming.

Final Thoughts and Wishes

Beneath the layers of conditioned thoughts and patterns lives the purest expression of your humanity. The strategies you developed in childhood were once useful, but they are now outdated. Once you start seeing the ways your current experiences are influenced by your past, you might want to rush your healing. On this journey of alignment, though, the only place to get is more in touch with what is alive within you right now.

Feeling the unfinished business that is housed in the body, you can open into deeper contact with your Self. As you do this, there will likely be barriers, numbness, urgency, and other mechanisms of self-protection that will also need your love and attention. May you bring compassion and validation to every layer you touch on the way to alignment, including your shame and shadow.

Once you remember your True Self, you will likely fall asleep to your Self again and again. The false-promise of security and certainty in the conditioned self can be alluring. May you know your patterns well so that you can find your way out of the matrix when you fall into it again.

My wish for you is that you are cleansed of all energy and constructs that are not part of your true nature. As you go through the great unlearning, may you hold yourself with tenderness and compassion. May you create a secure attachment with your inner young one, giving them the attuned attention, healthy boundaries, and empowered voice they've always longed for. May you honor yourself always, and may you honor others as you do.

May your relationships resonate with your most authentic Self, where you experience real love and real truth. May your presence on this planet bring more consciousness to the world, and may your undefended heart bless all whom you encounter. May your fullest expression empower others to also be fully expressed, and may gratitude and forgiveness touch every cell of your body.

When you want something, if it is aligned, may it be so. When you want something, if it is not aligned, may you easefully let it go.

May you honor your body with good food, kind thoughts, and loving touch. May you experience transcendent pleasure, where you feel safe to explore the full range of your sacred sexuality. May you devote yourself to your alignment with Source, and when you come off balance may you easefully come back to your Self again and again and again.

May your very presence on this earth bring the frequency needed for planetary healing and restoration. May your personal work of alignment empower you to participate in the collective work to dismantle systemic racism, environmental racism, and societal inequity. May the healing you experience in your body bring healing to the earth, to the atmosphere, and to our sacred waters. May every breath and every thought be a prayer for life, love, and truth.

From the Author

Dearest Reader,

Thank you so much for purchasing *Align: Living and Loving from the True Self.* I hope that your journey into alignment through this book has been as enlightening and deep for you as it was for me to write it. I've seen how hungry my clients and students are for deep transformation and deep connection, and I wrote this book to provide a comprehensive overview of how to bring this work into your daily life. If you found value in *Align*, I would deeply appreciate you taking a few moments to add a review on your favorite online bookseller's website.

I'm committed to supporting you on your sacred journey, and I have some gifts I'd like to offer you to continue to deepen into your inner alignment. I've created a companion journal and a unique alignment map for you to use in conjunction with this book. Visit my website to download both today.

In my first book, *Reveal: Embody the True Self Beyond Trauma and Conditioning*, I vulnerably shared my story of transformation in hopes of empowering you to discover your truest Self. *Align* is the "how-to" companion to *Reveal*, both of which are intended to let you know that you are not alone, you are already whole, and you have the capacity for deep transformation. It is my commitment to you that I embody the message that I teach, and sharing my story with you is part of that embodiment.

As a visiting instructor at Naropa University, I teach student therapists how to facilitate deep transformation with their clients using Gestalt Therapy. After 15 years plus as a Gestalt Therapist, I have developed a transpersonal framework for therapists and coaches called Spiritual Alignment Technique. Please visit my website to learn more about upcoming trainings with me.

May self-compassion and self-love be constant companions

on your evolving journey into alignment.

With Love,

Harmony

www.harmonykwiker.com

www.thespirituallyaligned.com

Vocabulary

Third dimension: Spatial reality of matter that has depth, height, and width, along with a quality of lifelikeness. It is something that increases the significance or vividness of a sequence of events, factual occurrence, and so on. "When our reality is based in the third dimension, we rely on measurable aspects of life."

Fourth dimension: In addition to the spatial reality of depth, height, and width of the third dimension, the fourth dimension is the non-material realm of time. There is time as it is regarded in linear dimensions, and there is time experienced as space in non-linear dimensions of spirituality.

Fifth dimension: Beyond space and time, the fifth dimension is a micro-dimension where there is a seamless tie between seemingly unrelated third and fourth dimension observations. It is the first of the higher spiritual dimensions where we experience oneness with others and unity with Source. It is a realm of consciousness with higher frequencies of energy.

Allopathic: Treating symptoms through conventional means.

Ancestral Trauma: Transgenerational or intergenerational trauma is a psychological term indicating that patterns of trauma can be passed down from previous generations; trauma patterns that live in our DNA as a chemical mark in our genes and are re-experienced by us in service of healing the lineage of our family; even if we do not have explicit awareness of the trauma pattern, it can still be expressed through us and experienced by us; trauma patterns that are inherited by each generation until someone in the lineage is able to transmute the epigenetic pattern.

Attachment Styles: The established ways in which a person relates to other people based on their formative experiences with their caregivers early in life; the ways in which a person relates to their intimate partners and their children based on their learned ways of relating to their caregivers: Secure, Insecure, Avoidant, and Disorganized are the four main attachment styles.

Attachment Wounds: An emotional wound where a breach of trust, misattunment, violation, or neglect caused harm to a child by their primary caregivers resulting in an attachment style that is either insecure, avoidant, or disorganized.

Attune; Attunement; Emotional Attunement: the ability to notice, comprehend, and respond to the emotional state of another person.

Bottom-Up Approach to Processing: This is the term used to describe information processing where incoming stimuli are first experienced in our bodies, then our emotions, then our intellect. When we process from a bottom-up, we form a perception of a stimuli from the body up to the mind. When we process from the top-down, we use ideas and models to create a perception, then move down into our emotions and our bodies.

Codependent: Characteristics of a person who takes responsibility for other people's actions; traits of a person who is self-sacrificing to a degree of enabling another person's harmful actions, including emotional immaturity, emotional abuse, poor mental health, and addiction; placing one's own needs as a lower priority to another's; codependency is typically a trauma response that provides a sense of safety and control when a person disowns their power.

Cognitive Bypassing: Intellectualizing our stress, trauma, and conditioned patterns to avoid feeling the painful experience housed in our bodies.

Conditioning; Conditioned Self; Mask of Conditioning: Learned ways of being that veil our authentic expression; personality structures that are guided by our identification with our false self.

Confluence: When an individual feels no boundary between themselves and others, taking on other people's thoughts, judgments, projections, and actions as an indication of their own sense of self.

Contact Boundary Disturbance: Habitual ways of relating to one's self and the world that originally were created as an adaptive response to a situation, yet the habits continue to emerge in response to environmental cues even though the original circumstances are no longer present or relevant; habits that prevent one from being present with their environment.

Core of your Being/Midline: In biodynamic craniosacral technique, the midline is where the potency of the neural tube and the central nervous system comes together with a surge of potential for health, order, and change; the midline corresponds with the energy center of the chakra system, which lives in the fascia and the subtle energy body; the midline is fluid and can be experienced as the core of our being, where we access our alignment with Source, our vital force, and the wholeness of our essence; having contact with the core of our being makes it possible to act from the deepest and truest place within ourselves.

Death Urge: The inner drive toward death and self-destruction, frequently expressed through self-harming behaviors, thoughts, and impulses, as first described by Leonard Orr; unconsciously thinking we need to die to get back to God. Our death urge is an unconscious drive to return to universal bliss; paradoxically it prevents us from embodying our True Self.

Deflection: Turning away from an external stimulus that causes internal discomfort; ignoring internal discomfort to prevent full awareness and recognition of relevant material, i.e., painful memory, shame, misbeliefs, and so on.

Distortion: Life force energy that has been twisted and altered from its original state.

Distorted narrative: Perception of factual events that have been filtered through our distorted life force and twisted into a warped version of reality.

Disowned; Disowned Parts: Internal thoughts, experiences, drives, and impulses that have been rejected and hidden by one's self; rejected and hidden aspects of one's self that are imbued with shame.

Dissociation; Dissociated: Disconnected or separated from one's experience and/or body; the separation of one's soul from one's body; the shutting down of awareness as a result of dysregulation and/or overwhelm caused by traumatic events and/or unresolved trauma.

Dysregulation: When conditions of stress compromise one's sense of safety are present, the autonomic nervous system can become dysregulated where an individual experiences an elevated heart rate, restricted breathing, hypo or hyper arousal, and dilated pupils; when unresolved trauma is active and the nervous system is off balance, the fight/flight/freeze/fawn/fix response can be an expression of dysregulation; spaced out, scattered, uncoordinated, forgetful, scared, angry, rigid, and overwhelmed are signs of being dysregulated.

Ego: Identity; a person's sense of self; a sense of self that is created as a necessary means of navigating the third dimension; identity that creates a perception of separateness and "other," with a need to control the third dimension in order to maintain a sense of self.

Embodiment: Having the quality of being in full contact with one's body, where one's soul is occupying their body in the full three-dimensional experience of one's physical form.

Energetic body: The five layers of energy that encompass the field around the human body; the layers of the human energy field that store the mental, physical, emotional, and spiritual characteristics of an individual; these layers can be in balance or out of balance, clear or blocked.

Enmeshed: Not knowing where the boundary point is between one's self and another; cause to become entangled.

Entangled: Becoming twisted together with another in

the habitual patterns of our distorted life force, making it challenging to see and know with clarity what is transpiring in the relationship encounter.

Epigenetics: The study of "modifications of gene expression rather than alteration of the gene code itself" (Canli, 2015).

Essential Self/Essence: The intrinsic wholeness of a person's spiritual self that is the unique vibrational characteristics of their true nature; the fundamental core of a person's being that has been with them throughout their entire life and remains untouched by experiences of this life.

Field Theory: We exist within a social context, and the meaning we create of an experience relies on what we keep our attention focused on and the context in which the experience occurs.

Felt Sense: A term created by Eugene Gendlin, creator of Focusing, which describes the process by which an individual places their attention on bodily sensations that are related to unresolved emotional pain; processing unresolved emotional pain by focusing on our bodily sensations as we loop in mental narratives that are limiting and painful, thus accessing the somatic intelligence that is deeper than our thoughts.

Fertile Void: When the mind ceases to focus on one thought or behavioral pattern, and no energy is being directed to awareness or sensation, a person is simply open to the infinite; when nothing in particular stands out to a person's mind and they are open to discovering and consciously creating new ways of being.

Fragmentation: A disruption of one's inherent wholeness, clarity, and wisdom; a division that occurs within one's personality and/or mind-body-spirit connection.

Gaslighting: Distorting objective reality, causing another person to question their sanity, memory, and perception; covert psychological manipulation where a person misuses their power in an attempt to undermine someone else and cause them to doubt themselves; a tactic in emotionally abusive relationship dynamics where a person twists the truth into a distorted story in an attempt to maintain power and control over another person.

Give our power away: We give our power away when we believe that the way other people treat us and what they think of us is indicative of our worth, enoughness, and lovability; believing that other people are the source of love, we give our power away by hiding our truth, our needs, our desires, our beliefs, and/or our values; we give our power away when we believe other people are more powerful than us and we defer to them as the authority of right action and reality.

God: God, as referred to in this book, indicates the theological concept of a deity outside of one's self that people have projected certain qualities onto, some of which are harmful and some of which are useful. "We make the other person God," is a phrase used to describe the way the unconscious drive to please the theological deity interferes with our relationships and sense of self.

God Consciousness: The higher consciousness that exists within the human mind that is capable of transcending ego, conditioning, and primal instincts.

High Vibration: Qualities of joy, love, compassion, and creation hold a higher frequency than qualities of fear, anger, lack, and blame; when we talk about "bringing in more high vibrational qualities" and/or "raising our vibration" we are referring to the measurable qualities of Source; intentionally inviting the essence of true joy, unconditional love, compassion, and creation into our bodies without bypassing our pain is useful in softening the subtle energy body and embodying our essential self.

Homeostasis: This refers to the way a person controls their internal environment in an attempt to ensure stability in their external environment; we create an internal homeostasis that is out of balance with our health when the field we are part of and/or grow up in does not empower us to be in our true expression.

I-Divine: A transpersonal relationship encounter between two or more individuals who are in contact with the higher dimensions of their essence while also being with the higher dimension of other people's essence; relating to one another as Divine-to-Divine, where we experience ourselves and others as sacred beings; words can often interfere with this sacred encounter, and silence can amplify the beauty of the I-Divine.

I-It: A relationship where two or more people reduce themselves and one another down to objects, characterized by separateness and detachment; relating as object-to-object, sometimes shifting to subject-to-object, as first described by Martin Buber.

I-Thou: A relationship between two or more individuals characterized by reciprocity of subject-to-subject, where each person's unique experience is honored, as first described by Martin Buber; a mutual encounter between two or more individuals who are in contact with their wholeness and in discovery of the other people's wholeness; a relational encounter that leads to clarity, contact, and lacks permanency.

In choice: When we are aware of our conditioned patterns, differentiated from our conditioned self, and have spaciousness around our thoughts, desires, and impulses, we have the power to select how we want to relate to ourselves and to life; aware of our habitual thoughts and patterns, we are in touch with alternative options that are aligned with our truth and honor ourselves.

Intrapsychic: An individual's internal psychological process; a psychological term to describe something that exists in a person's mind.

Introjection: Internalizing other people's words, ideas, and ways of being; when an individual takes in information from the environment without discernment and this information becomes part of that person's intrapsychic characteristics.

Integration: The process of unifying and incorporating all aspects of who a person is; bringing together any psychological fragmentations and combining them into one complete whole; bringing all aspects of one's self back to the wholeness of one's essence.

Leaving one's self: To disregard one's own state of being, desires, and truth; to place the majority of one's attention on another person; when the mind is consumed by thinking of other people; when the real or imagined desires, thoughts, and actions of other people occupy one's mind in lieu of contacting and honoring one's deeper felt sense.

Life Urge: The inner drive to be fully alive now; the embodied experience of consciously bringing more divine energy into our whole being as we ignite our vital force; cultivating higher vibrational frequencies that support the aliveness of our being through life-affirming thoughts and actions, which allow us to embody the energy and wisdom of Source.

Meta: Seeing the larger view of one's self; being self-referential from a higher perspective, where one's internal design, practices, processes, and actions are seen with clarity.

Misattuned; Emotionally Misattuned: the inability to recognize, understand, and engage with another person's emotional state; identifying, responding, and understanding another's emotional state incorrectly in a way that causes harm.

Mistuned: When the experience of life alters our energy body in such a way that our system is not tuned in accordance with our own true nature; energetic imbalance; internal discord.

Narcissistic: Regarding one's self as more important than others; acting in ways to ensure the perception of one's self-importance; exaggerated sense of one's own entitlement, talents, and success; excessive need for admiration while disregarding other people.

Personality: The character expressions of our learned ways of being that obscure our essence.

Projection: Putting our own emotions or traits onto another person; seeing someone through the filter of our past and not for the fullness of who they are; in an unconscious effort to ignore our own unpleasant or hostile qualities, feelings, and impulses we attribute them to another; attributing our own internal experience to another person.

Projective Identification: A defense mechanism in which a person is unable or unwilling to feel what is happening within themselves and unconsciously induces it into another person, causing the other person to think that they are appropriately characterized by the qualities that originate in the other person; acting in such a way that causes another person to feel our own unprocessed emotions and believe that they are theirs; for example, if a person feels scared of rejection but is unable to identify and feel that fear, they yell at the other person, causing them to feel scared and afraid of being left; this is the foundation of many relationship entanglements.

Resonance: The deep, reverberating feeling of vibrating at a similar frequency as another person, song, place, art, etc.; the experience of having the vibration of our own essence amplified in the presence of another who embodies qualities that we feel aligned and connected with; when our frequency matches the frequency of another in a deep and satisfying way.

Retroflection: When we withhold our authentic thoughts, emotions, and desired behaviors towards another and turn them back on ourselves; turning a feeling or behavior that belongs to another onto ourselves.

Self as Source: In attachment theory, psychologists look at securely attaching to another person as a healthy way to be in relationship. In transpersonal psychology, we look at creating a secure connection with our True Self as the key to feeling safe and secure in the world; Self as Source is a term created by Harmony Kwiker to signify the importance of attaching to Self as the Source of security, healing, wisdom, and power.

Self-Attunement: The ability to notice, comprehend, and respond to our own emotional state and experience.

Self-regulation: The ability to respond to our own internal states in real-time in such a way that we honor the full spectrum of what our nervous system activation is reacting against; self-regulation is not about "calming down," it's about feeling and processing the emotional information that arises within us and supporting the movement of our stored energy to metabolize to completion.

Shadow Work: When we are aware of what is hidden in our unconscious mind and what aspects of ourself we have rejected, working with what we have disowned and what lives in the darkness of our own blind spots is called "Shadow Work"; owning the darker, unacceptable aspects of ourself, that which society deems vulgar but is an authentic aspect of our own character.

Source: The supreme energy of creation, the vital force that proceeds us all, and the divinity of universal bliss; the infinite wisdom of higher consciousness that has the capacity of unconditional love, healing, and acceptance for all beings; the sacred essence of all life.

Soul's Contract: Prior to our own birth, our soul makes agreements about the purpose of our return to the third dimension; our soul's contract includes the family we choose to be born into, the lessons we learn while here at earth school, and the contribution we make to planetary restoration.

Somatic Intelligence: The inherent wisdom seated in bodily sensations, physical pain, and biological response to external stimuli, such as stress; the expression of our deeper truth and knowing as felt and expressed through physical sensations and bodily feedback; consciousness as it is expressed through the body.

Somatic Phenomenology: Utilizing the obvious, present-moment sensations in the body to access deeper consciousness wisdom, rather than relying on mental interpretation; being aware of and paying attention to the messages of the body rather than the analytical mind.

Sovereignty: Embodying one's authentic, powerful Self; having agency of choice in how one responds to a situation, acting from one's deeper truth rather than conditioned values and reactionary patterns.

Spiritual Bypassing: "Tendency to use spiritual ideas and practices to sidestep or avoid facing unresolved emotional issues, psychological wounds, and unfinished developmental tasks" (Welwood, 2002).

Subtle energy body: Neither solely physical nor solely spiritual, the often unperceivable energy that permeates one's being affects physical, spiritual, and psychological well-being; the life force that is centralized up the midline of one's being and infuses one's essence with vitality; made up of five layers of energy, with seven energy centers up the midline, the subtle energy body can become stuck, clogged, or off-balance and cause decreased vitality and lower levels of one's health; when aligned and clear, the subtle energy body flows in sync with the energy of the universe, vitality thrives, and mental, emotional, spiritual, and physical health is elevated.

Trauma: Any event that has an individual feel split from their connection with Source; examples of trauma include being born, observing conflict and emotional volatility in our caregivers, being judged as bad by our caregivers, experiencing neglect, physical violations, and/or emotional abuse.

True Self: The untainted expression of the vital energy of Source through any one individual; the manifestation of the high vibrational frequency of Source as expressed through the unique qualities of an individual; an individual's divinity as it's expressed through them in an unadulterated, pure transmission.

Window of Tolerance: As our brain and body react to adversity or recall stress and adversity as we process our unfinished business, there is an optimal zone of arousal where a person can tolerate the emotional waves as they come and go without becoming flooded or overwhelmed (Siegel, 2018).

Witness Mind: The conscious observer of our thoughts, actions, and state of being; the expansive consciousness within our mind that holds the capacity for self-awareness, choice, and right action; awareness of the mind itself.

References

Badenoch, B. (2008). *Being a Brain-Wise Therapist: A Practical Guide to Interpersonal Neurobiology.* W. W. Norton and Company: New York.

Barstow, C. (2017) *Right Use of Power: The Heart of Ethics: A Guide and Resource for Professional Relationships.* Many Realms.

Beattie, M. (1986). *Codependent No More: How to Stop Controlling Others and Start Caring for Yourself.* Hazelden.

Brennan, B. A. (1988). *Hands of Light: A Guide to Healing Through the Human Energy Field.* Bantam: New York.

Caldwell, C. (1996). *Getting Our Bodies Back: Recover, healing, and transformation through Body-Centered Psychotherapy.* Shambhala: Boston.

Campbell, S. (2001). *Getting Real: 10 Truth Skills You Need to Live an Authentic Life.* HJ Kramer/New World Library.

Canli, T. (2015). *The Oxford Handbook of Molecular Psychology.* Oxford University Press: Oxford.

Dale, C. (2009). *The Subtle Body: An Encyclopedia of Your Energetic Anatomy.* Sounds True.

DiAngelo, (2018), *White Fragility: Why It's So Hard for White People to Talk About Racism.* Beacon Press.

Dion, L. (2018) Aggression in Play Therapy: A Neurobiological Approach for Integrating Intensity. W.W. Norton and Company.

Gendlin, E.T. (1982). *Focusing.* Bantam; 2nd edition.

Heller, L. & LaPierre, A. (2012). *Healing Developmental Trauma: How Early Trauma Affects Self-Regulation, Self-Image, and the Capacity for Relationships.* North Atlantic Books.

Jung, C. G., & Storr, A. (1997). *The Essential Jung.* Mjf Books; 2nd ed.

Kaparo, R. F. (2012). *Awakening Somatic Intelligence: The Art and Practice of Embodied Mindfulness.* North Atlantic Books:

Berkely, CA.

Kendi, I. (2019). *How to Be an Antiracist.* One World Publishers.

Kendi, I. (2017). *Stamped from the Beginning: Racism, Antiracism, and You.* Little, Brown Books for Young Readers.

Korb, M.P., Gorrell, J., & Van De Riet, V. (2002). *Gestalt Therapy: Practice and Theory,* 2nd Ed., The Gestalt Journal Press.

Kurtz, R. (1990). *Body-Centered Psychotherapy: The Hakomi Method.* LifeRhythm.

Levine, P. (1997). *Waking the Tiger: Healing Trauma.* North Atlantic Books.

Levine, A. & Heller, R.S.F. (2012). *Attached: The New Science of Adult Attachment and How It Can Help You Find - and Keep – Love.* Penguin Publishing Group.

Mann, D. (2021). *Gestalt Therapy: 100 Key Points and Techniques.* Routledge: New York.

Miller, L. (2015). *The Spiritual Child: The New Science on Parenting for Health and Lifelong Thriving.* Picador: New York.

Menakem, R. (2017). *My Grandmother's Hands: Racialized Trauma and the Pathway to Mending Our Hearts and Bodies.* Central Recovery Press: Las Vegas, NV.

Mooney, C.G. (2009). *Theories of Attachment: An introduction to Bowlby, Ainsworth, Gerber, Brazelton, Kannell, and Klause.* Redleaf Press.

Morningstar, D. (2017). *Out of the Fog: Moving from Confusion to Clarity After Narcissistic Abuse.* Morningstar Media.

Naranjo, C. (2004). *Gestalt Therapy: The Attitude and Practice of an Atheoretical Experientialism.* Crown House Pub Ltd.

Ogden, T.H. (1977). *Projective Identification and Psychotherapeutic Technique.* Jason Aaronson, INC.

Orr, L. & Ray. S. (2007). *Rebirthing in the New Age.* Trafford Publishing.

Patterson, J. (2020). *The Power of Breathwork: Simple Practices to Promote Wellbeing.* Fair Winds Press.

Perls, F., (1973). *The Gestalt Approach and Eye Witness to Therapy.*

Science and Behavior Books, Inc.; 1st edition.

Porges, S.W. (2017). *The Pocket Guide to the Polyvagal Theory: The Transformative Power of Feeling Safe.* W.W. Norton & Company.

Rosenberg, M. B. (2015). *Nonviolent Communication: The Language of Life.* Puddle Dancer Press; 3rd edition.

Siegel, D.J. (2018). Aware: The Science and Practice of Presence. TarcherPerigee.

Siegel, D.J. (2011). *Mindsight: The New Science of Personal Transformation.* Bantam Books: New York.

Stanley, E. A. (2019). *Widen the Window: Training Your Brain and Your Body to Thrive During Stress and Recover from Trauma.* Avery Publishing.

Taylor, S.R. (2021), *Your Body Is Not an Apology: The Power of Radical Self-Love.* Berrett-Kohler Publishers.

Welwood, J. (2002). *Toward a Psychology of Awakening: Buddhism, Psychotherapy, and the Path of Personal and Spiritual Transformation.* Shambhala: Boston.

Wilber, K. (2000). *Integral Psychology: Consciousness, Spirit, Psychology, Therapy.* Shambhala: Boston.

Zinker, J. (1977). *Creative Process in Gestalt Therapy.* First Vintage Books Edition.

MANTRA
BOOKS

EASTERN RELIGION & PHILOSOPHY

We publish books on Eastern religions and philosophies. Books
that aim to inform and explore the various traditions that began in
the East and have migrated West.
If you have enjoyed this book, why not tell other readers by
posting a review on your preferred book site.

Recent bestsellers from MANTRA BOOKS are:

The Way Things Are
A Living Approach to Buddhism
Lama Ole Nydahl
An introduction to the teachings of the Buddha, and how to make use of these teachings in everyday life.
Paperback: 978-1-84694-042-2 ebook: 978-1-78099-845-9

Back to the Truth
5000 Years of Advaita
Dennis Waite
A demystifying guide to Advaita for both those new to, and those familiar with this ancient, non-dualist philosophy from India.
Paperback: 978-1-90504-761-1 ebook: 978-184694-624-0

Shinto: A celebration of Life
Aidan Rankin
Introducing a gentle but powerful spiritual pathway reconnecting humanity with Great Nature and affirming all aspects of life.
Paperback: 978-1-84694-438-3 ebook: 978-1-84694-738-4

In the Light of Meditation
Mike George
A comprehensive introduction to the practice of meditation and the spiritual principles behind it. A 10 lesson meditation programme with CD and internet support.
Paperback: 978-1-90381-661-5

A Path of Joy
Popping into Freedom
Paramananda Ishaya
A simple and joyful path to spiritual enlightenment.
Paperback: 978-1-78279-323-6 ebook: 978-1-78279-322-9

The Less Dust the More Trust
Participating in The Shamatha Project, Meditation and Science
Adeline van Waning, MD PhD
The inside-story of a woman participating in frontline meditation research, exploring the interfaces of mind-practice, science and psychology.
Paperback: 978-1-78099-948-7 ebook: 978-1-78279-657-2

I Know How To Live, I Know How To Die
The Teachings of Dadi Janki: A warm, radical, and life-affirming view of who we are, where we come from, and what time is calling us to do
Neville Hodgkinson
Life and death are explored in the context of frontier science and deep soul awareness.
Paperback: 978-1-78535-013-9 ebook: 978-1-78535-014-6

The Way of Nothing
Nothing in the Way
Paramananda Ishaya
A fresh and light-hearted exploration of the amazing reality of nothingness.
Paperback: 978-1-78279-307-6 ebook: 978-1-78099-840-4

Readers of ebooks can buy or view any of these bestsellers by clicking on the live link in the title. Most titles are published in paperback and as an ebook. Paperbacks are available in traditional bookshops. Both print and ebook formats are available online.

Find more titles and sign up to our readers' newsletter at http://www.johnhuntpublishing.com/mind-body-spirit.
Follow us on Facebook at https://www.facebook.com/OBooks and Twitter at https://twitter.com/obooks.